◆ When the Cheering Stops ◆

EX-MAJOR LEAGUERS TALK
ABOUT THEIR GAME
AND THEIR
LIVES

WHEN THE
CHEERING
STOPS

⬧ Lee ⬧   ⬧ Dave ⬧   ⬧ Bill ⬧
Heiman   Weiner   Gutman

MACMILLAN PUBLISHING COMPANY ⬧ NEW YORK
COLLIER MACMILLAN PUBLISHERS ⬧ LONDON

Macmillan Publishing Company
866 Third Avenue, New York, NY 10022
Collier Macmillan Canada, Inc.

Designed by Beth Tondreau Design/Jane Treuhaft

LIBRARY OF CONGRESS CATALOGING-IN-PUBLICATION DATA
Heiman, Lee.
When the cheering stops: ex–major leaguers talk about their game and their lives/by Lee Heiman, Dave Weiner, and Bill Gutman.
p.   cm.
ISBN 0-02-550765-6
1. Baseball players—United States—Biography.   I. Weiner, Dave.
II. Gutman, Bill.   III. Title.
GV865.A1H45   1990   89-12172   CIP
796.357′092′2—dc20
[B]

Macmillan books are available at special discounts for bulk purchases for sales promotions, premiums, fund-raising, or educational use. For details, contact:

Special Sales Director
Macmillan Publishing Company
866 Third Avenue
New York, NY 10022

10   9   8   7   6   5   4   3   2   1
Printed in the United States of America

♦ Contents ♦

♦ ACKNOWLEDGMENTS ♦

On a warm Sunday in mid-September 1987, I was privileged to spend several hours with retired Met great Ed Kranepool. The occasion was an annual New York book fair; my company had hired Kranepool to autograph a book about the Mets. During my conversation with him, I realized that this highly intelligent ex-ballplayer had prepared for the day "when the cheering stopped."

That night, after hearing my reflections and musings about Kranepool, my wife, Roberta, commented that there ought to be a book describing the trials and tribulations of ex-ballplayers during and after their careers. In that conversation this book was conceived.

Within a week I mentioned the idea to my longtime buddy David Weiner, a published author. David's immediate enthusiasm convinced me that there should indeed be a book and that he should be its coauthor. His knowledge of baseball and his unbelievable photographic memory for ballplayers and their statistics made him invaluable to this project.

The concept might have died if it were not for a casual conversation with Bill Rosen, who was then marketing director at the Macmillan Publishing Company. Bill immediately offered us a contract, with Rick Wolff as our editor. This was a coup since Rick, to my knowledge, is the only editor in publishing who actually played professional baseball. The relationship between editor and authors was sometimes stormy, as Rick would only accept first-rate material. This led us to another coauthor, Bill Gutman, a writer of almost ninety books. Bill gave the project an air of journalistic professionalism.

During my teen years in the forties and fifties, I had been a rabid Brooklyn Dodger fan. My dedication as a fan was sorely tested in the final game of the 1951 National League playoffs between my beloved "Bums" and the New York Giants. Bad enough that the then mighty Yankees had humiliated the Dodgers in postseason play again and again. Now the villain was Bobby Thomson, who, with one swing of his bat, started the winter of discontent for thousands of Dodger fans and ripped a hole in my gut through which a bitter wind blew all that winter.

Now fast-forward to October 17, 1987. David and I were driving out to interview the person I had hated all those years, Bobby Thomson. It was, of course, Black Monday, the day the stock market crashed. How coincidental! What had been a dreary day turned into a nostalgic evening. It was a long day's journey into a wonderful night. Thomson is one of the most charming and knowledgeable men I have ever met. Bobby is a helluva guy, as are the twenty other retired major league players interviewed for this book. Without the cooperation of these ballplayers and their families, this project would not have been possible.

Special thanks also go to Cathy Gutman and Kathleen Stymacks for transcribing the endless hours of taped interviews and to Jeanine Bucek, who, as assistant to the editor, guided us through book protocol.

—Lee Heiman
October, 1989

◆ INTRODUCTION ◆

The road through the major leagues was different for all of them. Some found their way into the record books. Others had the thrill of playing in the World Series. A few traveled a path filled more with disappointment and frustration than satisfaction. And a number were able to experience that special kind of moment, when they were a part of something that would forever be enshrined in the long and glorious history of their sport.

But whether they were hero or goat, had long or short careers, or played with winning or losing teams, these men have a common bond. They were big league baseball players. And that makes them part of a relatively small fraternity, whose member ship is but a mere dream for most of us, a fantasy camp that occupies the thoughts of nearly every American boy again and again during the course of his lifetime.

When the Cheering Stops is a book about baseball players by baseball players. The former big leaguers represented in the following pages talk not only of their lives in the majors, but also about how they got there, famous and not-so-famous teammates, the often traumatic experience of being traded, battles with management over money, the high and low points in their careers, and finally of that dreaded day when the ride was over. That meant coping with a sometimes unwelcome retirement and all that followed after the cheering had indeed stopped.

Those represented here played mostly from the postwar 1940s through the 1960s, with a few lasting into the 1970s when baseball began entering the modern, big-money era. Some have remained in the game, others tried but were not wanted, while still others left and never looked back, at least not until the nostalgia revival of the 1980s.

But no matter which direction their careers and the aftermath have taken, all twenty-one players who agreed to speak extensively of their lives in baseball have generously shared their memories and feelings, creating a book that will allow fans to relive a period that is now gone, having been replaced by a game where the rules on the field are basically the same, but the rules governing the structure of the sport are almost completely different.

None of the players interviewed is in the Hall of Fame. But many put together solid, memorable careers and left their marks. Others were less fortunate, their careers shortened by injury, circumstance, or by just not being in the right place at the right time. Each was, nevertheless, part of the big league scene, playing with and against those who went on to become legends and Hall of Famers during an era many consider one of the greatest in the history of the game.

What was it like to be among the first handful of black players signed into professional baseball? Or how about the intensity of the Dodger-Giant and Dodger-Yankee rivalries of the 1950s? What was the real effect of Willie Mays's great catch in the 1954 World Series? How does it feel to burn up the National League for half a season, then never get a full shot at a regular position in the big leagues again? This is just a sampling of what is to come.

There's more. How do yesterday's players feel about today's big leaguers—their skills, the money they make, the high-priced pension plan awaiting them upon retirement? What about those players whose sons are trying to follow in their father's footsteps? Or those involved in the great pennant races of 1948, 1951, and 1969, or the World Series of 1955, 1957, 1960, and 1963?

How does it feel to be the league's home run and RBI champ with a last-place ballclub? Or to be one of the highest-priced bonus babies ever and never become a regular? What is the feeling when the fans in the bleachers are the first ones to tell you you've been traded? And how does it feel to learn that the game you've always loved more than anything else just doesn't have room for you anywhere, leaving you barely into middle age with no idea of what to do with the rest of your life?

The wide variety of baseball topics appearing in the following chapters will seem never-ending. The reader will also learn what it's like playing with and against Ted Williams, Sandy Koufax, Mickey Mantle, Hank Aaron, Jackie Robinson, Roberto Clemente, Roger Maris, Bob Gibson, Al Kaline, Bob Feller, and other great players of the period. In fact, *When the Cheering Stops* is chock-full of all kinds of baseball—stories, anecdotes, opinions, and tales never before shared with such candor.

This is a book for both the diehard baseball fan and the newcomer to the sport, for those who remember the times and the players well, and also for those who have only read and heard about them, yet want to learn more. Baseball was surely a different game then, with a very different kind of player and a different kind of life. For each dramatic game-winning home run, there has been an equally disheartening strikeout. Like other institutions, baseball doesn't always give back what it takes. And while the numbers are radically different today, it was still a business forty years ago and it will always be a business. It just took the older players a lot longer to find that out.

But enjoy now, as Bobby Thomson, Mel Parnell, Al Smith, Clem Labine, Chuck Stobbs, Roy Sievers, J. W. Porter, Dale Long, Bob Boyd, Davey Williams, Bill Bruton, Bob Hazle, Ray Boone, Elroy Face, Dick Ellsworth, Gary Peters, Tom Tresh, Ed Kranepool, Jake Gibbs, Bob Veale, and Al Weis take you back to baseball as they knew it, how the game affected their lives and what happened to them when the cheering stopped.

TOM
TRESH

New York Yankees, 1961–1969
Detroit Tigers, 1969

Assistant baseball coach at Central
Michigan University; has served the university in a number of administrative capacities since 1971.

*Tom Tresh's rookie season was almost like a dream. When Yankee
shortstop Tony Kubek was called into the army in 1962, Tresh not
only became the shortstop on a New York Yankee team featuring
the likes of Mickey Mantle, Roger Maris, Yogi Berra, and Whitey
Ford, but he also won the Rookie of the Year award by hitting
.286, slamming twenty home runs, and collecting ninety-three
runs batted in. He then banged out nine hits and a game-winning
homer against the Giants in the World Series.*

♦ 4 ♦

Born in Detroit on September 20, 1938, Tom grew up around baseball. His father, Mike, was the long-time catcher for the Chicago White Sox, and also played briefly for the Cleveland Indians, so Tom saw both the good and bad sides of baseball at an early age. But there was never any doubt that he would follow in his father's footsteps.

Upon Kubek's return, Tom became a Gold Glove left fielder for the Yanks, and played in two more World Series. After that, however, he witnessed the Bombers' rapid fall from grace and saw his own career slowed and eventually shortened by a knee injury suffered in the spring of 1967.

After playing the second half of the 1969 season in his native Detroit, Tom was released, only to jump into a successful second career at Central Michigan University. With his son, Mickey, now in the Yankee organization, Tom may soon become part of the first three-generation family of major league ballplayers in the game's history.

My desire to be a major league ballplayer kind of evolved over the years. People were always asking me if I was going to be a ballplayer like my dad. And when you grow up always hearing that, it almost becomes the only choice. After a while, I never thought about doing anything else. As a kid, it seemed the only toys I ever got were baseball bats and gloves, but my dad didn't force me into baseball. Yet I was lucky because he was a player and I grew up in an environment that was strictly baseball— meeting players, talking baseball, and thinking baseball. Because of this I never felt I couldn't make the major leagues.

But having my dad as a big league baseball player made me acutely aware of something else. I knew there had to be something else in life besides playing baseball. That's because I saw my father turn thirty-six and suddenly become too old to play in the majors anymore. In those days they felt you were an old man as soon as you turned thirty and you'd better not have a bad season.

When my father left baseball, a lot of things changed very quickly. For one thing, he didn't have a college degree. Then, a lot of the people who always seemed to be on his side were suddenly on the side of the guy who took his place. In other words, when you're something of a celebrity, there are always a lot of people who want to hang around you. But they're only friends because of what you are, not who you are. When the what you are ceases to be a big deal anymore, a lot of them seek out other people. Even those people who had the jobs—you know, "'You can always come to work for us, Mike"—disappeared.

Then I saw my dad working at a job he enjoyed—plant security at the Ford Motor Company—but a job he didn't feel particularly proud of. And I think that's why my father always encouraged me to get a college education. It wasn't so much the money you could make, but how you felt about yourself, and how other people might feel about you. You know, the old stigma of the broken-down old jock. That was a label a lot of ex-players had back then. When they got out of baseball it was almost as if they went from being first-class citizens to being fourth-class citizens. Consequently, I was aware at a young age that if you played baseball, you still had to be thinking about what you would do after you got out of baseball.

The players from my era were very conscious of their image when they left baseball. They didn't want people thinking they weren't doing very well or feeling sorry for them. There was a lot of pride involved and that didn't make it easy. I haven't had that feeling because I finished my college education and that put me in a kind of title situation. It gave me more of a feeling of success than just being an ex-baseball player. It showed that I was college educated and was working for a university where I was the director of this or the assistant director of that.

Yet I remember when I first left baseball. I had a Kentucky Fried Chicken franchise that hadn't been doing well, so I felt my first job was to get that going again. And I did everything, including the cooking. People would come in and see my trophy case in the front, but when Tom Tresh the ballplayer would come out from the back he would be wearing an apron and have flour up his arms to his elbows.

By the same token, it wasn't always easy for the ballplayers in my time and those who came earlier to plan for a second career. They didn't make enough money. They'd have to come home for the off-season and go right to work. My dad, for instance, was a deputy sheriff for a couple of years. Then, during the war, he worked in a factory making tanks. He always had a job. But there isn't enough time during the off-season to really learn a trade or anything like that, unless you persist, year after year. So with a lot of players then, when they left baseball that was still all they knew—baseball.

Because I was intent on finishing college, I always went back to school in the off-season. It cost me a lot of money because I wasn't earning anything. Rather I was taking money out of the bank to live and go to school. But I had promised both my parents and myself that I would finish. It took a long time, but it was worth it, because it certainly opened a lot of doors for me that just wouldn't have been there otherwise. And I got my degree about a year before I left the game.

As I said, I grew up in a baseball atmosphere. I was born in Detroit, but my father played for the White Sox and later the Indians, so I always rooted for them. My family has a movie of me when I was about fifteen or sixteen months old running around our apartment in Chicago, throwing and hitting a ball. I once used it as part of a Wheaties commercial, so I know I was already playing ball at that age.

My father also took me out to Comiskey Park quite often when I was young and I would stay with him right up until the game began. I met a lot of his teammates and friends that way. Besides my father, my early idol was Luke Appling. Luke was my dad's roommate and we always did things with the Appling family. Plus Luke was a shortstop and that's what I wanted to be, even though my dad caught. I can remember my father telling me that if you play shortstop you can always play second or third, or even the outfield. He felt shortstop was the best position to develop if you wanted to learn the complete game.

Switch-hitting was also his idea. I started fooling around with it when I was just seven or eight. In fact, I often tried it when I was at the ballpark with him. I'd go out to the outfield and one of the players would pitch to me and I'd hit both ways. For years, however, I'd always hit righthanded in ballgames. The first time I really dedicated myself to switch-hitting was when I played in the Detroit Amateur Baseball Federation the summer before my senior year in high school. When I hit over .400 that summer, I decided to stick with it during the high school season.

I had to talk my coach into letting me try it. He finally said, okay, you can hit lefthanded for one game. Well, I hit for the cycle that day and convinced him I could do it. My father had always felt it was an advantage. As a catcher, he knew it was easier to hit a curveball breaking in to you instead of away from you. And by the time I began playing professionally they were really getting into a lot of platooning. So being a switch-hitter eliminated any chance of my becoming a platoon player. The funny part is that in later years I often wondered how I would have done if I had remained strictly a righthanded hitter, because my first few years in the majors I was always somewhere between .340 and .350 righthanded. Of course, about two-thirds of my big league at-bats were lefthanded, so I'll never really know.

Anyway, I was scouted pretty often in high school and during the summers with the Amateur Baseball Federation. But after high school I decided to enroll at Central Michigan University instead of signing. I already had my eye on a big league career, but I didn't want to sign then because of the old bonus restriction. That was the one that said if you signed with a team for more than three thousand dollars, you had to stay on the roster for two years before you could go to the minors. The result was two years wasted, because the players who signed under that rule just took up space and then a number of them never developed. The rule was changed at the end of 1957, after my freshman year, and that's when I decided to sign.

There was also no draft then, so you could sign with whichever team offered you the best deal. The funny part was that I always took a lot of ribbing from my Detroit buddies because I rooted for the White Sox and Indians. So after my father stopped playing I wanted to get even with them and I began following the Yankees. Whenever we played stickball type games back then, I was always Yankee players. I started in the early fifties, just about when Mickey Mantle and Gil McDougald were starting with the Yanks.

Pat Patterson was the scout who was following me and Pat reminded me that the Yanks had Tony Kubek at shortstop. Tony was Rookie of the Year in 1957 and that meant he'd probably be around quite a while. But I told Pat there were a lot of other positions besides shortstop and I wasn't afraid of being in that situation. Maybe it was the confidence my father had instilled in me, but I really didn't fear signing with the Yankees even though they had so many good players in the organization. And when we agreed on a figure—I think it was about thirty thousand dollars—I signed.

I was in the minors for three and a half years, starting in D ball, and I guess I made the usual progression. I went from St. Petersburg in the Florida State League to New Orleans in Double A, then to Greensboro, North Carolina. From there it was Binghamton, New York, Amarillo, Texas, and finally Richmond, in the International League. That was in 1961. I was hitting about .315 and in a race for the batting title with Ted Savage when the Yanks called me up. Ted got the hitting crown, but I was named International League Rookie of the Year and then got a taste of the majors.

Because I had been to spring training with the Yanks in 1961 and had met most of the players, coming up to the team wasn't that much of an adjustment. The veterans all treated me well, especially Bill Skowron. Bill was from Chicago and knew my father pretty well and my father had asked him to keep an eye on me. So he kind of took me under his wing. One of the things he told me was not to be too forceful with the other guys, just to do things in a professional manner and they would accept me. He was right, and it wasn't too difficult for me to do that because I was basically a shy kid anyway.

Then before the 1962 season Tony Kubek was called into the army and the shortstop job was left open. The two candidates were myself and Phil Linz, who was also a rookie. Phil and I knew each other well from the minors, and suddenly we were thrust into competition for the job. At least that's how the media portrayed it. And whenever either one of us was interviewed, they would try to get us to put the other down.

So Phil and I kind of got together and talked about it. We knew that Tony was gone and that his backup from the year before, Joe DeMaestri, had retired. There were two infield spots open and we figured we would both be able to make the team. We also knew that one of us would start and the other would be the utility man. We decided to let the chips fall where they might, shook hands on it, and we have been good friends ever since, even today. Plus we respected each other as ballplayers.

At that time I felt that Phil had quicker hands than I did and would probably hit for a better average. I had more power and we were both pretty good defensive players. For two young kids, I think we both handled the pressure pretty well. In fact, he and I were one-two in hitting during spring training. I was fortunate enough to win the job and get the chance to prove I could play every day. Phil was the utility man and I think that made it tougher for him.

In fact, in the long run it hurt him. For beginners, he was a guy who had never sat the bench in his life and all of a sudden he's sitting. I think he could have been a very good ballplayer if he had gotten with a team that played him every day. But it was one of those situations where the Yankees had a lot of talent and not everyone could play.

By the time Tony came back late in the season, I had already established myself as an offensive player who had to be in the lineup. At first, Tony went to the outfield and Ralph Houk left me at short. Finally, we had a talk. Ralph told me that the reason the team had a commanding lead in the pennant race was the way I played shortstop, but now he had a situation where he had to play the two of us. He said he felt that with my speed and arm strength I would make a heck of an outfielder and his feeling was to put me in left, where he had been alternating players, and to solidify the outfield with Mantle in center and Roger Maris in right.

I told him I hadn't played the outfield since junior high school, but he built up my confidence and told me he thought I could be one of the best defensive outfielders in the league. I thought he was just blowing smoke, but I decided to give it a try and felt good a few years later when I won a Gold Glove for my outfield play. So I guess Ralph wasn't blowing smoke after all.

But 1962 was like a dream season. I ended up Rookie of the Year, we won the pennant, then beat the Giants in the World Series in seven games. I had nine hits in the Series including a three-run homer off Jack Sanford that won the fifth game and gave us a 3–2 lead. And I was able to do all that with my father sitting in the stands and watching me. He had played all those years without getting into a World Series, so in a way I felt I was also doing it for him.

One funny thing that happened. Mickey Mantle had really become a good friend that year. He kind of took over for Bill [Skowron] and took me under his wing and was one of my biggest boosters. Anyway, a couple of weeks before the season ended Mickey told me that he made a bet with a local sportswriter, Phil Pepe, that I would hit twenty home runs. Well, I already had nineteen, but now I felt I had to get one more so Mickey could win his bet. It took me almost the entire two weeks and in that time my average dropped from about .300 to .286. But I got the homer for Mickey, who was always my idol.

As for the decision to move me to left field, I think it was a good one. Tony had three or four years more experience and had worked with Bobby Richardson, our second baseman. The ironic thing was that had I remained at shortstop and hit my twenty-fifth, twenty-sixth, twenty-seventh home runs, I probably would have been considered the best shortstop in the league. But when you're an outfielder hitting that many homers, you just become one of many.

Even though I hit twenty home runs as a rookie, I never saw myself as another Mickey Mantle. I just didn't see that much potential in myself and, in fact, felt I had pretty much achieved my potential as a rookie. Looking back, maybe that was a mistake, maybe I should have reset my goals higher. But to hit home runs in Yankee Stadium you have to pull the ball. And because I was hitting more home runs, and was later expected to hit them, my average suffered and I wasn't nearly the average hitter I could have been. In fact, once Mickey and Roger began to fade, Joe Pepitone and myself were looked upon to provide the power. And I guess that's when I really started thinking of myself as a home run hitter.

I had twenty-five in 1963, twenty-six in 1965, and then twenty-seven in 1966. That year I hit nineteen the second half of the season and I think for the first time felt I could hit thirty or more. But then in the second game of spring training the next year, I blew my knee out. After that, everything went dead. I just couldn't play over the knee injury.

It happened against Baltimore. Mark Belanger hit one down the line and I went over to get it. When I planted my leg to make the throw to second, the knee just gave out. I went down and was never in so much pain in my life. It lasted only for a minute, but then it seemed like forever. When they examined it, they said it was just a strain.

So I played 130 games that year with one of those knee braces with the iron hinges on both sides. I think my knee went out of joint five times and playing on it like that destroyed the knee pretty good. By the time I went into surgery that September they took the cartilage and other damage out of one side and just sewed it up. They said they'd have to do the other side later.

Had that happened today, they would have gone right in and scoped it out, and I'd probably have been playing in two or three weeks. But back then they couldn't even tell the extent of the damage without going in, and the doctors made the decision to hold off on the surgery. I really didn't have any choice, so basically my career was in their hands. If I had that choice today, I probably would have insisted on an operation, but the team was floundering at that time and they didn't want to lose me.

The other part of it was that my father had always taught me that if the manager wants you in the lineup you play, even if you're hurt. That's the way my dad and most players from his generation looked at it. He was called 'Iron Mike' and one year caught the complete schedule with the White Sox, every double-header, everything. So playing hurt was no big deal. It was what I was expected to do as the son of Mike Tresh. And there were a lot of other players who did the same thing then.

But as bad as it was, I never thought of it as career threatening. I figured whatever it was, they'd fix it. I remember one game at the Stadium that year, I hit a ball up the gap in left center and as I rounded first my knee locked in the up position. It wouldn't go back down to the ground and I went down like someone had shot me. I literally crawled back to first but didn't make it. They threw me out and I got booed by the fans.

I'll never forget that. I really felt bad inside because here I was, busting my heart out to get to second and because of a physical problem I go down, then struggle to get up and get booed for it. But the fans didn't really know about the injury and that's what makes it tough. They're out there booing because they think you're not as good as you used to be.

I came back the next year and played 152 games, and more than 100 of them were back at shortstop. That was in 1968. The knee was coming back somewhat and the team needed me there. Ralph asked me to come back to try to stabilize the infield. I wasn't 100 percent, but I could still make the plays that were right at me, the plays that had to be made. And that's the most important thing for a shortstop, not to bobble the easy ones. It's a pressure position and a lot of otherwise good infielders can't handle that. But as I said, I always considered myself a good defensive player and did it to help the team.

By then, of course, the Yankees had changed. In fact, the team changed very rapidly. I don't really know why, but the Yankees weren't the same Yankees. It started in 1965 and really bottomed out the next year. Part of it was the change in managers. Ralph Houk gave way to Yogi in 1964, then Yogi was fired and Johnny Keane came over in '65. So we went from a very stable team to an unsettled one. And the veterans like Mantle, Maris, and Ford were getting older, while the young talent didn't match up.

I also felt when Johnny Keane came in from St. Louis, he brought a different kind of philosophy to the team. He made us more of a bunt, hit-and-run type team, going more for stealing bases, and our club wasn't built to do that. The ballclub was set in its ways and didn't turn out to be very compatible with Johnny. I don't really think we accepted him as a team the way we should have. We had more talent than our achievement indicated in those years. But there were personality conflicts and I don't think we'll ever know why Johnny tried to change the team that way. He probably felt that was the kind of baseball that had made him successful. And, in a way, I think our ballclub was spoiled. We were too used to having it our own way.

None of us liked losing very much. Guys like Mickey and Whitey had played for a long time without ever losing. As I said, 1965 was a chaotic year. We had won it with Yogi in '64 and when they let him go after we took the Cards into the seventh game of the World Series, I think that's when the unsettledness started. But even when we lost in '65 we just looked at it as an off year and figured we'd be back the next season. I really think it took until about 1968 to convince us that we just weren't going to do it anymore. That's when they started to rebuild and trade, and it was the next year that I asked to be traded to Detroit.

Just to backtrack a second, I think there are still some people who point to the so-called harmonica incident in 1964 as one of the events that led to Yogi's downfall. That was when Phil Linz kept playing the harmonica on the team bus after Yogi told him to stop. The press corps were on the bus that day and after that they started writing that Yogi didn't have control of the team. Anyway, I was indirectly the one who brought that whole thing about. I used to enjoy singing, and so did Tony Kubek. In the minors, I took a guitar around with me, but I didn't do it when I was with the Yanks. So one day I bought a harmonica. Well, pretty soon Tony started playing it and decided he wanted one of his own.

We were in Chicago then and the team was struggling. Tony and I decided to go over to Marshall Fields and get him a harmonica. Well, we ran into Phil and when we told him he said he would come with us. Tony bought the harmonica for $2.50 and before we're out of the store, he's already playing "Streets of Laredo" on it. That's when Phil decided he wanted one. So I told him go ahead, it would only cost him $2.50.

Phil had been playing short in Baltimore because Tony was hurt, but in Chicago Yogi benched him again and put Tony back in. That didn't make Phil too happy anyway because he had been playing well. And when we lost four straight in Chicago, things got worse. It was on the bus ride back to the hotel after the fourth game when Phil and Yogi got into it. I guess after you lose four games you're supposed to be real sad. I never believed in that. You can't change what happened. But we should have been quieter because of the press and it wasn't smart for Phil to play the harmonica.

The funny thing is the team fined him $250 and I always kidded him about telling him the harmonica would cost him $2.50. I just had the decimal point in the wrong spot. Phil got a bit of the last laugh, I guess, because he eventually got a $10,000 contract from Hohner harmonica. But the whole thing was unfortunate because overall I think Yogi did a good job. He was just in a tough spot because he went from being a teammate and buddy to the boss in the space of a year. And that's not easy for anyone. If they had made him a coach for a couple of years, then let him take over the club, I think he would have been fine. And, as I said, that year was really the beginning of our troubles as a team.

Anyway, getting back to 1969. I had promised my wife years earlier that I would only play ten years in the big leagues. She never liked the baseball life, the traveling, uprooting the family, going here and there. So with my knee problems and many of my friends already gone, I asked for the trade. Playing for the Tigers I would be closer to home and I thought it would be nice to finish my career there. The Yankees accommodated me in June and I went over to Detroit. They really did me a favor and I thanked them for that opportunity.

Detroit had a good team. They had won in '68, but when I got there in '69 they were already thirteen games out. I don't know why. But I enjoyed playing there and played mostly shortstop again. I also made some fast friends. I still see Mickey Lolich, Al Kaline, Jim Northrup, and Mickey Stanley. And I was really close with Norm Cash until he died. In fact, since I'm still in the area, I see my Tiger buddies much more often than my Yankee buddies.

I didn't start playing for them until July, and I managed to hit fourteen home runs between then and the close of the season. I think only Willie Horton hit more in that same span of time. So it wasn't a bad year. Then, after the season ended, I went in for another operation. They finally had to fix the other side of the same knee I had hurt in New York. I took it real slow in spring training, just trying to get the leg in shape. I figured they knew what I could do and my goal was to be ready for the season.

Then, the day before we were scheduled to break camp and go north, I was released.

It was a shock to me and to the ballclub. No one had really seen me play all spring, but for some reason they decided to go with younger players. And because I hadn't played, the other teams must have figured my knee was really destroyed. That, and the timing of the release, made it almost impossible for me to hook up with another ballclub. In fact, because of the late release, they had to pay me my salary for the first sixty days of the season.

There's even an irony in that. When the pension plan was revised to go back a few years and pick up some additional people on the top line, the cutoff season was 1970. Everyone who played in 1970 and later got the top figure. Those who stopped playing before 1970, got considerably less. Well, because I hadn't played a single game in 1970, I didn't qualify for the top amount. Yet the ballclub paid me for part of that season. Some time later, there was an article in *The Sporting News* about the pension, and they used my case as an example. They estimated that had I played just one game that season, I would have eventually gotten some six hundred thousand additional pension dollars. That's projected over the life of the pension, with interest and all that. But a figure like that is enough to get you thinking.

Fortunately, I've been lucky, but there are plenty of ballplayers who could use extra money and today's players don't want to give it up. Yet the guys in my day were willing to bring everyone in on it. My father, in fact, helped to start the pension plan and we were always conscious of who came before us and who helped us. We felt the players were all part of a fraternity. Eventually, it won't be a problem, because the older players are gonna die off. But there are guys today sixty-five or seventy years old whose lives could be a whole lot easier with a few hundred dollars more a month.

Anyway, I would have liked to have played at least another season in Detroit, but it didn't work out that way. If I had been healthy and didn't have the knee injury, maybe I would have talked it over with my wife and continued. But I was also very family oriented and also believed in keeping my word. So I might have left after ten years as planned. As it turned out, I didn't have a choice.

Fortunately, there was no time to worry or fret about it. I went right from being released to trying to save the Kentucky Fried Chicken franchise I mentioned. I just jumped right in and did a lot of the work myself, often putting in twelve-hour days, and we slowly got the thing turned around to the point where it did quite well. And later the fact that I had persevered and had gotten my college degree began to pay off.

I went to work for Central Michigan University and have been there in a variety of capacities ever since. I started out as director of Corporate Giving, a newly formed department that raised money for the university. In a sense, I was trading on my name as a ballplayer then, but I felt that was something I earned, because I had always tried to present a certain image as a player and treat people fairly. Anyway, I did that for three years, then became involved in career placement and counseling, primarily in the business school. I helped youngsters from freshman to seniors, but mostly seniors, to decide what they wanted to do with a college degree in business and how to go about doing it. Part of that job was trying to attract businesses and corporations to the campus to interview students for jobs in marketing management and the computer sciences, all the business-related areas. I did that for twelve years.

Then about four years ago a unique opportunity came up. The baseball coach, Dave Keilitz, became athletic director, and his assistant, Dean Kreimer, became baseball coach. Dean and I were good friends and that gave me an idea. I was kind of anxious to get involved in some other things, one of which was getting back into baseball. I had started doing some fantasy camps and realized how much I missed the game. It was actually fun to go out and put the uniform on again. So I spoke to Dean about being his assistant, which was a half-time position. That was perfect. It gave me back baseball and it game me time. I took the job and have been doing that ever since.

We've got a great division I program and really get some good kids. In fact, we've won the Mid-American Conference title five years in a row. And since it's a half-time position, I have time for the fantasy camps, card shows, and some other things I am involved with now.

I've also had time to invent a portable sliding pad. Sliding is one skill we were never able to teach well. You can't do it indoors and even outdoors, repeated sliding takes a toll on the body. So I came up with a device, a twelve-foot mat with a loose surface on top of it, a tongue, that takes the friction when someone slides. There's a cloth between the person sliding and the pad itself. It works perfectly. With it we can practice tags at home plate, pickoffs, everything, indoors or out. Guys can slide all day. We call it Slide-Rite and right now it's in the patent pending stage. But it's something I'm really excited about, something that would be a great help with Little League right on up. It's not yet on the market, but we're getting closer. And because I went into coaching, I now have time for all these things.

I've also got a son, Mickey, who's in the Yankee organization. If he should make the majors, I guess we'd be the first three-generation family of big leaguers. Mickey's a shortstop and a hard-working one. But he's also got his college degree and a good off-season job with a large accounting firm. So one way or another, he'll be all right.

But there's still a great deal of pressure on him. I've tried to be a positive influence, but I know he's often compared to me, has people coming up to him and saying things like, you're not as good as your father and you don't have his power, or your dad was such a natural athlete. Things like that have really hurt him. But I love him so much and we have such a good relationship that I understand the pressure he's under. No one wants to play baseball more than he does. By the way, he's named after both my father and Mickey Mantle, the two people I really idolized the most. It's nice to remember both of them with one name.

The next year or two will probably determine whether Mickey gets there or not. As I said, I know he's under pressure and there have been times when I thought I was helping to relieve the pressures but instead I was only adding to them. So it's a tough situation, not as hard on me as it is on him, but hard nevertheless.

Yet with everything happening in my life, I still remember my days in baseball vividly. The Yankees were a great team when I joined them. Mickey, of course, was definitely the Yankee leader. Just his presence in the lineup made you feel you were going to win. Roger Maris was an outstanding individual as well, very close to his teammates and friends. It's too bad the public didn't really know him as we did. I've always felt there's no reason he shouldn't be in the Hall of Fame. Length of career shouldn't be the only thing that counts. Just the one act of hitting sixty-one homers should get him in there someplace. But he was also a great outfielder and a two-time Most Valuable Player. And the year he hit the sixty-one he was still sliding hard into second, taking guys out on double plays and diving after balls in the outfield. He wasn't just protecting himself so he could hit.

Elston Howard was also a class act. In fact, Clete Boyer, Bobby Richardson, Kubek, Whitey Ford, Hector Lopez, and Moose Skowron were all great guys.

The toughest pitcher I ever faced was Sandy Koufax. In the first game of the 1963 World Series, when he struck out fifteen of us, he was in a different league. I hit a homer off him for the only two runs that day, but he struck me out three times. He was simply the most overpowering pitcher I ever saw. I guess I just kept swinging the bat in the same place and he finally threw one there.

But the guy I really had the most trouble with in the majors was Stu Miller. He didn't throw very hard, but he would keep you off balance and was a real show to watch. There were so many great ones, though, I can't name them all. Guys like Jim Bunning,

Bob Gibson, Camilo Pascual, and Don Drysdale were all tough. I really feel I played the game in a great era. It's an era people really seem to remember. So many people still talk about it to me now, everywhere I go. There were so many great players then it was really fantastic, just unforgettable. And even though you can't take those memories to the bank, you'll always be able to take them to bed.

DALE
LONG

Pittsburgh Pirates, 1951
St. Louis Browns, 1951
Pittsburgh Pirates, 1955–1957
Chicago Cubs, 1957–1959
San Francisco Giants, 1960
New York Yankees, 1960
Washington Senators, 1961–1962
New York Yankees, 1962–1963

♦ **CURRENT STATUS** ♦

Represents the National Association of Professional Baseball Leagues, the governing body for all the minor leagues from Triple A down to Class A.

Like many players of his generation, Dale Long spent nearly a decade toiling in the minor leagues and waiting for his chance.

When he finally got his shot in 1955, he responded with sixteen homers, seventy-nine RBIs and a .291 batting average. He also tied the great Willie Mays for the National League lead in triples with thirteen.

During the next several years, the six-four, 205-pound native of Springfield, Missouri, proved himself a solid power hitter in the National League. In 1956, he set a record by hitting at least one home run in eight consecutive ballgames.

Traded several times over the next few years, Long was lucky enough to wind up as a member of the New York Yankees in both the 1960 and 1962 World Series. But he is often remembered more for being the man chosen by Branch Rickey to be the first left-handed catcher in the major leagues.

Born on February 6, 1926, Dale Long played ball in an era that produced a number of great ballplayers, and he was fortunate enough to be teammates with Roberto Clemente, Mickey Mantle, Ernie Banks, and Willie Mays. He was back in the news in 1988 when the Yankees' Don Mattingly tied his thirty-two-year-old record of eight homers in eight days.

There's an old saying that a pat on the back is just a few vertebrae away from a kick in the ass. One thing you didn't do was kick me. Pat me on the back and I'd go through the wall for you. And I guess that attitude often determined how I reacted to things during my baseball career.

A lot of it had to do with the handling of people. Baseball is not a friendly sport. The way people were treated, the way trades and releases were handled, those things caused me some bitterness when I left the game. When your productivity was done, they put you out to pasture. And I don't think it's any better today in that respect. The difference is that the players today are making a lot of money. For that reason alone, they should realize how lucky they are. They come into the ballpark with just their shoes and their glove and their jockstrap. That's the only thing they own, that and a little talent. But sooner or later, everyone finds that pitcher who'll get him out and that hitter who'll drive the ball down his neck. So it's best to always be a little humble.

I was always aware how people were handled throughout my career. Take managers, for instance. Playing for Casey Stengel was much different from playing for a Bob Scheffing or a Mickey Vernon. Those guys would just say, "Get a bat. Pinch-hit." But with Stengel, he would send you up there with goose bumps on your back. He'd say, "Hell, you can hit this guy. He's got good stuff, but that's what we got you over here for. Now go on up there." He'd make you want to do it.

It was this same kind of insensitivity that led to my being traded by the Pirates. The general manager of the team was Joe Brown. He was the son of the old comedian Joe E. Brown. Well, Joe and I got along good, because we had come up through the minors together. But he irked me one day and I told him where the bear shit in the buckwheat. In the long run it didn't turn out very good.

Joe had a bad habit of coming into the clubhouse when we won and staying out when we lost. And then when he did come in he'd shake the hands of the guys who did well and walk right past the guys who didn't. And all you needed at a time like that was a pat on the back and some encouragement to hang in there.

But he really shouldn't have been in the clubhouse in the first place, and I had it up to my ears with his routine. Then one day I put together a really good game and he came in to shake my hand. By then, everybody knew how I felt so they were agitating me. Bob Friend and Dick Groat began telling me that my pal was coming in to see me. So I said some things I shouldn't have said to Joe about his visits to the clubhouse. I apologized later and he said he'd forgive me. I told him, yes, he might forgive, but he wouldn't forget. And he didn't.

It happened again a few years later when I was with the Giants. The team was supposed to go to Japan to play at the end of the season. But a short time after the trip was announced, management began fingering out guys who weren't going, replacing some veterans who could have used the extra money with young players who hadn't been with the team all year. So Dave Philley, another veteran, and myself went to see Chub Feeney about it and raised a little fur. And on the next road trip to Chicago, I was traded to the Yankees and Dave Philley went to Baltimore.

Raise a little hell with the front office in those days and they would get you out of the way. That's what I mean when I say it wasn't always a friendly game.

But don't get me wrong. There were some good times, too, even though I had a long, ten-year haul to make it to the majors. I was born in Springfield, Missouri, but grew up in Green Bay, Wisconsin, home of the Green Bay Packers. In fact, it was because the Packers were there that I got my start in baseball.

I had joined the Navy in 1943 when I was seventeen, but I was in only for about nine months when I hurt my back and was discharged. So in the summer of 1944 I was back in Green Bay. I had played all three sports—baseball, football, and basketball—in high school, and while I enjoyed baseball, football was always my first love. I was pretty big already, about six-three, 190 pounds, and even had a chance to work out with the Packers that summer.

The Packers had an assistant coach then by the name of Red Smith. He was a pretty popular guy and they decided to hold a day for him. One of his friends who came up for the day was Casey Stengel. Casey was managing the minor league Milwaukee Brewers then, so he wasn't very far away. I just happened to be playing for a local team that night, the Green Bay Press Gazette. Funny thing was I didn't really want to play, but they needed a right fielder.

Well, that night I hit a home run and Stengel asked me to come to Milwaukee for a tryout with the Brewers. I could swing hard then, but I'd also miss a lot. I guess they saw something, though, because they signed me. The next year I went to spring training with the Brewers before ending up in Class D, where I began my long trek through the minors.

It wasn't unusual for players to stay in the minors six, eight, ten years back then. You almost had to go class by class as you slowly got a baseball education to the point where every phase of the game became a habit. A lot of the minor league teams were independent then, and they could trade you or release you. Or you might even be drafted by another team. So during the course of drifting through the minors, a player might be with teams affiliated with three or four major league organizations.

Milwaukee, for example, was independent, but they worked with the Cubs. Then in 1945 I was traded in Class D from Middletown, Ohio, to Lima, Ohio, and I landed in the Cincinnati organization. I was there in '45 and again in '46 when they decided I wasn't gonna make it and released me. So I went up to Massachusetts where my father was living, and contacted the Red Sox. They got me a tryout with a team in Lynn, Massachusetts, and after they signed me for 1947, they sent me to Oneonta, New York.

That's the way you could be dealt around the minors back then. At Oneonta I played for Red Marion, Marty Marion's brother, then went back to Lynn in '48 and from there was drafted in 1949 by Williamsport in the Eastern League. But you could be drafted only if it was a higher league. Lynn was Class B, Williamsport Class A. After that I was drafted again the next two years. Williamsport was affiliated with the Tigers, then Kansas City in Triple A drafted me. They were a Yankee farm team. And after they sent me back to Binghamton, I was finally drafted by Pittsburgh in 1951. That's when I met Branch Rickey and that's when he decided to make me a baseball oddity, a lefthanded catcher.

Billy Meyer was the manager of the Pirates in '51 and I think on the second or third day of spring training he walked up to me and said, "Mr. Rickey wants you to become a catcher." Just like that. I had never caught before. Besides, I was lefthanded and I told Meyer. He didn't even know it, so he called Rickey and said the kid's lefthanded. And Mr. Rickey said, "I know. That's what I want."

The news broke right away and I guess it was a pretty big deal back then. But Mr. Rickey always was an innovator and was probably looking all along for someone to turn into a lefthanded catcher. Because I started that very day. And before I knew it, he had ordered me three brand new catcher's mitts.

He also had a kid from the Cardinal organization in camp that year, a kid named Bobby Thomson, but not *the* Bobby Thomson. This Bobby Thomson had apparently struck out about 195 times batting righthanded. Mr. Rickey said he couldn't do worse left-handed and told him to switch. So this kid would get in the batting cage to face the pitching machine lefthanded and I was the catcher. He'd either miss or foul tip almost every pitch and I would keep getting hit. I used to catch two hundred balls in the morning, then back up Ralph Kiner—who was trying first base that year—in the game. Ralph would play two or three innings and I'd play six or seven. Then, after the game, I'd catch two hundred more balls as the kid Thomson tried to hit the pitching machine.

The hardest part of catching for me was the throw to second. Lefthanders seem to have a natural slider when they throw a ball any distance. The ball just wants to move. Outfielders allow for it, but I had problems with that throw. I remember Bill Dickey telling me the big problem would be handling a righthander's curveball in the dirt with a guy stealing third. I said, "Hey, Bill, that's a hard job for anybody."

Well, the experiment didn't last that long, but I still think that someday we'll see a lefty catcher. It's strictly tradition that's stopping it. Because everyone catches one-handed today there's no reason why it couldn't work, as long as he could handle that throw.

I started the '51 season with the Pirates, played ten games with them, and then went to the St. Louis Browns on something called a look-see option. They'd look at you for thirty days and if they liked you, they'd keep you. But if they didn't, they'd send you back. The Browns used to train with us in California and every time we played them I beat their heads in. I'd knock their pitching all over the place, so I guess they figured I was a pretty good deal. But by the time I got there Bill Veeck had bought the club and then you didn't know if you were on any roster at all. They had three teams—one coming, one going, and one playing. You had to buy a scorecard. And they were bad.

I played just thirty-four games for the Browns and then they shipped me back to the Pirates. And the Pirates sent me outright to New Orleans. It was discouraging. But my wife and I had a baby and I was driving an old Studebaker. I didn't want to quit, and when I hit thirty-four home runs at New Orleans in 1952, I thought again that I could do it. The next year I was at Hollywood [California], where we won the pennant and I was the MVP. But when Mr. Rickey sent me back to Hollywood in 1954, it was time to take a stand. I threatened to quit.

Mr. Rickey called me in and asked if I wanted to be placed on the voluntary retired list. I said, "That's right, sir." So he told me to put a letter in the mail to that effect. I said okay, and that's when he told me not to be hasty. He ended up paying me an additional two thousand dollars to stay in Hollywood that year, and the next spring, 1955, the Pirates told me the first-base job was mine until I proved I couldn't handle it. This time I stayed.

It wasn't unusual to see rookies my age back then. I was twenty-nine years old when I finally won a regular job. But people assumed in those days that you had to put in so much time in the minor leagues just to learn how to play the game. That's why these kids today make so many bad mistakes. It's strictly a matter of maturity. Careless mistakes, mental.

I had a pretty good rookie year. In fact, I tied Willie Mays for the league lead in triples with thirteen. The catching thing had ended when they sent me off to the Browns. When I returned I was strictly a first baseman. But Ralph Kiner always said that Mr. Rickey set me back four years with the catching and all that went with it. I even gave the three catcher's mitts away. Guys would use them for cushions on the bench.

If I had a weakness then it was the inside pitch. I could always hit the ball away from me. You have to know your own faults and I just knew I couldn't hit the ball in on me. Couldn't hit it with good mustard, anyway. The guy who helped me the most was George Sisler, the Hall of Famer. He got me to the point where I could handle them inside pretty well.

George was a Pirate coach then, though he didn't dress. But he could do a lot with you verbally. He knew hitting and I loved the guy. That's another thing you don't have today, kids listening to the older players. Some of them don't even know who Ted Williams was. But the old-timers liked to teach. Pie Traynor was always around the park in Pittsburgh; so was Paul Waner. And I remember Honus Wagner sitting in the dugout. He couldn't move around much, but we had a lot of respect for him and the other old-timers.

In Chicago, Rogers Hornsby would help us out. He was probably the worst batting instructor of the bunch for the simple reason he wanted everyone to hit like him. And no two people hit alike. I remember when Lou Boudreau was broadcasting for the Cubs he gave me some help and I really started hitting good. But when I gave him credit on a TV interview, he suddenly stopped talking to me. I asked him what was wrong, and he said the Cubs told him not to talk to me anymore because they already had a hitting instructor. Ain't that a crock.

Anyway, by 1956 I was established and had a real good year. That was also when I set the record with eight homers in eight straight games. I guess it started making news when I reached about five. When I got the sixth a photographer came out and took some pictures with seven bats and seven balls. I asked him what he'd do with the pictures if I didn't hit one. And he said probably throw them away. I'd been around the farm enough by then to know that if you do, you're a hero; and if you don't, you're a goat.

One reason I was able to set the record is that I had Frank Thomas, another home run hitter, behind me. All big home run hitters should have someone behind them. Ruth and Gehrig, Maris and Mantle, Mathews and Aaron, and Canseco and McGwire today. It always seems to work better that way. Then the pitchers can't go around them, they have to go through them.

The real good thing about the streak was that the Pirates were winning and I was also hitting over .300. Everything seemed to be going right. I was seeing the ball real well and my timing was perfect. I hit the seventh off Ben Flowers of the Dodgers, then the eighth off Carl Erskine. And the next day against [Don] Newcombe, I blasted one a mile to center field. But in old Forbes Field it was over 450 feet to center and Duke Snider circled under it and caught it. In most parks today, it would have gone out.

Unfortunately, things didn't last. In June, I fouled two pitches off the same spot on my ankle in two straight at-bats against a little lefty named Jackie Collum, who threw a screwball. I rolled around on the ground like a wounded elephant, but I kept playing. In those days there was no disabled list. I was black and blue from my knee to my foot, but I missed only four games. It turned out to be my misfortune because I went right down the drain after that. I heard Bobby Bragan, who was our manager then, saying that the big guy is hurt and that the team would have to scratch for one or two runs and then hold 'em. That's when I said I was all right and I'd play. That was the way guys did it in those days. They played. It wasn't the right way, but we did it. In my case I couldn't turn my foot when I'd stride and I just lost everything.

The next year, after just seven games, I was traded to the Cubs, the result of my run-in with Joe Brown the year before. But

I used to come back and beat the Pirates silly. I think I hit about .375 against them. The switch to the Cubs was easy. Mr. Wrigley, the owner, was a good person and it was fun playing the day games there. And that's when I finally got to catch in the major leagues.

It happened first in 1958. They pinch-hit for Sammy Taylor, who was the starting catcher. Then Cal Neeman came in, a quiet guy who rarely said anything. But on the first play he got into an argument with the umpire and was thrown out of the game. Bob Scheffing, the manager, looked around and realized he didn't have another catcher. Then I guess he remembered hearing about me. So I got back there with my first baseman's mitt.

Bill Henry was pitching, a lefthanded reliever. Wild Bill Henry. He was fast and every time he'd throw I'd blink. I remember he used to open his mouth when he threw, like he was going Ooooo. I asked him why he opened his mouth all the time and he said, "My arm goes by my ear so fast I have to let the pressure out."

But life goes on back there. I wouldn't call for a curve because I was afraid I couldn't catch it. After that first game they got me a glove. Rip Collins, the old Cardinals first baseman from the Gas House Gang days brought it out to me. He worked for the Wilson Company. I could catch anyone's smoke, even with the first baseman's mitt. Only if you caught it in the wrong spot your hand was in trouble. But catching is not an easy job. It's a rough, rough thing and that's why I give guys like Gary Carter, who sit back there day after day and year after year, a whole lot of credit.

Even though I enjoyed being with the Cubs it wasn't always easy being on a losing team, and there were times when I wondered if I'd ever get with a winner. You were still motivated because you had only a one-year contract. So all of us tried like hell to get some figures on the board to use in contract talks for the next year. And we also enjoyed playing the spoiler to the teams running for the pennant. That was fun. But then in 1960 I finally got my wish. In fact, I got it twice.

I was with the Cubs in spring training and one day Charlie Grimm told me he had good news. I had been traded to the Giants. I said thanks a lot. My wife was at the hairdresser, the car was in the garage, and my kids in school. When you're traded, you've suddenly got to change your whole outlook on where you're going. Instead of going east, I was suddenly going west.

At first, I enjoyed being there. We were in second place and doing well. Then they fired Bill Rigney and hired Tom Sheehan, a scout who used to hang around with [owner Horace] Stoneham. That upset me, because Rigney was doing a good job. Then the flap over the Japanese trip started and things were never the same. I was just pinch-hitting for them anyway. One day in August I was in the bullpen warming up Johnny Antonelli during the first game of a doubleheader. There was a perfect situation for a lefthanded pinch-hitter and Sheehan gave the sign for a hitter to come in from the pen. I start toward the dugout and he says, "Not you. Antonelli."

Well, Mays almost flipped. He said, "God damn, Tom. We're trying to win this game." He was really upset. But I found out later I had already been traded to the Yankees and they didn't want to announce it yet. Know how I heard about it? The people in the stands started yelling, "Hey, Dale, you just got traded to the Yankees." And I'm telling them they're full of shit. Later, Sheehan told me and said they didn't want to use me as a pinch-hitter because they didn't want me to get hurt and nullify the deal. I told Sheehan I could go out and get hit by a streetcar and it wouldn't make any difference. That's how stupid it was.

But it was a beautiful transition to the Yanks and I got to play in the World Series against my old friends from the Pirates. Casey was a great manager to play for and guys like Mantle, Maris, and Ford, their big stars, were all great. Then the next year I got caught in expansion and end up with the new Washington Senators. They platooned me with a kid named Bud Zipfel and a year later traded me back to the Yanks. Ford and Mantle told me I'd better behave or they'd trade me again. But I got into another World Series, this one against the Giants. Let me tell you, being the World Champs is a very special feeling.

In 1963 I was with the Yanks almost all year, but I didn't play much. The first time I had backed up [Moose] Skowron, now I was backing up [Joe] Pepitone. Then in September they decided to change the roster and they asked me to be a coach. So I was a coach when they lost the '63 Series to the Dodgers in four straight. I went home after the season, and one morning I was sitting down having a cup of coffee when I read in the paper that I was released. No phone call. Nothing. I was the last to know.

During the off-season I made a typical dumb ballplayer move. I bought a bar and restaurant in Adams, Massachusetts. It was the kind of thing where it looked good from one side of the bar, but not so good from the other. I did go down to Jacksonville in '64 when the Cardinals called me, but there were troubles with the bar and I just went home. My eyes were starting to bother me anyway. Plus my wife was getting sick and I had two kids in school. So it was time to make a decision. I was thirty-eight years old. How long could I play?

As I said, I did have some bitterness when I left. I missed spring training come March, going in with the guys, getting in shape and staying in shape. Things like that made it tough, as well as simply playing the game. Just swinging the bat. Those are the things you miss. And I guess in our minds we all think we can still play. But it just doesn't work that way. You body says, who me, I can't do that stuff anymore.

Looking back, I guess I was always awed by the outstanding players—Musial, Williams, DiMaggio, Mays, Mantle. Just the caliber of their talent, their productivity, what they could do. I played with Clemente when he was just a kid. He was erratic then, but he was producing. He could fly and he had an arm like a rifle.

Mays was probably the best ballplayer I ever saw. He was something else. I would pay the price of admission to see him play because he'd beat you in so many ways. Mantle was a fierce competitor who was so dedicated that he would hate himself for not producing. There wasn't a time when I didn't see him give every bit he had, even when his knees were shot.

Last year [1988], of course, Don Mattingly went out and tied my record of eight home runs in eight games. Another great player and a nice kid. To tell the truth, I kind of enjoyed the whole thing. The record had sat dormant for so many years. When he got to five or six, they started looking for me. I called him in Texas and congratulated him when he tied it, but I guess in some ways I was glad he didn't break it.

For six years after I quit I was completely out of baseball. I had the bar for a time, then went into sales. After that I was an ironworker for a while. I did a lot of different things to try to put bread on the table, and I was bitter because I felt I had something to show someone, but never had the opportunity to do it.

I wrote a lot of letters trying to get back into baseball and got a lot of Dear Johns in return. They'd say they were keeping my letter on file. And a lot of them were people who knew me. I think there are many former players who would like to get back in and just don't get the chance.

So for a while I was just living in Florida on my baseball pension. My wife had gotten sick and things were not easy. Then one day I was visiting St. Pete and talking to Lou Gorman of the Red Sox about getting maybe a scouting job. As usual, they were filled up. But Johnny Johnson happened to be sitting there. Johnny was with the Yankees when I was there and he asked me if I'd be interested in working for him, doing PR work. I said I'd love it.

It took nearly a year for it to happen, but the following March I became full-time. I work for the National Association of Professional Baseball Leagues, which is the governing body for all the minor leagues from Triple A down to A. Johnny Johnson passed away in January of 1988 and my boss now is Sal Artiago. Don Lee, a former big league pitcher, does the job on the West Coast and I'm on the East Coast.

I usually travel about eighteen or twenty thousand miles a year. We do PR work, speak to the kids about how to act as ballplayers. We help the clubs sell tickets by going to Rotary or Kiwanis lunches, and we run clinics. We also evaluate the ballparks, reporting on everything—the clubhouses, the fields, the restrooms, the concessions. We even check the lights. The price of a minor league club is outrageous today. Some of them are making a fortune.

So are the ballplayers. For that I say God bless them. But I also find a lot of them are selfish individuals. I got a fan letter recently from a guy who said it's a shame that the players today don't conduct themselves like the players of yesteryear. So what else can I say? They should remember that if they don't have the fans, they have nothing.

But the money must be there or they wouldn't pay them. They're very fortunate and shouldn't say anything bad about it. In fact, I'd love to play one more year, but not back in the 1960s. If I could play one more year, I'd much rather play it at the going rate of today.

MEL
PARNELL

♦ **MAJOR LEAGUE EXPERIENCE** ♦

Boston Red Sox, 1947–1956

♦ **CURRENT STATUS** ♦

Owner of pest control company in New Orleans, Louisiana.

To many baseball people of the time, Mel Parnell was an oddity, a lefthander who could win consistently at Fenway Park. But pitching in the old ballpark with the short left-field wall never bothered Parnell. He had his own way of pitching there, and it enabled him to win twenty-five games in 1949 and twenty-one more in 1953.

Born in New Orleans on June 13, 1922, Parnell's first pitching idol was Hall of Famer Herb Pennock, a player he saw only in photos and later in films. But he quickly found his own style and won fifteen games in his first full season, 1948. A member of the powerful Boston teams of the late 1940s and early '50s, Parnell was a central figure in several tight pennant races.

He pitched especially well against the rival New York Yankees, beating them five straight times in 1952 with four of the wins via the shutout route. An arm injury suffered when he was hit by a pitch helped to shorten a career that saw Parnell as one of the American League's most stylish pitchers for five seasons.

Even in his final year, Parnell had enough left to pitch the only no-hitter of his career, an achievement he still remembers vividly today. When his career ended he became first a minor league manager and later a Red Sox broadcaster, noting that the game looked infinitely easier from the broadcast booth than it did on the playing field.

I never had trouble pitching at Fenway Park. Like every other lefthanded pitcher, I had heard that Fenway was a graveyard for southpaws, mainly because of the Green Monster in left field. When I first came up people were always telling me that the short distance in left gave the hitter the advantage and that I should work righthanded hitters outside. But I had another theory.

For years, I think I was the only lefthanded pitcher who worked them inside. I always felt it was best to come in tight, because if I tried to hit the outside corner of the plate and missed to the inside, then I was down the middle where the hitters could swing with their arms extended. And that's where their power comes from. But by throwing inside I was still making it tough for the batter to get good wood on the ball, even if I missed the corner. And since I was a lefty and throwing on the angle to a righthanded hitter that way, the left-field wall never became a factor. I can't remember ever giving it a thought and I threw very few home runs there.

In fact, I always worked all the Yankee power hitters that same way. By keeping the ball tight on them, I would force them to swing with their elbows as close to their bodies as possible. And by doing that, I'd be taking away most of their power. After a while, they knew I'd be pitching them that way, yet they still couldn't do anything about it, because my slider would move in on them. The result was always a lot of broken bats, and they used to complain about it to me. I can remember them breaking six or seven bats in a game. Hank Bauer used to really get sore about it and give me the business. I think Bauer and Mantle always broke the most bats, and through it all I'd just keep throwing my slider inside.

Most times, my slider was my out pitch. I also used a fastball, curve, and sinker, depending on which one was working the best on a particular day. The slider wasn't as popular in the late 1940s and early fifties as it is today. In fact, I think Don Newcombe was one of the few pitchers who used it in the National League back then. But I basically mixed the slider with the other three pitches. What I would do was use the slider to back a righthanded hitter off the plate a bit, then come back with a sinker outside. If he moved up again, I'd return to the slider. So I kept working in and out, always giving the hitters a lot of movement and changing speeds.

Lefthanded batters, in a lot of cases, seemed to have a mental thing about facing a southpaw hurler. Some of them just quit. I remember Ferris Fain, when he was winning two straight batting titles with the old Philadelphia A's. He was mentally whipped whenever he faced me. He would give me a friendly hello before the game and I could tell he was already on my side.

Because a lot of teams pitched righthanders in Fenway, Ted Williams never felt as if he saw enough lefties. So he'd often ask me to pitch batting practice to him, but to pitch as if it were game conditions, throwing the pitch I wanted. I always felt this helped me a lot because if I could figure out Ted Williams, the rest of the guys would come a lot easier.

Ted was the greatest hitter I ever saw. Of course, I didn't get to see some of the earlier greats of the game, but just watching him was always a great thrill. He simply could handle the bat and he had tremendous concentration. I remember one day we were playing the Yankees in Fenway and Ted was called out on strikes against Frank Shea. He was pretty upset when he came back to the dugout and he got into an argument with our manager, Joe Cronin. Ted insisted that home plate was out of line.

I was sitting with a couple of other pitchers and we started laughing. We thought he was making a strange excuse for striking out. Well, he kept insisting that someone take some measurements. And the next morning he got Cronin and the ground crew to come out early, about 9:00 A.M., to measure home plate. I'll be damned if he wasn't right. Home plate was out of line, a little to the left of where it should have been. It just showed how much he would concentrate up there. To all of us pitchers, the plate looked perfectly normal. Ted didn't forget, either. He always insisted he would not have struck out if the plate hadn't been out of line.

My own pitching career didn't begin until I was in high school. I was born in New Orleans and had been in love with baseball from the time I was seven or eight years old. We had a Class A team in the Southern League then and I used to go out to the park to watch them play. There were a number of future big leaguers playing there, guys like Tommy Henrich, Roy Weatherly, Joe Dobson, Bill Zuber, and Denny Galehouse.

The first pitcher I came to idolize was Herb Pennock and most of that came from articles I read as a kid. I knew he was a big winner and I saw pictures of him with that high kick and smooth delivery. Yet I was mostly a first baseman and outfielder in the neighborhood. The pitcher was always Howie Pollett, who also went on to a big league career. I became a pitcher once I started throwing batting practice in high school. My ball seemed alive and the players began to complain to the coach. That's when he asked me to pitch. Of course, I said I'd do anything just to play.

Even though I pitched only about six games in high school I was scouted by the Red Sox and Cardinals, and I chose to sign with the Red Sox. They came to look at a hitter named Ed Levine one day, and I happened to strike out seventeen batters in that same game. I got peanuts for a bonus, but it had always been my dream to play in the majors, so I didn't care at the time.

I was in the low minors in 1941, then started 1942 at Scranton in the Eastern League. But shortly after the season began I was drafted into the service and didn't return to baseball until 1946. Fortunately, I played a lot of ball in the service, and the caliber of play was so good that it was almost like playing in the minors. In fact, while I was pitching in the service, a veteran pitcher from the Phillies, Hugh Mulcahy, saw me and told me if I could get a release from the Red Sox he could get me seventy-five thousand dollars right quick from Philadelphia. So I called Joe Cronin and asked for a release and he said, "Don't be ridiculous. There's no way we're going to release you." Of course, I didn't tell him why I wanted a release then, but when I told him about it later he just laughed and said he figured something was up.

When I came out in 1946 the Red Sox had so many good players they didn't know what to do with them all. I played with Scranton in the Eastern League, and I think that team was even better than the Sox' Triple A team at Louisville. We won the pennant by nineteen and a half games and I was something like 13–4 with a league-leading 1.50 earned run average. We had future major leaguers like Sam Mele, Sam Dente, and Al Kozar, and a pitching staff of Tommy Fine, Mickey McDermott, Jocko Thompson, and me. And by the end of the season I felt I was getting close. The comments from the scouts and opposing managers told me my day was coming.

It came the next season. The Sox had two openings on the pitching staff in 1947 with six guys vying for the spots. It was the two rookies who made it, Harry Dorish and myself. That didn't make us the most popular guys on the team, because the four who didn't make it were veterans, and the other vets looked down on us because their buddies were cut. When we broke camp and headed north I was rooming with Frankie Hayes, the old veteran catcher. I was almost afraid to go to bed at night because I half expected him to try to throw me out the window. Frankie was a dyed-in-the-wool veteran and not thrilled that his pals were gone. This wasn't unusual then, and there was a lot of hostility.

But despite that, it was a thrill being there, being at the top of the profession. But it lasted only half a year in '47, because Cronin decided I needed regular work and sent me back to Louisville in midseason. Wouldn't you know it, I broke a finger there and didn't get the work anyway.

I was up again to stay in '48, went 15–8, and we lost the pennant to the Indians by one game. The next year, 1949, everything started to fall in line for me. I was pretty much of a slow starter in the cool weather. But in '49 we had a warm spring and I got off to a good start. I avoided injuries, didn't have any arm trouble, and wound up winning twenty-five games. I think I led the league in five different categories that year.

Ellis Kinder was right there with me. He won twenty-three and everything was almost perfect until the final two games of the year. We led the Yankees by one and had two to play against them in New York. I pitched the first game and left with the score tied at 4–4. They tied it when DiMaggio hit a ball back through the middle that just went off the end of my glove. A game of inches. If I had caught it I would have been out of the inning. Joe Dobson came in and Johnny Lindell wound up beating us with a home run. Ellis then pitched the last game and they won it 5–3 when Jerry Coleman hit a little blooper over second to drive in the winning runs. Al Zarilla made a dive for a ball and tore up his knee on the play. Believe me, it was long train ride back to Boston that night.

We were down, really disappointed that we didn't win, but we still got a great reception from the fans in Boston. I didn't realize how much all those innings [295.1] had taken out of me until I got home. I was about twenty-five pounds underweight and my doctor told me I looked terrible. Because of the pennant race, Ellis Kinder and I were either in the game or in the bullpen the last nineteen days of the season. That had a telling effect and that's when we pretty much drained ourselves. There was a lot of physical fatigue. We'd often pitch on three days' rest and I recalled on one occasion starting with only two days' rest and once relieving against the Yanks on two days' rest.

Back then I really didn't worry about what it might be doing to my arm. You did what you had to do, and when you got called on you went out and did the job that was expected of you. If there was a problem I would have said something, but my arm felt good all year and I just did what I was being paid to do.

Winning the pennant then was important for two reasons. Our salaries weren't that high, so naturally we wanted the money. But we also wanted the ring. That was the big thing. It was something to be proud of. Even right now I'm wearing a ring from the 1949 All-Star Game and the World Series ring would have even been better. But money also plays a big part and if anyone says it doesn't they're not being truthful.

The Red Sox back then were a pretty close-knit ballclub. In fact, they were that way during my entire stay in Boston, a great bunch of guys. We were often called the Country Club Ballclub because of [owner] Tom Yawkey's kindness to us, but that really wasn't the case. I think the press abused Mr. Yawkey with that. He was a good person and a great fellow to play for, but he never spoiled any of us. We just had a very good team.

Mr. Yawkey did pay real well, but because of that we always felt we had to give him 1,000 percent. We knew we had to go overboard and play the very best we possibly could. The man was simply deserving of it. He appreciated our efforts, but he would never come down to the clubhouse or do anything to spoil a player. After I pitched my no-hitter he did offer me a new contract, which I graciously signed, but that was the only thing he did out of the ordinary for me.

Of course, having Ted Williams drawing a large salary helped the rest of us. It kind of pulled our salaries up and gave us a little more to argue about or request. My top salary was seventy-five thousand dollars and we had some other great names on the ballclub, guys like Dom DiMaggio, Bobby Doerr, and Johnny Pesky, who were also drawing top dollar. So we did have a high payroll on the club. But all of those guys could play.

Bobby Doerr in my opinion was the greatest person I ever met in the game of baseball, on or off the field. He was a perfect gentleman and a great player to have behind you. You could always depend on Bobby making that play for you. He was one of the best pivot men on the double play and a player very deserving of being in the Hall of Fame.

Johnny Pesky was a great shortstop. Johnny and Dom DiMaggio were one of the best one-two punches at the top of a lineup. Dominic was good at getting on base, while Pesky had the bat control to move him over. He could pull the ball or go the other way with it. Good ballplayers. And John formed a great double-play combination with Doerr.

Dominic was the most underrated center fielder I've ever seen. You always hear names like Terry Moore and Joe DiMaggio mentioned as great outfielders, but I think Dom was just as good as any of them. He played a little more shallow than the others and was the only one I knew who could come in and reach down for a line drive without breaking stride. That's hard to do. He didn't really have a rivalry with his brother, but he did resent being called Joe's little brother. He didn't like that at all and would tell people to just call him Dominic.

Ellis Kinder was a different type of pitcher than I was, so I guess we made a good combination. Ellis had one of the best changeups in baseball and a good, live fastball. Plus he was a gutty individual who wouldn't give in to any hitter. He also had what we called a rubber arm, never came up with an ache or pain. He could walk out of the dugout, grab a ball, take three or four warmup pitches and be ready to go into the ballgame. He had an arm like I've never seen, and in that way was unbelievable.

There were plenty of good pitchers in the league back then. I guess the Yanks and Tigers had the two best staffs that we faced. Whenever I went up against the Yanks I knew my opponent would either be [Vic] Raschi or [Allie] Reynolds, especially in Fenway. Whitey [Ford] didn't have good luck there and after a while wouldn't pitch in Boston. Casey would bypass him in Fenway. [Eddie] Lopat would pitch there on occasions, depending on how they could work their rotation. But he was a different type of pitcher than Ford. He would throw a lot of soft stuff and could spot a pitch on a needlehead. He had perfect control.

Reynolds on certain days was as fast as any pitcher in baseball. He wasn't as consistently fast as a Walter Johnson or someone of that type, but on certain days he was quick. He pitched a no-hitter against me in New York and on that day his fastball made us look bad. That was the game where Ted fouled the ball to Yogi for what looked like the final out. But Yogi dropped it, and no one ever wanted to give Ted Williams a second chance. But Reynolds got him to foul one in almost the identical spot and this time Yogi caught it.

The Tiger staff had some hard throwers. Both Virgil Trucks and Dizzy Trout were fastball pitchers. If they had good placement—I guess they call it location today—they had no trouble. Hal Newhouser had the best curveball I'd seen. You could see it right out in front of the plate, but when you'd swing at it, it wasn't there. It would break in front of the plate at the last moment.

Another great lefty who didn't pitch much in Fenway was Herb Score. He dropped some games there early in his career and after that they bypassed him. But I remember the first time he pitched there as a rookie in 1955. I was pitching against him and the first time I went up to hit the guys told me to be ready because he was real fast. I was a pretty good hitter and I went up there with my hands down the end of the bat. Well, he threw me a fastball and I started to swing. But before I could get the bat around—POW!—I thought the catcher's glove exploded.

Now I realized that this guy was even faster than I thought, so I choked up about a foot on the bat. On the next pitch I threw the bat out in front of the ball, got a piece of it, and it went off the left-field wall for a double. I went back to the dugout and told the guys that Score wasn't so tough, that I just ripped the wall off him. Of course, it was his speed that was responsible for the double, and he got me three straight times after that. But I played that hit for all it was worth.

After 1949, things didn't go quite as well. I had a pair of eighteen-win seasons, then fell to twelve–twelve in 1952. I had a little knee problem that year and was concerned about it. I was only thirty, but I began to wonder if my career might be coming toward the end. But when that happens you just have to get on with it and try to make adjustments. I never talked to coaches much. I always preferred talking to other pitchers, someone who might be going through the same thing on the mound.

I also didn't work out in the off-seasons. Instead, I would try to rest and regain my strength because I pitched a lot of ballgames. So I tried to get back some of the weight I'd always lose and just played softball on Sundays. Then in 1953 I came back and won twenty-one games. I felt real good about it, especially because I beat the Yankees in all five starts, and four of them were shutouts. I took a lot of enjoyment in that, because the Yanks were a great team and heated rivals. Pitching against them always brought a little more out in me. If you pitched against a team like the St. Louis Browns, you were supposed to win. But beating the Yankees was something extra.

It was always a great rivalry. The cities were fairly close together and the crowds often seemed split fifty-fifty. There were times I remember going into Yankee Stadium when we actually felt like the home team because we got the greater applause. And sometimes in Fenway it was just the reverse. It was always a foregone conclusion that we would play extra hard against them. No one had to come out and say it. But as heated as the rivalry was back then, there was always a lot of kidding between the teams.

Yogi, of course, was a good one for that. And there were times when some of them would try to get me into a conversation to find out what kind of pitches I'd be throwing. Tommy Henrich was another one who often did that. He'd sometimes take a pitch and then ask what in the world that was. I'd say, "I don't know. It probably got caught in a little cross wind that made it move that way." I wasn't about to tell him.

But 1953 was a great year. I felt that I was all the way back. But baseball can be a funny game. It didn't take long for things to change. One of my teammates and friends from 1948 to '53 was Mickey McDermott. Mickey was a lefty with one of the best arms I'd ever seen. But he never really matured, stayed a kid all through his career, and it hurt him. He never seemed to take the game seriously enough. Then in 1954 he was traded to Washington and early in the season was pitching against me.

We were planning to have dinner together after the game. That was before he hit me. Mickey threw me a fastball that looked as though it was headed for the inside of the plate. I started to swing and the ball suddenly sailed up and in. I threw my arm up to protect my face and it broke a bone just above my left wrist. Mickey was so upset he came into the clubhouse as soon as the inning was over. I think it hurt him more than it did me then. He had tears in his eyes, but I told him to forget it. It was just one of those things.

I was out a couple of months, but then tried to come back too soon and it really messed me up. The club was hurting for pitching that year and they asked me to throw. I really shouldn't have, but sometimes you don't realize these things until it's too late.

So I came out of it with some shoulder problems and that was really the beginning of the end. I took it slow in spring training the next year, looking to be ready by opening day, but the effectiveness just wasn't there. I had lost some velocity on both the fastball and slider. Then I tried to change my style and the more I tried, the worse it got. I still wasn't thinking about retirement, but I knew the twilight was nearing and I wanted to try everything to stop that from happening, or to find something else that would be helpful.

I had a bad year in 1955 [2–3, 7.83 ERA in thirteen starts], but then did a little better in '56. That was the year I pitched the no-hitter. Everything worked perfectly that day. I had a great sinker and could put it anywhere I wanted. I remember during the seventh inning Jackie Jensen came up to me and said, "Look, fella, you're pitching a no-hitter. Don't let someone hit the ball to right because I don't want to be the guy to mess it up." I think he was just kidding, trying to keep me loose, because Jackie was a great athlete and very competitive. But the no-hitter was a highlight, something I still think about today.

Then, after the 1956 season, I needed elbow surgery. I had a nerve that got caught between the bone and the elbow and also a muscle that was torn from the bone and had to be wired back. I don't even know how it happened. But it just took more away. I didn't have the good liveliness in my arm anymore, the good snap in it. I tried to get into shape during spring training, but the club had put me on the disabled list. I kept working, but it didn't really improve. Finally Joe Cronin and I decided that was it.

The whole thing was very depressing. I'd go on the road with the ballclub, but my heart wasn't in it because I knew my time was up. My teammates tried to be encouraging, but most of them knew what was happening because we had all seen it so many times with other guys. So it's not shocking or surprising, and I was pretty much prepared for it. I had tried my best and it just wasn't there anymore.

I simply left the team quietly in the middle of the season. We were on the road and I went back to Boston to gather my stuff and then went home. Before I left I said goodbye to everyone and wished them luck. Believe me, the immediate transition wasn't easy. I followed the team religiously through the rest of the season and caught them on TV whenever I could. I had also made quite a few good friendships in Boston over the years, and I'd call people constantly so they could bring me up to date on the team.

For the first year I kind of stayed home and tried to readjust. I had an association with a Plymouth dealership in New Orleans, where they would use my name and I got a royalty in return. But I really didn't work. Then in 1959 the mayor of New Orleans asked me to manage the New Orleans Pelicans in the Southern League. They were trying to save the franchise and I did it for a year, but the team folded anyway.

After that, the Red Sox asked me to manage in the minors for them. I managed in Texas, Pennsylvania, and Seattle. I enjoyed it, but after three years decided it wasn't what I wanted. The lower minors were more enjoyable. The higher I got, the more disciplinary problems I found and I didn't want to be mother-father-doctor-lawyer-policeman.

After that I began broadcasting for the Red Sox, doing color with Curt Gowdy. One thing I noticed was how easy the game looked from the booth. You couldn't really see the movement of the ball. Now I knew how people in the stands could watch a pitcher and say, "I could hit this guy." You can't see that sharp movement. Anyway, I stayed with the Red Sox until 1969, then went over to the White Sox for a year. But by then it was getting to be monotonous and I was tired of the travel. It was time to go home and be with my family.

Because I had a year to go on my contract, I had to find an acceptable replacement. I finally got Billy Pierce, because they wanted another former ballplayer. That was in 1970 and was my last association with baseball. Then I had to look for a new career.

I had done some public relations work for a pest control company in New Orleans with Al Hirt and Pete Fountain, two great guys. Anyway, I thought I'd like the business and I decided to start my own pest control company. It's gone well and I've had it ever since.

Of course, I still think of my career quite often. Sometimes I wonder what would have happened if I hadn't put my arm in front of that Mickey McDermott fastball. I also think about the hitters I faced, guys like Mantle and DiMaggio, who I did well against, and a guy like Jim Hegan, who wore me out. The toughest guy to fool was Luke Appling. He was the easiest guy in the world to get two strikes on. But just try to get that third one.

The pitchers today seem to rely more on speed than anything else. A lot of the younger ones just want to throw the ball past the hitters. You can get away with it now and then, but after a while it's gonna catch up with you. Every good pitcher changes speeds and spots the breaking ball. A guy who just stands out there and pumps it can be effective on the day he has his real good stuff. But on the day when he loses a little bit of it, then he becomes nothing more than a batting practice pitcher. And that day comes for all of us, sooner or later.

JAKE GIBBS

♦ **MAJOR LEAGUE EXPERIENCE** ♦

New York Yankees, 1962–1971.

♦ **CURRENT STATUS** ♦

Head baseball coach at Ol' Miss, the University of Mississippi, in Oxford, Mississippi.

Jake Gibbs came out of the University of Mississippi as an All-American quarterback who led his team to a 29–3–1 record over three varsity seasons. But with a possible pro football career in the offing, Gibbs surprised a lot of people by signing with the New York Yankees for a one-hundred-thousand-dollar bonus in 1961.

Three years later, in 1964, he was a last-minute addition to the Yanks' World Series roster, only to break two fingers in the final inning of the final game of the year. So Gibbs missed his only chance to participate in the fall classic. For he had joined the

Yanks at a time the Bronx Bombers were beginning their fall from grace.

Yet he became a solid catcher for the team, and during his career played alongside such Yankee greats as Mickey Mantle, Yogi Berra, and Whitey Ford. He observed firsthand how difficult it was for these Hall of Fame players to experience losing for the first time. It was also difficult for Gibbs, who had also played for winning teams all his life.

A throwback to the old school of hard-nosed athletes, Jake Gibbs always gave a 100 percent effort on the field. He ended his baseball career prematurely when he received an offer to return to his alma mater as head baseball coach, but the Yanks showed their appreciation by giving him a "day" at Yankee Stadium, a memory he has treasured ever since.

About a week before the 1964 season ended, Tony Kubek hurt his throwing hand and had to be taken off the World Series roster. I had been in the minors the entire year until September, but Yogi Berra and his staff decided I would take Tony's place. The Yanks were about to clinch their fifth straight American League pennant, and the whole thing was almost unbelievable to me.

We clinched the pennant the second-to-last day of the season against Cleveland and I said to myself, "Looky here, this ol' boy is going to the World Series!" Then the last day of the season Yogi puts me in as his catcher. The game goes thirteen innings and in the thirteenth and final inning, I take a foul tip and break two fingers! So I get pulled from the Series roster and Mike Hegan gets put on.

But I had a good attitude. My first impression was, the hell with it. We'll win the pennant again next year and then I'll get in the World Series. But it never came; it never came. Six years later it never came. So I missed by one inning. I got my ring out of it, but I didn't even go with the team. Instead, I went back to Mississippi.

I guess you could say I came to the Yankees at the end of an era. Everyone knows how the team totally dominated baseball for so many years, and I got there just as the ballclub began to go downhill. But that didn't make it any less of a thrill to be a Yankee. That will never change.

I signed with the Yankees on May 25, 1961, and went to New York that very same day. I had only been in New York City one time before. That was when I was on the *Ed Sullivan Show* as part of the *Look* magazine All-American football team. I came up with guys like Joe Bellino, E. J. Holub, Bob Lilly, people like that. But my second trip was to join the Yanks.

The plan was for me to spend about eleven days with the ballclub before going to the minors and I can remember the plane flying right over Yankee Stadium before it landed. I looked down and didn't believe it. It was like a fantasy thing. You wish, you wish and you hope. And all of a sudden here it is.

I didn't know much about the Yankees then except that they were the best team in baseball. That was probably the reason I chose them over Milwaukee and Houston, two other teams that were interested in signing me. The Yankees were the best team in baseball and at that time Ol' Miss was probably the best football team in the South. During my time there we were 29–3–1. And I think that was on my mind as much as anything. I was leaving a winner and going to a winner.

The picture of walking into Yankee Stadium for the first time is still clear in my mind. Ralph Houk was there to greet me. Then I met Mickey Mantle, Whitey Ford, Yogi Berra, Moose Skowron, people like that. In fact, Moose Skowron told me not to pay any attention to the ribbing I might get. "If they say anything it's just in friendship," he told me, and that made me feel good. And when

I met Yogi he said to me, "It's about time you got here." Stuff like that made me feel right at home.

But it was scary, as well. You know, country boy comes to New York, walks into Yankee Stadium and meets guys like that. Just the feeling that all of a sudden you're a New York Yankee can be frightening. But everyone went out of their way to be nice, and after I was there a short time I actually felt comfortable, really at ease. By the end of that first day I knew I had made the right choice.

It's funny, but even though I came from football country in the Deep South, baseball was always a big part of my life. I probably started playing on the sandlots when I was about eight years old, while I didn't play football until I was a freshman in high school. I was born in Grenada, Mississippi, in 1938. They had a semipro league in the area back then, and I really used to live at the ballpark. My brother and I would come home after the game and try to imitate the styles of the guys we saw. That's really how I learned some of the fundamentals—like fielding a ground ball and turning my hips into a throw—by watching the semipro players and imitating them.

But I think the one thing that really started me dreaming about baseball was the Game of the Day radio broadcasts that we used to hear in Grenada when I was a kid. This was about 1950 or '51, when I was about twelve or thirteen. Al Helfer was the announcer and it seems now that every game was between the Yankees and Detroit Tigers. I remember hearing about guys like Hal Newhouser, Vic Wertz, Dizzy Trout, Virgil Trucks, Johnny Lipon, DiMag, Yogi. But I became a Tiger fan back then and could name the entire Detroit team. In fact, I met Hoot Evers years later and told him how I used to listen to him play the outfield. He laughed.

We sometimes watched pro football on Sundays back then on our old black-and-white sets, but I never had the same exposure to it as I had to baseball. The Game of the Day really planted the seed and I used to sit there and dream about playing major league ball. And looking back, I think that really had a lot to do with my choosing baseball over football.

The first choice I had to make came during my senior year in high school. I had made the high school team as a second baseman when I was in the seventh grade. In fact, my brother was the shortstop and my cousin the third baseman and two brothers who lived in our neighborhood played first and the outfield. So we kind of had a monopoly on the team.

Anyway, I saw my first scout when I was a senior. One of the first to come down was Dixie Walker, who had played with the Dodgers. Dixie was scouting for the Braves at the time and he came to Grenada to see me play. He went up to the top row of the bleachers to get a good view, I guess, and leaned back to watch the game. The problem was there was no backrest and he fell all the way to the ground and broke his collarbone. So while I was playing, Dixie was in the Grenada hospital.

I guess I could have signed with someone out of high school, but I knew all along I wanted to go to college. Mother and Daddy had talked it over and they wanted their sons to go to college. That was a good thing in my mind. I felt it was important to have that education behind me. Plus I wanted to play college football anyway and only had to choose between Ol' Miss and Mississippi State. I picked Ol' Miss and went up to Oxford, which was only about fifty miles from Grenada.

I played a lot as a sophomore and won the starting job as a junior. That year I led the Southeastern Conference in total offense and the guy who finished second was Fran Tarkenton at Georgia. My senior year, Fran was the total offense leader and I was second to him. We had a play action offense with a lot of bootlegs and sprintouts. So I had a lot of options to either throw or run.

There was never a problem with my arm. I could always stand on the fifty yard line and throw the ball through the goalposts. When I thought about playing pro football I never worried about my size, either. In fact, Fran and I were about the same size, and everyone knows the kind of pro quarterback he became. I knew the pro people wanted bigger quarterbacks, but I was still drafted.

The Philadelphia Eagles called me during my senior year and said they were thinking of making me their number-one draft choice. But I told them I wasn't going to choose between football and baseball until I had played my final season as a third baseman at Ol' Miss. When they heard that they hemmed and hawed around, then said they might pick me up on a later round. I guess they wanted a definite commitment from me.

I had a great year in 1960. I was an All-American, the MVP of the Sugar Bowl. [Jake scored both Ol' Miss touchdowns in a 14–6 victory over Rice.] And I finished third in the Heisman Trophy voting to Joe Bellino of Navy.

Even though I wound up choosing baseball, I still feel there's nothing more exciting than college football. Back then in Mississippi it was football, football, football. It got most of the publicity and was the thing down South. Even today, more people remember me for football even though I played seven years with the Yankees. People still say to me they wish I had gone into pro football.

College baseball was a different atmosphere, a different kind of environment. Football was intense all the time, rah rah, big crowds. And I always felt I couldn't have a bad Saturday. I was fortunate to play for a guy like Coach [John] Vaught. We had a powerhouse team, a dominating team, and there was a lot of prestige involved being a part of it. Yet somewhere deep down inside, baseball still had that hold on me.

I was an All-American for three years, though my junior year was actually my best. I think the pressure got to me as a senior, because every time I looked up there were ten or fifteen scouts in the stands. You know you should shake it off and just play your game, but the subconscious thing comes into it. So that was the pressure, not deciding between baseball and football.

I'd say the old Houston Colt 45s and the Braves were most interested in me. The Yanks didn't come along until my senior year. Although I was told later that they also had their eye on me for five years. But Houston and Milwaukee saw me play the most and after my junior year the Braves offered me one hundred thousand dollars to sign. I turned it down.

It may sound crazy, but I just felt I could not leave Ol' Miss at that time. They were counting on me as their number-one quarterback and I guess it was loyalty to the school. My family didn't have a whole lot of money. Daddy made enough to get us by, and an offer of one hundred grand was like a gold mine. So it was a big decision, but we turned it down. I stayed and got my degree, which meant if I didn't make it in pro ball I could always come back, get a coaching job, and make a living. But then the Yanks came along and gave me the same money as the Braves had offered.

So I joined them in '61 and spent that great eleven days with the team. After three or four days at the Stadium we left by train for Boston. I hadn't ever been on a train before and I remember sitting in the lounge car with Mickey, Tony Kubek, and some of the other Yankees. They were asking me all kinds of questions about football . . . until I crossed my legs. Before I left Mississippi I had bought about six new pairs of argyle socks and had one of them on that day. When I crossed my legs, Mickey looked over and said:

"Jake, you all got a lot of rattlesnakes in Mississippi?"

I said, "Yeah, we do, Mick."

And he said, "Well, you can take them damned socks off because we don't have no rattlesnakes up here."

So I got indoctrinated real quick about my dress. Those socks had some wild colors in them. Like I said, my first eleven days with the Yankees were a real experience.

From there, I went to Richmond to begin my minor league career. Dan Topping, who was one of the Yankee owners then, flew me down personally in his own private jet, me and Jesse Gonder, who was with the team then. I was still playing second and third. It wasn't until I came out of a six-month stint in the

National Guard in the spring of 1963 that they decided to make me a catcher.

The whole thing was Ralph Houk's idea. Yet when I was at Fort Gordon in Georgia, in 1962, an army captain saw my name and asked me if I was the Gibbs who played baseball. When I said yes, he said, "I hear you're gonna be a catcher come spring training." I couldn't believe it. I didn't know this captain from Adam and he knows I'm gonna be a damned catcher in the spring. So I said to him, "Captain, that's the last thing I'm gonna be, a catcher." He said he got it from the general manager at Augusta, which was a Double A team of the Yanks. I said, no way.

Don't you know the first day I walk into Fort Lauderdale Ralph Houk pulls me aside and says he wants to make me a catcher. Right away I thought about that army captain at Fort Gordon. Anyway, he said they had Elston Howard with John Blanchard behind him, but nobody else. No good young catchers coming up. He also told me it was a way for me to get to the big leagues faster and to stay longer.

I think Ralph felt that in some ways a catcher was like a quarterback, giving signs, running the show, and being a leader. He said they all felt I could do it and he asked me to try it for a week. Then if I didn't like it, they'd put me back in the infield.

Well, it wasn't easy. First I got a mitt. It was the kind Jim Hegan used, with one pocket in the middle and no break in it. You had to catch with two hands. I just warmed up the pitcher for the first two days, but the third day Ralph wanted me to catch batting practice. So I got all the stuff on to catch and you talk about a man blinking. Every time the ball came in, I blinked. But when the week was up, I agreed to try it a second week, and that did it. From then on, I worked to be a catcher.

Don't get me wrong, it was still a tough road. I broke a couple of fingers in '63 and was concentrating so hard on being a catcher that my batting average went down. In fact, at one point I told my wife, Tricia, that I was gonna call Blanton Collier and see if he wanted a beat-up old quarterback. Blanton had been the coach at

Kentucky in our conference and had just been named head coach of the Cleveland Browns. That was the closest I ever came. But I didn't call him, and after catching thirty-five or forty games in the Instructional League during the winter of 1963, I finally began feeling comfortable behind the plate.

I was up for part of 1965 and then in 1966 for good. And by that time the team had started losing. Johnny Keane had come over from the Cards to manage the ballclub in 1965 and I think he kind of changed the philosophy of the team. The Cards were more of a hit-and-run, bunting, and base-stealing ballclub, while the Yanks were a power-hitting team that played for the big inning. Keane tried to make the club more like the Cards and we finished under .500. The next year we got off to a horrible start, something like 4–16, and Ralph Houk took over again. But I don't think the team ever recovered from that start.

It's hard for me to say what happened to the team because I hadn't been there for that long. But guys like Mantle, Maris, Ford, Kubek, Howard, Bobby Richardson, they were all winners. In fact, before '65 they never knew what losing was. And the younger guys like me looked up to them. They were our example. But once the ball started bouncing wrong in 1965 there was a lot of frustration on the team. Nobody wanted to lose.

I was only there for half a season in '65, but the feeling on the team was that we'd regroup and be right there again the next season. But something just didn't jell, just wasn't clicking in 1966. We got off to that terrible start, but when Ralph took over from Keane we thought we'd pick up. But we didn't.

It also bothered me a great deal to lose because I was used to winning. I never liked losing at anything. It also concerned me that we were the Yankees and people expected us to win. Yet we didn't. We'd lose, lose, lose, and pretty soon you began to get that losing atmosphere. And I didn't like it.

Of course, I always played very hard. But the one guy who sometimes made me play even harder was Mickey Mantle. When I first came up Mickey didn't like to lose to anyone. And when his legs were sound, I never saw him when he didn't play hard. And I think watching him made a lot of guys play a little bit harder. He was always out there busting his ass, even when he was hurt. Being his teammate and knowing how he still went 110 percent despite the condition of his legs was always an inspiration to me.

After Elston was traded in 1967, I was probably considered the number-one catcher for the rest of that year and for all of 1968 and 1969. Then in 1970, Thurman Munson came in. I knew right away that he would be the Yankee catcher simply because of the way he hit the ball. I think I always hurt myself a little at the plate because of the pressure I put on myself. And part of that was because I was a Yankee.

When you play in New York you always want to do well. If you talk to players they'll tell you that putting on pinstripes gives you a little more prestige. And when you're a Yankee you want to play well before Yankee fans. So I think you put a little more pressure on yourself playing at Yankee Stadium. I know that happened to me when I became the number one. I'm not saying I was gonna be another Bill Dickey or Yogi Berra. But I wanted to do well because I was aware of the tradition. Because of that, I probably hit two times better on the road than at the Stadium. I felt more relaxed on the road. The pressure I put on myself at the Stadium really hurt. It wasn't until 1970, when Munson came, that I decided to forget about the pressure and relax. I should have done it sooner.

That was the difference between me and Munson. Thurman hit, and you've got to hit to really be a number-one catcher. I never had arm or leg trouble and could still catch and throw. And that's what people wanted in a good backup catcher, somebody to throw and catch, maybe sixty or seventy games a year. I always felt I was a good defensive catcher, could work the pitching staff and throw people out. That's why I think I could have stayed another four or five years in the majors.

For a while, in fact, I really wanted to manage. Ralph told me I was the one guy on the team he thought could become a man ager. And I used to sit in the bullpen and practice, watching both teams and thinking like a manager. But since 1965, I had also been returning to Ol' Miss every year to coach the quarterbacks, and about 1967 or '68 Coach Vaught asked me to come back full-time and be on his staff. But at that time I had to decline because I wanted to get five years in the big leagues for my pension. So I told Coach Vaught I would love to coach under him, but I had to stick with baseball. Plus I was just starting to play a lot then.

Then in early June of 1971 my wife and three boys had just left Mississippi to join me in New Jersey. They always did that at the end of the school year. We were staying at the Holiday Inn in Paramus and sitting by the pool when the phone rang. It was Bruiser Kinard, the athletic director at Ol' Miss. He wanted me to come back and be the baseball coach, as well as a football recruiter.

I knew that not too many college jobs came open, especially back in your home state where you played ball. So it was kind of a dream come true. And even though I was only going on thirty-three and had thought about staying in baseball as a manager, I knew this was an offer I couldn't turn down. And I told Ralph right away that 1971 would be my last year.

He accepted it well because he knew how I felt about Ol' Miss. Then he told me that the Senators wanted to trade Mike Epstein, the big first baseman, for me that spring and the Yankees had turned it down. They tried it again before the trade deadline and Ralph said the Yanks didn't want to let me go.

It was a true story, because when we went into Washington for the last three games of the year, I went to see Ted Williams, who was their manager then. I told Ted I was going back to Ol' Miss in a few days and he said, "What the hell you doing getting out of pro baseball?" When I told him why, he said, "Hell, we tried to trade for you twice this year. We wanted you to be our catcher." I told him I appreciated that, but it wouldn't change my mind.

So I finished 1971 catching about fifty games behind Munson and then called it quits. But before I quit, the Yanks did something that I'll never forget. They gave me a day at the ballpark. How many times has the Yankee organization honored a player with a .233 lifetime average? Among other things, they gave me a beautiful oil painting showing me swinging the bat in my uniform in Yankee Stadium. And I had to stand out there right behind home plate and thank the people, just like Babe Ruth did, like Lou Gehrig did, Mickey Mantle, and the rest of those other greats. I've never forgotten that.

The toughest part of retiring was not playing. I really enjoyed playing the game. I didn't miss the road trips and things like that, but I missed the guys and the playing. I saw a lot of great ballplayers during my time. Besides my teammates, there was Al Kaline on the Tigers. Never saw him loaf. He always gave 100 percent. Frank Robinson, great ballplayer, great power. Tony Oliva, Boog Powell, Carl Yastrzemski, Harmon Killebrew. They all came to play baseball. Hell, you can just start calling out names and you're gonna leave somebody out.

But I've also enjoyed coaching. I like to teach and get real satisfaction from watching kids improve. There's some pressure, because you still gotta win ballgames. That's number one. I've had four of my kids from Ol' Miss make the majors. Steve Dillard played about eight years with several different teams. Tucker Ashford played about the same amount of time. Jeff Calhoun belongs to the Phillies now after a couple of years with Houston, and Pete Ladd pitched for Milwaukee in the '85 World Series.

Two of my own boys, Dean and Monte, have both played for me. And the third, Frank, is at junior college and will probably play for me in a couple of years. So things have worked out well.

Besides coaching at Ol' Miss, I still work with Mickey and Whitey at their fantasy camp every year. Those two are both near and dear to me. Moose [Skowron] works with them, as do Hank Bauer and Mike Ferraro. We all have a good time.

So while I played only seven full years, the entire experience was a satisfying one. I wish I could have relaxed a little more and perhaps hit better, but I know the Yankee organization liked me and respected me for what I gave them. And that means a lot to me, even today. But I also realize that all of that is in the past. And if there's one thing I learned a long time ago, it's never to look back.

AL
SMITH

◆ **MAJOR LEAGUE EXPERIENCE** ◆
Cleveland Indians, 1953–1957
Chicago White Sox, 1958–1962
Baltimore Orioles, 1963
Cleveland Indians, 1964
Boston Red Sox, 1964

◆ **CURRENT STATUS** ◆
Retired after eighteen years with the Chicago Park District running the city's baseball programs.

Born in Kirkwood, Missouri, on February 7, 1928, Al Smith didn't think much about the big leagues as a youngster because blacks weren't allowed to play. But he became an all-around athlete, achieving renown as a sensational high school running back, who once scored ten touchdowns in a game, as well as a Golden Gloves boxing champion.

He was fortunate in that by the time he began playing baseball with the old Cleveland Buckeyes of the Negro American League, Jackie Robinson had been signed by the Dodgers and the color line was coming down. Al was signed by the Indians in 1948, the same year the legendary Satchel Paige inked a contract with the Tribe.

A steady if not spectacular player with both the Indians and White Sox, Al played in both the 1954 and 1959 World Series. In 1960, his .315 batting average was second in the American League to Pete Runnels's .320, an average Al says was partially the result of a friendly rivalry with teammate Minnie Minoso, who hit .311 that year.

In 1961, Al had career highs with twenty-eight homers and ninety-three RBIs, the same year Roger Maris broke Babe Ruth's record of sixty home runs. But Al says that Sox owner Bill Veeck proved that the baseball was juiced up that year, a controversy that never seems to go away. Al Smith retired after the 1964 season with a .272 lifetime average and nearly fifteen hundred career hits.

I was traded three times during my career; two of those times I heard it on the radio while I was sitting in a barber shop. But it didn't bother me hearing it like that because I always looked at it this way. If you own the club and you trade for me, then you must want me. So I didn't care where I went. It made no difference because I was gonna play ball. Wherever I went I was always gonna do the best I could.

But something did happen at the end of my career that really left a bad taste in my mouth, something I've never really talked about before. I had come back to Cleveland in 1964, the team I had started with eleven years earlier. I was thirty-six years old then, but felt I had a little time left. And I was happy to be going there because Birdie Tebbetts was the manager. He had been my last minor league manager at Indianapolis in 1953, and I hated to leave him then. I really loved the guy.

Birdie would tell you what he wanted you to do and then leave you alone. He'd say it was up to you to be in the castle or the shithouse. If you gave it your best shot, okay, the castle. But if you didn't, you were in the shithouse. So when Birdie got me back I really thought I would finish my career there.

Then Birdie had a heart attack in the spring and George Strickland took over as interim manager. George had been a teammate of mine when I first played for the Indians, but when he took over as manager I wasn't playing much. We were in Minneapolis around the middle of the season playing the Twins and George called me into his room one afternoon. He told me the team had decided to go with younger players and they were going to release me.

I said, okay, do what you have to do. I understand. That night, they put me in the lineup and I hit two home runs and drove in five runs. I had already told Sam Mele, the Twins' manager, that the Indians were going to release me and he said that if they let me go, he wanted me for the Twins.

So after the game Mele and Calvin Griffith, the Twins' owner, were waiting when I came out of the dressing room. They wanted to see if I were available. And suddenly Cleveland denied the whole thing. Strickland claimed he never said I was being released. And then I found out why. The team just learned they were going to have an unexpected hole at first base that they couldn't fill. So they decided to move [Tito] Francona in from the outfield, and needed the extra outfielder.

Because of that, I started playing some outfield. They kept me until September 1. Then they released me. I finished the season with the Red Sox and retired. I never did hook up with the Twins. It just wasn't the best way to go out. Strickland had been a teammate and I felt close enough to tell him that Mele wanted me. It was our last game there. We were leaving town and I said if you're releasing me I want to talk to Mele. But they denied the whole thing.

That's why I loved playing for Bill Veeck when he owned the White Sox. He was a helluva guy, one man I will never forget as long as I live. Whatever he told you he would do, he did. And he never wrote anything down. If he told you he was gonna give you a ten-dollar or fifteen-thousand-dollar raise, he'd give it to you. He spent a lot of time with his ballplayers. He would always come down to the clubhouse and talk to the guys. And in the winter some of us would go around with him, promote the team and try to sell tickets. He was always trying something new and he'd make you feel you were part of it, no matter what it was.

I remember when he put the exploding scoreboard in at Comiskey Park. I hit the first home run to set it off. Bill loved to do stuff like that. In 1961, when Roger Maris broke Babe Ruth's record and everyone else in the American League was hitting home runs, Bill got a 1961 baseball and another ball from five years earlier and dropped both of them off the second tier at the ballpark. The 1961 ball bounced about twice as high. Bill had suspected that ball was juiced up that year. It must have been, because I hit twenty-eight home runs that season and my previous high was twenty-two six years earlier.

The White Sox were my second team. I started with the Indians back in 1953. I think I was somewhere around the sixth black player signed by a major league ballclub. I signed with the Indians in 1948, the same day they signed Satchel Paige. But Satch was a little older than I was.

I was born in Kirkwood, Missouri, in February of 1928. Kirkwood was just a hop, skip, and a jump from St. Louis. So as a kid I used to see the old St. Louis Browns and the Cards when they were known as the Gas House Gang. I started playing ball early. I always say I had a gift, because I could watch something, then go out and do it. My older brother, Alonzo, who has since passed away, used to take me along and let me be the batboy for him and his friends. I must have been about ten or eleven years old then and pretty soon I began filling in when they didn't have enough players.

These guys were grown men, maybe twenty-five or thirty, and I was fourteen and playing with them. But I was pretty big for my age, about 165 pounds and tall. As much as we enjoyed playing, none of us thought much about the major leagues back then because we knew that blacks couldn't play. But as I got older there was a feeling among us that sooner or later there would be black players in the big leagues. I was just eighteen when Jackie signed with Montreal in 1946, so I was lucky. But there were some awful good ballplayers who were already thirty or thirty-five, some older than that, and they knew they would never get a chance. Satch was unfortunate, too, because he was already in his forties. But he was uncanny and still pitched some good ball with Cleveland and St. Louis. But guys like Josh Gibson, Cool Papa Bell, and others like them never had a chance.

When I got a little older, I went to Douglas High School in Webster Grove, which was about six or seven miles from my house. I couldn't go to the high school in Kirkwood because it wasn't integrated yet. At Douglas I played three sports, but back then football was the main one. In fact, around St. Louis I was ranked as the best football player from the 1930s and 1940s. I was a halfback and weighed about 185 pounds. The high school didn't even have a baseball team, so baseball then was confined to the weekends. And that was just sandlot.

I had some scholarship offers, but there weren't many blacks at the major colleges then. There was one guy from the University of Mississippi who saw me play one day. For some reason, he hadn't known beforehand whether I was white or black. After the game he came into the dressing room and said he'd never seen a fellow run the ball like I did, but there was no way he could bring me to Mississippi back then.

Boxing was another sport where I had some success in those days. We had a little church group in town and this fellow used to come down and help the boys out. He used to teach us boxing. At first, I didn't want to get into it because I had a perforated eardrum, but one day one of the other guys started calling me a sissy, so I put the gloves on and whipped the devil out of him. After that, my mother gave me permission and in 1944 I became the St. Louis AAU champ and the Golden Gloves champ at 160 pounds. But I never really wanted to take it any further than that.

So it was finally back to baseball. I started playing more around St. Louis with different pickup teams, and eventually played some with the Cleveland Buckeyes of the old Negro American League. I played shortstop with them beginning in the summer of 1946 and that was just about the time the big league scouts were looking at players in the Negro Leagues. Sad Sam Jones was on the team, and so was Sam Jethroe. I also met Minnie Minoso for the first time. He was playing with the New York Cubans.

We played a pretty good brand of ball and had a good team. Our home field was old League Park, where the Indians once played. Because we played in Cleveland, the Indians would scout us quite often. They were pretty interested in Sam Jones, but they asked me to come out there with him. Satch was with the Kansas City Monarchs then, and he came out too.

They had a lot of people looking at us. Tris Speaker was there, Hank Greenberg, Lou Boudreau. They put me in the outfield because they saw I could throw pretty well. Then they had a lefthander named Sam Zoldak, who was with the Indians then, throwing batting practice, and when it was all over they signed Satch and me to contracts.

This was in 1948, and I stayed with the Indians and worked out for about three weeks. The problem then was where to send me. They had a farm team in Oklahoma in the Texas League, but they couldn't send black players there. They didn't want to send me to San Diego because I was young and the Coast League was a helluva league then. There were a lot of ex–big league ballplayers out there. So I finally went to Wilkes-Barre [Pennsylvania] in the Eastern League.

Even in the Eastern League things weren't always easy then. I met the team in Elmira, New York, and they had a lot of players from the South, from places like Alabama and Mississippi, who had never played with a black man before. The manager there was Bill Norman, who later managed the Tigers for a while. He told the team that he was there to do a job and he was gonna play me. If anyone there didn't want to play with me, he could get right up and leave. I was the first black player in the Eastern League and I really appreciated what Bill Norman did when I got there.

At first, most of the guys kept to themselves and I kept to myself. In most places, I couldn't stay with the team and had to go to other hotels. I think Elmira was the only place where we all stayed together. But after a few months, more and more of them began coming up to me and shaking my hand or patting me on the back after a home run. I also finished second in the league in hitting with a .388 average, if I remember, and that helped, too.

The next year I was back at Elmira and Suitcase Simpson, another black, joined me there. Suitcase, God bless him, he led the league in homers and RBIs, and I was third in hitting and led the league with seventeen triples. Then in 1950 I finally got to the Coast League, as a shortstop with San Diego. By this time I began to feel I was going to make it to the majors sooner or later because I kept having good years in the minors. They also kept moving me to different positions—third, short, the outfield. As soon as I'd learn one, I'd go to another.

I was called into the army after the 1950 season ended, but I was there only nine months when I was discharged because of my perforated eardrum. When I got out in July of 1951, I called Hank Greenberg and he wired me the money to fly to the Coast and meet the San Diego club in Sacramento.

The Coast League was still a dropping-off point for ex–big leaguers and there were a lot of them there. It was a strong league that played a two-hundred-game schedule, starting in mid-March. We used to play one whole week in each town, night games during the week and day games on the weekend. So we'd go from Portland to Los Angeles, to Hollywood, back home, that kind of thing. We finished second that year and then they sent me to Indianapolis for 1952.

I played third there and had a solid season at the plate. The next year I went to camp with the Indians, but they had Al Rosen at third, so they moved me again, this time back to the outfield. They sent me down to Indianapolis to begin the season and I got hot. I think I drove in nearly one hundred runs by July, and soon after that they called me up. It was exciting, all right. You're finally there and you figure you might stay around.

The club had three other black players when I arrived—Larry Doby, who was the first black in the American League; Luke Easter, and Suitcase. So that made me feel a little more comfortable. The other vets were all pretty good, guys like Early Wynn, Bob Feller, Mike Garcia, Al Rosen. They were all established players and didn't see a rookie as any kind of threat.

I finished the season with the club in '53 and became just about a regular the next year. That 1954 club was one of the best ever. We set a record by winning 111 games in the regular season and finally managed to beat the Yankees in the process. But it was really a combination of things, guys having great years, and the club changing its style just a little bit. And that was something I helped to happen.

Al Lopez was the Cleveland manager then, and while he was an easy guy, he was still the Rock of Gibraltar. He never said much, but he knew every damned thing that was going on. And once he saw that you knew what was happening on the field he would give you a little bit of range. For example, when I first broke into the lineup he would always tell me to study the pitchers. At that time the Yankees had a lefthander named Ed Lopat. Good pitcher, especially against the Indians. I used to say that Ed Lopat could throw his glove out on the field and beat us.

But one day I told Lopez that no one ever bunted on Lopat, that we should move him around. So he put me in the leadoff spot and I started bunting. We had a play where if I got on first I would take off and Avila would bunt down the third-base line. I'd round second and just keep going to third. And it was that kind of thing that enabled us to chase Lopat, because he was a little slow off the mound.

The same kind of thing happened in the '54 World Series. I was standing next to Al while they were playing the National Anthem because I led off. He said to make [Giants' starting pitcher Johnny] Antonelli pitch to me. I said, "Skip, you know Antonelli. Once he gets two strikes on you he always goes to the screwball." And just as I was stepping out of the dugout to hit he said, "Al, go up there swinging." And I hit a home run off Antonelli's first pitch. After that, he kind of felt I knew my way around from studying the pitchers.

As I said, everything came together in '54. The team really improved itself, especially on defense. Al Rosen, for example, worked very hard to become a good third baseman. He used to go out and have [Coach Tony] Cuccinello hit him two hundred or three hundred ground balls, and in '54 he had a real fine year with the glove. George Strickland moved in at short and covered a lot of territory, so that made the entire left side of the infield solid. Avila won the batting title that year and also fielded well, and Vic Wertz came over from Baltimore to play first. Jim Hegan, God bless him, was one of the top defensive catchers in the game. He made our pitching even better.

I think Larry Doby played the best center field of his career in 1954. He always used to tell me to watch him. "If I take two or three steps to the right, then you take two or three steps to the right," he would say. He also taught me to learn our own pitchers. Mike Garcia, for instance, would throw sinkers so you wouldn't get a lot of fly balls when he pitched. But Early Wynn was a high-ball pitcher and he threw a lot of fly balls. Those were all things you had to study once you got up to the majors, especially if you wanted to keep playing.

Anyway, in '54 we just figured we couldn't be beat. I think we took the Yankees 13–9 that year. And I also think that Avila and I helped the team click because of the kind of running we did. It gave the club another dimension. They worried about walking me, because they knew Avila would either hit behind me or we'd work the bunt play, and then we had Doby and Rosen coming up behind us. We didn't steal a lot of bases. It was the other little things we did when we were on.

We also had a veteran player named Hank Majeski. He was near the end of the line, but he used to talk to me a lot and give me a lot of pointers about batting leadoff, taking pitches and making the pitchers work. Hank's advice paid off the next year, 1955, when I had 186 hits, 93 walks, and led the league with 123 runs scored.

But getting back to 1954, we went into the Series with people telling us that once we got by [Sal] Maglie and Antonelli [the Giants' two top pitchers] we had it won. Unfortunately, it didn't work that way. Rosen was playing with an injured foot and some of our other hitters had gone cold. Only Vic Wertz was swinging the bat well.

The first game was probably the key to the Series. I was on second base when Mays made his great catch off Wertz. I didn't think he'd get it when it was first hit, but he just outran the ball. I also think it was a kind of dead area out there, the way the ballpark was built. If the ball had been hit another ten to fifteen feet toward right field it would have been all she wrote. In fact, I always said if that one ball rolled in we'd have won the Series. It would have cleared the bases, and that would have been it. Instead, Dusty Rhodes hit a three-run homer in the tenth and they won it. Any time you get beat like that it's tough. Everyone felt bad about it, and they just got hot and won the next three.

Most of us really thought we were going to repeat the next year, but we lost to the Yanks by three games. I think the White Sox helped knock us out. They gave us a hard time all year, and so did the old Washington Senators. And some of the guys just didn't have as good a season as the year before.

I had a good year, but I must have played five or six different positions. Lopez would tell me that my versatility would keep me in the big leagues a little longer, but being moved around used to bother me then. In fact, I've always wondered what it would have been like to play just one position. I think I would have hit a little more, because when you're moving from the outfield to third, or third to second, you've always got to stop and think about your defense, and what you do in certain situations. That can take away from your hitting. But there's no sense crying over spilled milk. In one way, moving around could hurt you, but in another way it could help.

We were second again in 1956 and then in 1957 it all more or less came apart when Herb Score got hurt. I really think Herb would have been another Koufax if he hadn't gotten hit with that line drive. I was playing third that night and was the first to get to him. He was bleeding from the nose and ears, and his face looked like he just had a fight with Joe Louis and Rocky Marciano. His eye was already closed, but he never lost consciousness. Mike Garcia was a real good friend of his and Herb asked Mike to go to the hospital with him.

When [the Yankees' Gil] McDougald first hit the ball it looked as if it would go back through the middle. But then it trickled over to me and I picked it up. McDougald had stopped running halfway when he saw Herb crumble. Then I almost threw the ball in the seats. Vic [Wertz] had to jump to get it, but McDougald never started running again so he was out. And then I ran right to the mound.

I remember when Herb came back the next year. It was like he was shy. He was still throwing hard, but it was almost as if he was still thinking about someone else hitting the ball back through the middle. He'd have to tell you that. But he just never found himself again.

I was also having a couple of subpar years. My mother had passed away in 1956 and it took me awhile to get over that. I was hitting well over .300 when it happened and the rest of the year just wasn't the same. Then in 1957 I jammed my ankle sliding into home plate early in the year and it bothered me on and off for nearly two years after that. But back then you didn't want to get out of that lineup because someone else would get in there and you didn't know whether you'd get your job back. So you played through the injuries, and this one affected my hitting because it was on my right leg and I couldn't put weight on it when I was up.

Then in December of 1957 I was traded to the White Sox. Al Lopez had gone over there and he wanted me. So they traded me and Early Wynn for Minnie Minoso and Fred Hatfield. Minnie was a big favorite of the fans there and they didn't take too well to me in 1958 because I took his place. Plus my ankle was still bothering me and I couldn't run that well. So they used to boo me a lot when I came onto the field. It got better the next year because I was running well again and because the White Sox won the pennant.

The Sox were a different kind of team than the Indians. They were known as the Go-Go Sox and didn't have much power. But the club played good defense, played together as a team, and helped each other. We had a solid infield with [Nellie] Fox and [Luis] Aparicio, and some solid pitching with Wynn, Billy Pierce, and Bob Shaw. We always felt we would win the close ballgames, and I think we won something like thirty-six of fifty-two one-run games that year. We clinched the pennant at Cleveland and I hit a home run in that game and threw out Minnie at the plate. That was a big thrill for me to do that.

We lost in the Series to the Dodgers that year. They were playing in the Los Angeles Coliseum, which was the funniest ballpark you'd ever see in your life. And it was hard playing there because it was really a football stadium. Plus we got beat by a guy no one expected to beat us. That's when Larry Sherry got hot out of the bullpen.

It was also the Series in which I got the cup of beer spilled on me while I was chasing a Charlie Neal home run. I look at that picture quite often. When it happened I went to the umpire right away and he told me it was an accident. The guy in the stands was trying to get up to catch the ball and his coat knocked the beer down. I guess he had the cup balanced on the top of the wall. And I mean it hit me square. But I didn't even make any money out of it. I don't know why some beer company didn't pick it up and do something with it.

I had a real good year in 1960, hitting .315 and finishing second in the batting race to Pete Runnels. There were two reasons. First, my ankle was fine again, and second, Minnie Minoso had come back to the Sox that year. Minnie and I had a kind of friendly rivalry, and he had a great year, too, hitting .311 and driving in more than one hundred runs. The next year, 1961, I had career highs with twenty-eight homers and ninety-three RBIs, but as I said before, we were pretty much convinced that the ball was juiced up.

It's funny, but the last few weeks of the 1961 season was the only time I ever changed my batting style. I began pressing, because I wanted thirty homers and one hundred RBIs. Of course, when you begin going for home runs, nothing works. I think I was close to .300 entering the last few weeks and I finished at .278. So much for pressing.

I had another good season in '62, but this was the first time I think I began to feel my age. It was harder getting into shape and all the bumps and bruises from playing the outfield and running into walls or jumping over them were beginning to take a hold on me. Then in January of 1963 the White Sox shipped me to Baltimore. Veeck was gone by then. I think he was sick and I had some words with Ed Short, the general manager. He was just an unreasonable guy. You know you had a good year and you ask for maybe a ten-thousand-dollar raise. But he wanted to give you only what he wanted to give you.

So I went home and changed my phone number. Then the paper ran a story that the team didn't know where I was, but I just didn't want to talk to him any more. We were still $2,500 apart and I finally offered to split the difference, take $1,250 and a ticket for my wife to come to spring training. He still said no, and the next thing I knew I was in the barber shop and heard I was being traded.

That was more or less the beginning of the end. With the Orioles I wasn't really a regular, even though I didn't have a bad year. The club was trying to win a pennant, but once they saw they were out of it they began bringing in the young players and I didn't see much action the last part of the year. I still had the best batting average [.272] among the regulars. Then in December I went back to Cleveland and had that bad experience over my release.

Anyway, I finished the 1964 season with Boston, going there for the final month, then I was unconditionally released. I had already made up my mind that this was going to be it. I also saw that year how much tougher it was to play well when you were in and out of the lineup. I probably could have stayed around another year or so, but by then I just didn't want to. Somewhere along the line you see the writing. It's on the wall. You also begin to see how they treat you when you start getting older, and that's when you should start getting yourself prepared. I was prepared.

Looking back now, the 1950s and 1960s was a really good time for baseball. There were just eight teams in each league before the expansion and there were good ballplayers everywhere, even on the bench. Now, maybe there are just a handful of good players on each team, but back then I think there were more damned good ballplayers around. I even think the managers today over-manage, and they don't have the material.

I can remember being at the 1955 All-Star Game in Milwaukee. Ted Williams was there and we dressed next to each other. Ted loved to talk about hitting and he really helped me out that day. He talked to me from breakfast right up to game time. He always used to say if you go into a slump, aim to hit the ball back through the middle. Don't try to pull, just take everything back at the pitcher and sooner or later you'll start pulling again. He was one of the best hitters I ever saw.

Things also got better for black players during my time in the big leagues. In my early years there were a lot of places I couldn't stay. Even in Chicago and Baltimore, and in Florida during spring training. But guys like Hank Greenberg and Bill Veeck did a lot to change that. They would tell the guys who owned the hotels that if everyone couldn't stay there, they would move the entire ballclub.

I still think that every ballpark should have a picture of Bill Veeck someplace. He was a ballplayer's man. He loved every guy who played for him. He would never, never cut a player's salary. Before he would do that he would let him go. If a guy didn't have a good year, he'd keep his salary at the same level.

My only connection with the game since I retired is working with some twelve-, thirteen-, and fourteen-year-olds. A friend of mine sponsors a team and I coach a bit with him. But I've only seen maybe five big league ballgames in twenty-five years. I just don't go. And the reason is the pension plan. We started that plan and there are some ballplayers who aren't getting a damned thing. I'm fortunate because I don't really need the money. But these ballplayers today won't even vote to give the older players any more.

We went back and got some money for guys who played before us, like Joe Medwick, Pepper Martin, and Whitey Kurowsky. They don't get much, but at least we got them something. But take a guy from my time who was a real star, and he's getting only maybe eighteen hundred or two thousand dollars a month. A guy playing today can retire with sixty or seventy thousand dollars a year, maybe more. That's why Early Wynn is so angry today. He's really taken this thing to heart and he won't come to old-timers' games.

The funny part is the people want to see the old ballplayers. A team that might be drawing sixteen or eighteen thousand a game is gonna draw forty thousand when the old-timers come in. Like I said, my situation is all right. I'm more concerned with guys who played maybe eight or ten years before me. Some of them aren't getting a damned thing.

I'm retired today. I've never gotten a single call or one offer to do anything in major league baseball from the time I retired. I worked eighteen years for the Chicago Park District, running the baseball programs all over the city. I worked with Dick Drott, who used to pitch for the Cubs. Dick died of cancer in 1985. I retired so my wife and I could travel. We both like to play golf and do that whenever we can.

When I look back at my career I sometimes wonder what would have happened if I played only one position. But I was fortunate enough to play with some damned good players and some damned good teams, so I'm not gonna cry over that.

After the Red Sox released me in 1964 I took a long nail, about six inches long, almost a spike, and I nailed it into a wooden beam going through my house. I hung my baseball shoes and glove on that nail and I told my son if they fall off I'll go back [for another try], but it they don't fall I'm not gonna play anymore.

Well, they never fell and I never worried about it from then on.

AL
WEIS

♦ **MAJOR LEAGUE EXPERIENCE** ♦

Chicago White Sox, 1962–1967
New York Mets, 1968–1971

♦ **CURRENT STATUS** ♦

Shipping and receiving manager for a furniture company in Chicago.

In the words of Al Weis, the 1969 World Series "made my career." It's not difficult to see why. After spending eight years in the major leagues as a utility infielder and defensive specialist, the light-hitting second baseman exploded for five hits in eleven at-bats against the powerful Baltimore Orioles, hitting .455 with a home run and three RBIs.

Before that, the Franklin Square, New York, native was known primarily for a 1967 collision at second base with Baltimore superstar Frank Robinson. Robby was sidelined for a while with a *concussion and Weis had to undergo knee surgery. The result of the surgery was his trade to the Mets in 1968, setting up his World Series heroics.*

A small and unscouted player in high school, Al Weis had no thoughts of a big league career until the White Sox spotted him playing for a naval service team. He joined the Go-Go White Sox team of 1962 that featured the likes of Luis Aparicio and Nellie Fox, and he fit right in with the speed and defense philosophy of that ballclub.

Ironically, his unexpected World Series stardom may have led to an early end to his career. Having given Weis a substantial raise after the fall classic, the Mets decided his salary was just too high for a part-time player and he was released after playing just eleven games in 1971 at the age of thirty-three.

Being a utility player is no picnic. In many ways it's much easier to play every day. When you're a utility player you almost always have to go in cold. You may sit for seven or eight innings in a close, 2–1 game and suddenly you're told to get in there. The game is on the line and you're expected to make the plays. It's a tough job.

Speed and defense were my strong suits, and I think that's why I became labeled as a utility player. My hitting was always suspect, and maybe because I was a small guy they questioned my stamina. I remember a lot of times sitting on the bench in Chicago and in the eighth or ninth inning [Manager] Al Lopez would tell me to go in there to pinch-run for somebody and to steal second on the first pitch. He had the impression I could do it and quite a few times I did.

So I think it reached a point where there was just a kind of understanding that I was going to be a utility player. After a while, I could sense when I would be used. It was a feeling of how the game was going, the score, the situation, the inning. So you begin to know when you have to be ready. Come the seventh inning I would get up and move around. And if it was cold, I'd work the legs and try to get myself in a frame of mind to play.

A utility player has to do a lot of it himself. Because you're not playing that much there's a tendency to slack off a little bit. So you have to keep yourself in good shape. When I was with the Mets, [Manager Gil] Hodges used to gather all the guys who were not playing much and always run us before a game. So he made sure we kept in shape.

My job was mostly defense and that's probably why I stayed in the big leagues. I had some pretty low batting averages, another thing that doesn't make a ballplayer look good. But, again, I think this is sometimes the result of being a utility player. It's hard to maintain an average when you don't get many times at bat. When you hit one day, then go three or four days before getting another at-bat you really can't get in any kind of groove.

I'm not making any excuses for the low averages I had, but it is hard going in during the late innings and just picking up one or two at-bats. You have only a fraction of a second to make up your mind if you're going to hit that pitch or not. And once you decide to swing you've got to make good contact. Other sports take skill also, but I don't think there is that fraction-of-a-second decision that there is in hitting. And it's just very difficult when you don't get the at-bats.

Actually, I didn't even play that much baseball as a youngster, not the morning-to-night stuff you sometimes read about. I was born in 1938 in Franklin Square, New York, which is only about ten miles from Shea Stadium. In 1950, my parents bought a house in Bethpage, on Long Island, and that's really where I grew up. In fact, my parents are still living there

The first organized ball I played was with the PBC [Police Boys Club] in Bethpage, a few years before I went to high school. I played both baseball and basketball at Farmingdale High, but basketball was definitely my favorite. I even ran a little track.

But I was very small back then. My senior year I was about five-ten, but weighed only about 140 pounds. And even though I made the all-scholastic baseball team as a senior, I wasn't anything exceptional. There weren't any scouts offering me contracts or even a tryout. So I really didn't give professional baseball a second thought.

Like a lot of other kids, I didn't know what I wanted to do when I got out of high school. I had taken a general business course but couldn't find a job right away, so three of us buddies decided to enlist in the Navy. I was at the ripe old age of seventeen and a half when I joined. That was in 1956 and playing ball was the farthest thing from my mind.

In the Navy I became a structural aviation mechanic, learning my skills at bases in Norman, Oklahoma, and Memphis, Tennessee. I wasn't planning to be a career man, just to see the world, as the old expression goes. Well, I never did. I was assigned to a division in Norfolk, Virginia, where I worked as a structural mechanic. And I stayed there.

Then one day I learned they were having tryouts for a basketball team and I went out and made it. After that, I got transferred to what they called a special service. I started playing basketball and then tried out for the baseball team and made that, too. They had some good service sports teams then and recruited some good baseball players. We traveled down to Florida and up to New York, always kept on the move.

I don't think there were any other players on the team who made the majors. The only guy with a connection to the majors was Walt Dropo's brother. He was a catcher, and a real big guy like Walt. I remember he never wore any protective gear, except maybe a shin guard. He was like a gorilla. Nothing could hurt him.

When I was playing on the service team I was finally scouted for the first time. There was a White Sox scout in the area and he had me come out for a tryout, running and fielding. Then they began watching some of our games. The only other team that looked at me, as far as I know, was the Dodgers. They also saw me when I played for the service team. The difference was that the White Sox offered me a very small contract, but the Dodgers wanted me to go down to spring training on purely a tryout basis. No contract.

This happened in 1958. I was a shortstop–second baseman and I think what caught their eye was my defensive skills and speed. And, as I said, that's just what carried me to the big leagues. Anyway, when I got the contract I was due to get out of the Navy and figured I'd try it for three or four years to see what would happen. I really didn't think I would make it to the big leagues, but I had nothing else to look forward to when I got out, so why not try?

I was discharged from the Navy in the spring of 1959 and went to play in the Rookie League in the Midwest. There were five or six teams in the league for recently signed players. It was quite an experience. I had been raised close to the big city and I can remember taking the train to a little place called Holdrege, Nebraska. We all lived with families who took in ballplayers. It was a good way to get your feet wet in baseball.

It also gave me a chance to see another part of the country. So while it was the lowest you could go, I'm glad the White Sox started me off that way. I got experience and I began to get confidence. I don't now how long they planned to give me, but I did well and must have caught someone's eye, because the next year they moved me up to Class B ball. I played in Lincoln, Nebraska, and again had a pretty decent year.

If you remember, the White Sox had a team that stressed speed and defense back then. When they won the pennant in 1959 they were known as the Go-Go Sox and I guess that was the type of ballplayer they were still looking for. I was lucky in that I spent just one year at each level, then moved up. I finally got to Triple A at Indianapolis in 1962 and had maybe my best year in the minors. I think I hit .300 and stole a lot of bases.

That was also the first year I started switch-hitting, and I think that was a major factor in getting me to the big leagues. The year before in Class A I didn't hit that well, and I think they figured with my speed I would get a lot of leg hits if I batted lefthanded. So I tried switching in the Instructional League during the off-season, then continued it at Indianapolis.

When I played at Indianapolis in '62 there weren't a whole lot of young players there. Luke Appling was the manager and he encouraged me to keep switch-hitting. Most of the other players had either been in the minors a number of years or were former major leaguers on the way down.

Becoming a switch-hitter was not easy for me. In fact, it was very discouraging at first. But I kept at it and continued to do it during my time with the White Sox. But when I came over to the Mets I was just doing it off and on, and finally Gil Hodges said he didn't want me hitting lefthanded because I wasn't getting enough at-bats. He wanted me to hit only righthanded, my natural way.

But anyway, my big league debut came at the end of the 1962 season, when the big league clubs could expand their rosters. And it was something I'll never forget. I got the call to report while I was still in Indianapolis and was told to meet the team in Washington, where the Sox would be playing the old Senators. The call really took me by surprise, so I didn't bother to write down the name of the hotel or anything else. All I could remember was that I had to get to Washington.

When I got to the airport I began asking around, but no one knew which hotel the White Sox were at. So I started making phone calls and finally got lucky. Then everything was fine until the first game. It was against the Senators and I started at shortstop for Luis Aparicio. I had a real good day—I went oh for four, struck out twice, and made two errors in the field. Everybody likes to get a big hit his first game, get the ball to take home and all that. But I think I knew the situation at the time. If the team had been in any kind of pennant race I wouldn't have played.

I don't even remember if I played anymore in that series or not. But I know it felt strange going from a minor league to a major league environment. It's like night and day. Triple A had some good playing surfaces and lighting, but by and large it was much better in the majors. The playing conditions were much better. And for those few games that I was up there I felt like I was in another world. There were a lot of adjustments.

The next year I had a good spring and made the team as a utility infielder. I took the place of a guy named Sammy Esposito and that was a hard thing to do. He was with the team for about ten years and it's hard to see someone like that get cut. You know you're taking his job and he's out of one, but I guess that's the way life is.

None of the veterans seemed to resent it. I guess they all knew that was how things went. In fact, one of Sammy's best friends on the team was Nellie Fox. They used to pal around a lot, but Nellie never showed me any hard feelings. He had had some great years with the Sox, but I knew his days were numbered. As it turned out, he was traded to Houston after the 1963 season and I started at second in his place in '64.

I hadn't done badly my rookie year, hitting .271 as a switch-hitter, so when Nellie was traded I knew I had a real shot at taking his job. And I got it. It wasn't a bad year for me until I had an unfortunate accident at Tiger Stadium, the result of some foolish clowning around.

In Detroit, there is a low overhang on the dugout that is made of cement. You have to duck to get into the dugout. Anyway, I was clowning around, ran into the dugout, slipped and hit my head on the cement. I needed six or seven stitches and missed the game that night. Don Buford took my place and also took over the job. I don't think I started a single game after that. It was pretty early in the season and for the rest of the year I split time between short and second. But I did learn a lesson about fooling around, the kind of stuff where you're pushing and shoving each other. I didn't do it after that.

Aparicio had been traded to Baltimore after the 1962 season and Ron Hansen was the new shortstop. Ron was an established shortstop, tough and a smooth ballplayer. His only drawback was that he couldn't run and he lost a lot of points on his batting average because he rarely beat out an infield hit. I think that was another reason they kept me around, because Hansen didn't really fit into their long-range plans. But balls he could reach he gobbled up, and he had one of the most accurate arms I had ever seen. So I was already playing a lot of late-inning defense and picking up one or two at-bats here and there.

The Sox weren't a real power team in those years. Hansen hit some home runs, and so did Pete Ward, but neither was a real home run hitter. The team was still based on pitching and defense. We got runs whenever we could, but playing for the Sox in those years your heart was in your stomach all of the time. We had very few easy games. It seemed it was always a one-run game, 2–1 or 3–2. Never high scoring. But we had a competitive team with a lot of young players and few key veterans.

There were guys like Hansen and Ward, Floyd Robinson, Tom McCraw, Mike Hershberger, Jim Landis, J. C. Martin, Dave Nicholson, Gary Peters, and Joe Horlen. One of the veteran players was Bill Skowron, who was with the Yankees in the 1950s and early 1960s. I roomed with Bill and he was an exceptional guy. When he was with the Yanks, he said, a veteran player had more or less taken him under his wing and that's what he did with me. When we went out to eat, he would never let me pay for anything. He'd take me out shopping and introduce me to people. Finally it reached a point where I told him if he didn't let me pay for something, I wouldn't go out with him anymore. Just a great guy. In fact, I'm the godfather of his daughter.

I had a pretty good year at the plate in 1965, hitting .296, though I didn't have a whole lot of at-bats. And while the team didn't come right out and tell me, this is the point where I began to get the message that my job was being a utility player. But even if you were unhappy, in those days you kept your mouth shut. I don't think too many players would ask for a trade back then. The contracts were really binding. You played for the White Sox or you didn't play for anybody.

Even though I wasn't completely happy with the situation I figured I was getting in my years of service and was getting closer to getting the pension. So I kind of accepted being a part-time player with the feeling that in another situation I could be an everyday player. I felt I had the ability.

It stayed that way until 1967. That was the year I had the collision with Frank Robinson and tore up my knee. And in a strange way, it was the best break I ever had, because the result of the whole thing was that I got traded to the Mets. It happened around midseason. I was playing second that day and Frank was on first. Brooks Robinson was up and he hit a slow grounder to Dick Kenworthy at third. Dick came to me at second and because I knew Brooks didn't run well, I tried to turn the double play. That was my first mistake.

I should have just taken the force and gotten out of the way. But it was a bang-bang play at second and I never did get the throw off to first. In fact, I don't even think I recorded the out at second. I had my left leg planted to make the throw when Frank hit me. I think my leg was on the infield side of the base and I guess he rolled into my left knee. I saw the replays of it and it didn't look that bad. It wasn't an intentional thing and I had no bad thoughts about it then or now.

But I remember lying on the ground and not yet realizing that I was hurt. I didn't have much pain but when I got up to walk it off, my leg kept giving out on me. Finally, they carried me off and took me to the hospital. They took X-rays and the doctor told me right away to forget about playing the rest of the year. I had torn ligaments and my only options were to have the operation right there in Baltimore or to fly back to Chicago for the surgery. I said I wanted to go back to Chicago, so they put it in a cast until I got there. And after the operation I had it in a cast for another two weeks. But as soon as it came off I started working out with the team again.

Frank, of course, came out of it with a concussion and had some double vision for a while. But we never called each other to discuss the play. Years later I had some pictures taken with him and there were no hard feelings. I look at it as good, rough baseball, the way the game is supposed to be played. I just didn't get out of the way fast enough.

Anyway, I was working out with the team at the end of the year and the Senators were in town. Gil Hodges was still managing them and my old friend Bill Skowron was playing over there. I guess Gil started making inquiries about me then. I also played winter ball that year to help rehabilitate the knee, and Gil saw me again. Besides playing, I did a lot of leg raises with a weight on my foot while sitting on the end of a table. But we didn't have all the fancy machines they have today.

The trade was made in December of 1967. I really don't think the White Sox felt I was capable of coming back and performing at the big league level. And, in truth, as hard as I worked to get the leg back in shape, it wasn't quite the same. I wasn't as fast. So I definitely lost something, but I still did an adequate job.

Anyway the Mets sent four players [Tommy Davis, Jack Fisher, Billy Wynne, and Buddy Booker] to the White Sox for Tommie Agee and myself. Tommie was a center fielder and the key man in the trade, but I heard later that Gil wouldn't have made the deal unless I was included. He had Bud Harrelson and Kenny Boswell playing short and second then, and both of them had National Guard commitments that caused them to miss time during the season. So the club needed someone who could fill in at both spots.

I was doing promotional work for the White Sox during the off-season when the Mets called and told me about the trade. My job was talking to season ticket holders, trying to convince them to renew their tickets. In fact, I had just bought a house in the

Chicago area that October, the same house I live in today. And here I was being traded to a last-place club. I had even spoken with Ed Short, the Sox' general manager, a few days earlier and he hadn't mentioned a thing. So I had no inkling of a trade. But the Sox called later in the day and I'd say the whole thing was handled pretty well. I even continued to promote the Sox for the remainder of the off-season. I felt I had an obligation and it was bringing in some extra money.

Even though I had come close to getting into the World Series with the White Sox and was about to go to a team that was usually last, I had no thoughts about quitting. Baseball was my life by that time and I also had a family to support. Besides, it was a good life. Basically, you were treated well. But it's tough on a player to get traded and to have to pack up and move, and then readjust. Fortunately, my kids weren't old enough to be affected by changing schools. In fact, I think it was good for them to be associated with kids from different parts of the country. They went to schools in Florida, Chicago, and New York.

What I didn't want to do was relocate. So I would rent my house in Chicago to my White Sox teammates, or former teammates. Ron Hansen lived in it, then Hoyt Wilhelm, and they just gave me enough to pay the mortgage. I didn't want to make money on them.

I knew that my role with the Mets would be no more than that of a utility player, a fill-in. I really didn't hit well [.172] my first year there and I found going from the American to the National League a big adjustment. I think a lot of players find this their first year in a new league. The National League had a lot more hard throwers then and you didn't see all the curveballs and off-speed stuff you saw in the American. And, again, not getting the at-bats doesn't help. Having a coach throw batting practice to you at seventh-grade speed isn't the same. But I don't really know the answer, because I never really hit well in the National League. The next year, the pennant year, was the highest and I only hit .215.

The Mets had a good nucleus of players in 1968 but I really didn't think the team would turn it around the way they did the next year. Maybe it was the rub-off effect of the team always being last. It was hard to believe it would change. I felt that maybe the team could get up to fifth or sixth place, but to win the pennant . . . I don't think too many teams have gone from the bottom, or near the bottom, to the top in one year.

We probably started believing about the middle of the next season. There was a series against the Cubs at Wrigley Field midway through the year in which I hit the only two homers I had all year. In back-to-back games. We won both and that had some effect on the team. After that, we began to feel we were going to win, even if we were two or three runs down.

But it was really a combination of things—pitching, relief pitching, good defense, good hitters, and a good balance between young players and veterans. But the veterans weren't really old. In fact, I was one of the older players on the team that year and I was just thirty-one. That was also the year Gil really went to the platoon system. Clendenon and Kranepool at first, myself and Boswell at second, Charles and Garrett at third, Shamsky and Swoboda in right, Jerry Grote and J. C. Martin behind the plate.

I really think that was a factor, because it kept us fresh. The Cubs pretty much went with their starting nine the entire season and playing all those day games in the July and August heat of Chicago took a toll on them. Plus we were a loose team. We had leaders like Grote, Harrelson, Ed Charles, and there wasn't any dissension about playing time because Gil was such a strong leader and had established the system he wanted to use. And he stuck with that all the way. As a rule, Gil was quiet, but if you saw the veins on his neck popping out, better watch out. He was a very physically strong man with huge hands that looked like they could strangle a bear.

The second half of the season, of course, we played extremely well, and I don't think we were playing over our heads. We were just playing sound baseball. We probably won some fluke games that we shouldn't have won, but we also had a good ballclub that was well deserving of being in first place and going from there. And that was the feeling among the entire club.

Strangely enough, I hardly played against Atlanta in the playoffs. That was the first year they had the divisional playoffs before the Series, so we had to win an extra three games. Because the Braves had all righthanded pitching I got only one at-bat. Then came the World Series against Baltimore and two of their starters, Dave McNally and Mike Cuellar, were lefties, so I got to play.

As it turned out, that Series made my whole career. People remember me for the things I did in that Series. Every time the 1969 World Series came up, even years afterward, I would get phone calls from someone wanting an interview. Funny part was when it happened, I almost didn't get the chance to enjoy it because it all happened so fast. My family was there and other friends from Chicago and there wasn't even much time to sleep. We played all day games then and by the time you would have dinner with your family and friends, then talk for a while, there was barely time to catch a few hours sleep before it was time to get up and go to the ballpark again.

But we really had confidence. We knew Baltimore had a great team and that anything could happen in a short series. But that feeling we had during the season, that we were somehow going to find a way to win, carried over to the Series. Our pitching was great and so was our defense. Agee and Swoboda made those great catches and Ed Charles made some fine plays at third. We were just high on winning.

And because I played several games in a row I just started feeling good at the plate. My timing felt better and once you play in a big game like that and drive in a key run, then it's almost like a steamroller effect. Like I said, that Series made my career. Donn Clendenon was the MVP, but the New York baseball writers voted me the outstanding player in the Series and I flew back to New York for a black tie dinner to get my award.

The Mets also doubled my salary the next year, putting me up to about thirty-thousand dollars. I felt that was excellent money for the amount of time I was on the field. But the funny part is I think that salary was one of the contributing factors in my being released two years later. They got somebody else to do the same job for less money.

I didn't play much at all the next year and the team didn't repeat. I guess I had about half as many at-bats as I had during 1969, but I still figured I'd be back in 1971. They kept me for about half the season, but I hardly played at all. Then, when Wayne Garrett came off the injured list, they released me. And it was a total shock. Gil told me that it had to be done, that they had to go with younger players. Years later, Joe Pignatano, who was one of the coaches, said that Gil told him my release was one of the toughest decisions he ever had to make.

But that didn't make it any easier at the time. I was thirty-two years old and suddenly going from a job to no job. And that was tough. Plus it happened at a time of year when all the rosters were filled and it was tough catching on with another team. I made some calls, but was told by everyone that there was no point talking until the winter. I tried again then and Cincinnati asked me to come to spring training because they had a young shortstop in camp and they weren't sure how he was going to pan out.

I had a good spring, even hit a couple of homers. Then about a week before the season started they made their decision. They decided to go with the young guy. That didn't give me much time, and I finally came home, figuring that was it. And that's when I made perhaps one of the worst decisions I ever made in baseball. The White Sox wanted me to play with their Triple A team and I said no!

You know, once you're in the big leagues . . . Maybe part of it was pride. I felt they knew what I was capable of doing. The money wasn't really a factor. It wasn't near what I had been making, but it was adequate. It was just a mistake on my part. If I had gone down there and played, they would have called me up as soon as there was an injury, or an extra roster spot, and I might have had two or three more years with them. Of course back then I probably didn't regret the decision, at least not for a year or so, but what can you do? I just felt then that being an established player I shouldn't have had to go back to the minors to prove myself.

As I said, I was just thirty-two years old. And you know, within that same year I went to an old-timer's game at Shea Stadium. At age thirty-two. And it hurt. I don't know why I did it. I guess because they asked me and I had no hard feelings against the Mets. But after that I had no intention of doing it again.

All in all, though, I had a good life in baseball. I got to travel around the country, met a lot of nice people, and had a lot of good times. I got a nice ring [for the 1969 World Series] that I wear occasionally. So I don't regret getting into it and spending thirteen years of my life doing it.

But leaving the game wasn't easy. First of all, the money wasn't the same. I didn't miss the traveling. I had had enough of that. I'm basically a low-key, private person and I enjoy my private time. I never really enjoyed giving interviews. That was just something we all had to do. But it took a while to adjust after I knew it was over.

Fortunately, I've been with the same company since I left baseball. It's a local furniture company and I'm in charge of shipping and receiving. It's a different way of life and not always easy. Sometimes I do physical work and I'm not ashamed of that. I make a good living; my wife works, and we've put a kid through college. My son graduated from Northern Illinois with a degree in finance.

I do some card shows now and go down to Mets Dream Week, the fantasy camp. So I keep in touch that way, even though I don't go to ballgames very often. It's funny, on the whole I think the ballplayers today are superior to those in my day. They're bigger, faster, and stronger. Yet at the same time I don't think there's a player in the game who can compare to a Mantle or a Mays or an Aaron. Those guys would still be superstars today.

People who know I'm an ex-ballplayer will ask me questions about the game and the guys I played with and against. I don't mind talking baseball at all. After all, I did get to the top of my profession, the major leagues, and I played in a World Series, something a lot of players with more credentials never did. And that's something I'll always be proud of.

CLEM
LABINE

♦ **MAJOR LEAGUE EXPERIENCE** ♦

Brooklyn Dodgers, 1950–1957
Los Angeles Dodgers, 1958–1960
Detroit Tigers, 1960
Pittsburgh Pirates, 1960–1961
New York Mets, 1962

♦ **CURRENT STATUS** ♦

Bank officer with the Eastland Bank of
Rhode Island.

*Clem Labine says he was born and bred a Dodger, and his deep
feelings for the organization continue today, as he is a regular
participant in the Dodgers' fantasy camps at Vero Beach, Florida.
First coming up in 1950, Labine was a big part of the powerful
Brooklyn teams of the decade, teams that won four National
League pennants and added another in Los Angeles in 1959.*

Used primarily out of the bullpen for most of his career, Labine had a penchant for pitching outstanding games in spot starts. He threw a shutout against the Giants in the second game of the 1951 playoffs, then whitewashed the Yankees after Don Larsen's perfect game in the 1956 World Series.

After leaving the Dodgers early in the 1960 season, Clem pitched briefly for the Detroit Tigers, then helped the Pittsburgh Pirates to the 1960 National League pennant. But he said that Pirate team could not compare to the great Dodger teams of the early and middle 1950s.

Like many of his Dodger teammates, Clem Labine hated leaving Brooklyn for Los Angeles in 1958, and calls the Los Angeles Coliseum, where the Dodgers played for two years, an insult to baseball. He made it a point to return to Brooklyn to watch the wrecking ball reduce Ebbets Field to rubble, and managed to rescue a large picture of himself from the rotunda of the legendary old ballpark.

W hen the Dodgers traded me to the Detroit Tigers in 1960, Buzzy Bavasi [the Dodgers' general manager] told me he was sending me to the best ballclub in the American League that he could find because he wanted me to go to a good club. I couldn't argue with that. The Tigers were a fine ballclub that year. Back then, you had seventy-two hours to report. So I came home first, then went to Detroit to meet some of the guys.

The first night I was eligible I went to the bullpen and watched Jim Bunning pitch. It was either a ten- or eleven-inning game, I can't recall which, and Bunning allowed just three hits . . . and lost, 1–0. God, do you know how you feel when you watch a loss like that? As I walked into the dressing room I got hit with a bag of peanuts in my left hand and a can of beer in my right. I said to myself, what the hell is going on here? It was as if they had won the game.

If you had ever walked into the Dodger clubhouse after a 1–0 loss like that, everything would have been tied up tight. Yet the Tigers lost and it was as if they won. The ballclub had an attitude that I couldn't believe. It was not a winning attitude, a "we-have-to-win-ballgames" attitude. And I really think that's the sort of thing that separates a good team from a great team. The Dodgers of the 1950s were a great team.

Last year I attended a thirtieth reunion of the 1959 Dodgers, just about the time the regular pitchers and catchers were reporting to spring training. It wasn't hard to see the difference between us and them. They're big. My God, are they big. I'm a shade over six feet and weigh over two-hundred pounds, but these guys are tremendous. To shake hands with the pitchers you have to look upward. Some of them are six-four and six-five and I hold nothing but respect for them in that they're probably as good as, if not better than we were.

But none of them talk to each other. They talk some on the field, and then they're gone. They don't seem to have any conception of what the hell it is to talk about the things they do. Can you imagine sitting down with your teammates and not being able to talk about last year when you surprised everyone and won the [1988] World Series? To me, that would be the most important thing I could talk about. Just to relive it again. Instead, all they were talking about was $7.9 million for Hershiser, $7.5 million for Clemens. Hey, come on. Money is important. But there are other things involved here, including loyalty to your teammates and the fact that no one player can do it alone.

The players today don't seem to understand that they walk in with such an edge that it's not even funny. If anything, I resent the edge these guys have. I resent the fact that they can go home during the winter and not have to work for a living, that they can stay in shape and don't have to worry about their families. If they're the type of people who get good advice, if they're intelligent enough to save their money, within a few short years they should be in a very good position.

We had no way that could happen to us. They get an incredible pension and they reflect upon the old ballplayers by saying screw the veterans. That's what they've told each and every one of us about improving the pension plan. I don't want their plan. I don't want anything from them. But how dare they not give it to the people who really need it. They are a very selfish group of people led by very selfish people. There are too many things going on today that shouldn't be happening, and nobody can do anything about it.

But I really don't mean to vent my anger. I appreciate today's athletes for being good athletes, and the fellows at the top of their field today are as good as, if perhaps not better than some of the people who played during my day. But they do come in with an edge.

I came in with a lucky break. Had it not been for a locked door I might have never signed with the Dodgers. I was born in Lincoln, Rhode Island, and I guess played some kind of ball as far back as I can remember. In New York it was stickball; in Rhode Island we used to play with a tennis ball against steps, making up our own games.

My thing then was also keeping box scores of everybody. My brother and I were both sports oriented and we kept two radios in our room. One above the bed to turn off when our mother would tell us, and the other under the bed so we could go down there and listen to the games. And I'd keep the box scores whenever I could. My brother was five years older than me and he's the one who first showed me how to throw a curveball. I started with a tennis ball and as soon as I learned how to throw it I could twist the ball better than he could. So I could beat him at some of the silly games we played, but it was kind of fascinating that I was better at certain things than he was even though he was older.

Back then I used to follow players on the Red Sox. They were the area team, and I remember liking Bobby Doerr and Ted Williams as a youngster. But I also liked the Dodgers. With the Dodgers it was the team, not individuals, and they were a bad team then. Maybe that's kind of why I liked them.

I had a great high school coach, the best you could get in my area. His name was Gus Sabaria and he was a football All-American at Lehigh. Yet because he saw my ability in baseball, he wouldn't even let me play football for him. He's the guy who really helped me develop and get confidence in myself. I played everywhere then, but I enjoyed pitching more than anything else, except maybe hitting. When I got to the major leagues I changed my mind about the hitting part.

The majors then might have been a dream, but I still never thought that I might ultimately have that kind of ability. Yet it reached a point in high school where if I didn't strike out at least sixteen or seventeen batters in a game it was a bad day. Maybe then, I started thinking more about the big leagues. But I was never scouted in high school.

By then I really loved the Red Sox and would have loved the chance to get into their organization. But I never even had the chance to get a cold shoulder from them. My lucky break came, I think, during or right after my senior year. My coach knew a trainer for a minor league hockey team who was also a scout for the Boston Braves and he took me to see him. It was sort of like a racetrack atmosphere. I pitched to this guy on a crowded parking lot, but he was impressed enough to feel I warranted a tryout with the Braves.

On the day I was supposed to have the tryout my coach and I went out to old Braves Field, but we couldn't get into the dressing room. It was locked. To this day, I don't know why. Maybe they just didn't know I was coming. Anyway, my coach went to look for someone to let us in and all of a sudden Charlie Dressen came by. Charlie was a Dodger coach then under Leo Durocher, and the Dodgers were in Boston to play the Braves.

Charlie asked me what I was waiting for, and when I told him a
tryout with the Braves, he said, "Come on, let's go." So instead
of a tryout with the Braves, I got one with the Dodgers.

I wasn't signed on the spot, but Dressen told me I had the best
slider he ever saw. And I can tell you that in twenty-one years of
baseball, I never threw a slider, not a single one. I think I had a
kind of ball that sank a little. Later, I started throwing my sinker
by splitting my fingers and throwing it like that magnificent pitch
they all say was just discovered the last few years—the split-
fingered fastball. It's also a lot like throwing a spitter without the
spit on it.

But after the team went back to Brooklyn I got a call from
Branch Rickey, Jr., asking me if I wanted to play for the Dodgers. They wanted me and my father to come to Brooklyn. So we
went and it was an overwhelming experience for me. They gave
us a contract to take home and it included a five-hundred-dollar
bonus, a few less zeroes than today.

My minor league career didn't start until 1946 when I came out
of the service. I was getting $250 a month to play at Newport
News, Virginia, a Class B team then. It was tough. My wife was
expecting and I rented the first floor of a house for $125 a month.
So that didn't leave us much. I was one of the few players who
had an automobile, an old Ford. But we had no Blue Cross then,
so I had to worry about my wife having the baby. And if I was on
the road at the time, there would be no one to take care of her. I
remember my manager moving into the upstairs of the same
house and telling me in no uncertain terms that he should have
had the first floor. I told him I didn't care what he thought, that I
got it first.

But it was a tremendous league with a lot of guys who ended
up in the majors later. Great athletes. Unfortunately, I just didn't
perform, maybe because I had so many other things on my mind.
So they shipped me to Asheville, North Carolina, to another B
team and once there my wife went home to have the baby and I
didn't lose a game. I was a hard thrower then with a real good

overhand curve. But I still didn't throw the sinker yet. Anyway, I made the usual progress through the minors, going to Pueblo in Class A and finally to St. Paul in Triple A.

This all happened about the time Jackie Robinson was breaking in with the Dodgers. There were still very few blacks coming into the minors then, and it really took a few years before they came in any real numbers. We finally got Jim Pendleton on our team at St. Paul and then we began having some problems, particularly in Louisville, Kentucky.

There were a couple of fistfights when we played there, including a big one when I ended up getting blackjacked by a policeman. There were a lot of drunk people in the stands that day and they kept asking us how wc could play with niggers. That started it and a couple of us ended up on top of the dugout with the fans. Then the cops came to break it up and I got blackjacked.

But as for the players in the minors, most of them were too busy fighting for jobs to worry about anything else, because the competition was fierce and there were far more players in the farm systems than there are today. I think the Cardinals had twenty-eight farm clubs then and the Dodgers twenty-six. They were probably the most. But imagine what it's like to be out on a field with 220 pitchers, let alone other people. That's how it was at spring training. They had so many people that they used colors, instead of numbers, on the uniforms. That's what the competition was like.

So we're talking about maybe 400 ballplayers and 220 pitchers. You begin to wonder how you'll ever make it. And you somehow always think you're the smallest guy there, even though you aren't. They gave me a one-game cup of coffee early in the 1950 season. Back then they could keep some extra players until the end of April. They had three options on you then, so they could bounce you up and down and play with your salary as they did it.

I really think the teams took tremendous advantage of the ballplayers. They would often offer to lend you money, then incorporate it as part of your new contract. And they had the reserve clause to hold over your head for ransom. If you don't sign, you don't play. They also had the waiver rule then that was supposed to protect the players. But they also had telephones and would make deals. Let my player through waivers and I'll let yours through. There was really a great deal of collusion taking place between the owners then and all at the expense of the players.

I'll always remember what happened after the 1953 season. I was coming off a pretty good year and I had an agent named Frank Scott who used to try to help me get endorsements. He wasn't a lawyer, but he knew that most players didn't get what they should and he suggested he go with me when I negotiated my new contract. We met in Brooklyn and took the elevator upstairs to see the owner, Walter O'Malley. When we walked in together, someone asked who Frank was, and when I said he was gonna represent me in negotiations they said, whoa, wait a minute.

Then Buzzy Bavasi, the general manager, came out and said that Frank Scott was not going in. And when I said he was going to represent me in my contract, Buzzy said nobody could represent me. He said either Frank went on his own or they were going to get security to take him out bodily. That's when Frank decided it was best that he leave. And this wasn't just my story. There are others.

But getting back to baseball. I got called up again in 1951, only I broke my ankle sliding into home the same day they called me. I went anyway, and finally started to pitch sometime around August. Even though it was really my first time up, I already knew most of the players from spring training and there were no problems. I also had an ego like you wouldn't believe then. Like a stone wall; you couldn't get through it. I thought I could get anybody out.

To tell the truth, I don't think you can play this game of baseball until you have that type of ego, that type of confidence within yourself that says there's nobody who's gonna step up there who's better than you. Because once you take a fatalistic attitude and say, well, I can't do it anymore, then you're dead.

When I finally started pitching in 1951 I was smack in the middle of a great pennant race. At least it became a great race once the Giants started winning in August and September. You know, I think the Dodgers made the supreme mistake that all clubs can make when they're going well and have that superiority complex. We played the Giants a three-game series sometime in July or maybe early August, I don't remember. But we beat them three straight. Now the walls between the two dressing rooms at Ebbets Field were really thin. I remember, after the third game, the players screaming and yelling.

There was [Ralph] Branca in his loud bass voice, Dressen, and Robinson with his tenor voice, and they were all yelling out "The Giants are dead!" "The Giants are dead!" "The Giants are dead!" And I know they could hear it. Boy, could they. You know the old saying about letting sleeping dogs lie. If that didn't wake those guys up. After that it seemed they couldn't lose. We didn't play bad ball, but it was such stupidity to do what they did that day. I can tell you, don't ever say a word. That would be like me going up to a hitter after I struck him out and laughing in his face.

I loved starting then. I had picked up the sinker I mentioned in Venezuela when I played winter ball there in 1950. I was fooling around with a spitter without the spit and the ball started to really drop. It became one of my main pitches and I think because of it I was often accused of throwing a spitter. But I never did. Honestly. I could admit it now. But that pitch always looked like a spitter.

Anyway, relief pitchers were not exactly glamour boys at the time and I started when I began throwing in August. I completed five or six starts, but had one bad ballgame and Charlie Dressen got mad and sat me for two or three weeks. I couldn't get my curve over at all that day and in the second inning the bases were loaded. I felt I'd have better control if I pitched from the stretch, but Charlie didn't like that and ordered me to take a full windup. I went into the stretch anyway and some guy named Jones hit it out of the park for a grand slam. And I didn't pitch for three weeks. Charlie was a vindictive guy in one way or another. It had to be his way or else. He was a good manager with good baseball sense, but he didn't handle people well.

It's funny, but the time that he sat me was when the Giants were making their run. I had won five of the six games I started and . . . how do I say this with humility . . . I probably had the best stuff of anybody on the staff at that time. Our other starters were all tired. Yet Charlie's ego was such that he wouldn't use me. He wanted to make sure that I paid the penalty of not listening to what he said. And everyone knows what happened after that.

He did start me in the playoffs and I was fortunate to get ten runs and pitch a shutout. Any time you get ten runs a shutout is easy. But then we lost the final game and it was a tremendous letdown. But maybe it was just preordained and would have happened no matter who was pitching. We were the best club without a doubt, but I can't fault the Giants, because they played us right down to the hilt. There's no way we should have lost that final game with a 4–2 lead in the ninth inning. But that's baseball.

Of course, our biggest rivalry was always against the Giants. It was intense. Part of the reason was the managers, Durocher against Dressen, his protégé. Charlie had been a coach under Leo at Brooklyn earlier. So the battle cry was knock them down or it's gonna cost you. We had this thing that you'd better do it or else. There were a lot of pitchers who could knock guys down with no trouble. But others had difficulty doing it. But when the Dodgers met the Giants, you'd better do it.

There was a lot of headhunting back then, even among the other teams. And although they had the caps with the liners, a lot of guys wouldn't wear them. It wasn't the macho thing to do. Of course, there were no batting helmets then.

The Dodger-Yankee rivalry was not as intense as our rivalry with the Giants. There weren't all the knockdowns. That wasn't even part of it. And, of course, we met only in the World Series. We had greatly matched teams, and while they beat us more than we beat them look how many times the Series went to six and seven games. But it was a pleasure to pitch against them. In fact, I think a pitcher's greatest challenge is to pitch against great teams and great players. Not against mediocrity.

I had been both starting and relieving, but gradually I began working out of the bullpen more because I had a strong arm and could pitch more than once every four days. I think that's the main reason I ended up primarily a relief pitcher. I did have some shoulder problems in '52 and tried to work through them. Finally, toward the end of the year it came around and I was as good as ever by September. But Charlie wouldn't use me. I used to pitch batting practice and Duke Snider used to come up to me and say, the way you're throwing how can anybody hit you? But Charlie wouldn't listen and he made me sit out the entire '52 World Series.

He said he didn't want to risk hurting my arm and wouldn't go with me. You can't imagine anything that breaks your heart more than watching a World Series, feeling you could contribute, and being held out. Yet I was 8–4 during the year with only a curveball. I couldn't throw the fastball until September. Then he wouldn't use me. I guess he didn't have the confidence that I could do it. I understand it now, but I didn't back then.

It was the next year, 1953, that I really became a reliever. And I liked it. You know, if you really love the game of baseball, you've got to enjoy doing it more often than once every four or five days. I also look at a relief pitcher as an orchestrator. He has charge of the situation. It's in his hands and if he has a little bit of ham in him, that's a helluva place to be. I always liked to walk into a ballgame knowing what I was going to do would have a lot to do with the outcome, if not everything. That's what relief pitching is all about. It's a great situation if you love to play baseball.

In 1955 we finally won the Series from the Yankees. Before that we always seemed to start badly, do well, then end badly. If we started well, we'd go badly and end badly. It looked like the same thing in 1955 until Johnny Podres won that final game. I was warming up in the bullpen during the last three innings, but my roomie took care of them and that was okay. I'm glad I didn't have to go in.

I remember the next year, when Larsen pitched his perfect game against us. It was a funny feeling. We were almost pulling for him in a strange kind of way. You know, if we're gonna get beat, let's get beat that way because it's at least something that nobody will ever see again. He sure had one heckuva day. I had never seen this guy throw slow curves over the plate consistently before. But he had absolutely perfect control, and was changing speeds in a way he hadn't done before. I think it's wonderful that he did it, really.

Then the day after Larsen's game, I went out and threw a shutout. It was another one of those spot starts I used to get. Again, I think [Manager Walter] Alston went to me that day because I had the strongest arm on the club, as well as the ability to pitch and recover. I always felt I could have been a big winner as a starter. It was merely the series of events that took place that made me what I was.

Of course, I couldn't pass through this period without talking about the Dodgers, even though so much has already been said and written about the team. There was a real togetherness about the ballclub. Some cliques, naturally. But the togetherness was stronger than the cliques. We spent a lot of time together, on and off the field, and I think it was the closeness between the black and white players that really made our club.

Jackie Robinson, of course, was the catalyst, and in more ways than one. Jackie couldn't step onto the field without creating excitement. He didn't even have to play, because of the vocal things that would take place while he was there. I've always said there were very few ballplayers I'd go out to see, and while Jackie was my teammate, I was always anxious to go to the ballpark just to watch him, even in batting practice. He was a ball of fire.

Campy, for instance, was a great ballplayer, too, but he didn't have Jackie's excitement. Jackie was a cosmopolitan personality, a worldwide personality, somebody presidents would come out to see. They may have loved watching Roy and the rest of the guys, but they wanted to see Jackie first. And you had to appreciate that about him. He was such a newsmaker.

But there were a lot of leaders on the ballclub. Pee Wee [Reese] was a peacemaker, always telling people to take it easy, calm down. He kept things on an even keel. But you can't have a good ballclub without having many great leaders. There might be one or two who stick out, but we had many guys who could take over when things began going badly. Gil could do it, Furillo could do it, even Billy Cox. And they could do it defensively as well as offensively. That's what a good ballclub is all about.

Newcombe, Erskine, and Roe were all fine pitchers. Newk was the power pitcher, Carl had a sneaky fastball and great overhand curve, while Preach was a finesse pitcher with great control; he would drive batters crazy by taking so much time, like a slow golfer. A lot of people have made Newk the fall guy in the World Series, but I'll forgive him for anything he might not have done in the World Series for what he did for us during the regular season.

He was the type of pitcher made for Yogi Berra. Yogi could hit anyone who had a good fastball and a curve that didn't break much. This was Newcombe, and Newk loved to pitch high and Yogi loved to hit high. Yogi was the guy who usually wrecked him in the World Series. So I don't think Don Newcombe ever has to bow his head in shame.

We all used to kid Duke Snider as being the luckiest guy in the world. We had a righthanded-hitting club and he was the lefty. So he saw all the righthanded pitching. But Duke was a natural hitter, almost like Ted Williams with that great swing. He was also a great outfielder with a great arm and terrific accuracy. He's right up there with Mantle and Mays and I think it really levels out for all three of them. They were all such great guys and great players that to put one ahead of the others is a shame. I would have loved to play with any of them.

In 1958 we all went West. We had to go. There was no other thing to do. While it didn't take us by surprise—there had been rumors for a long time—we didn't really like it. We were all comfortable in Brooklyn. It had been our home and while it was a large borough, in some ways it was very small. And, of course, the Dodgers could do no wrong. So it was an emotional thing to leave.

Baseball-wise, I think it hurt guys like Erskine and myself the most, because we were getting toward the ends of our careers. We knew how to pitch, but all of a sudden we were put into a ballpark that wasn't a ballpark. It was a football field with a fence just 215 feet away in left. We all lost our mode of pitching, tried to do things differently than we had been doing them for years. The hitters, too, changed their styles. A lot of them were trying to put everything over that short fence. We deserved better and ended up in seventh place.

The following year we adjusted somewhat. We started pitching inside and getting guys out. We might have won the pennant, but there was no way you could be a pitcher and pitch in a park like that. It was an insult to baseball, but probably a necessity for the Dodgers. The only alternative, Wrigley Field in Los Angeles, held about twenty-eight thousand fans.

I remember going back to Brooklyn to watch the demolition of Ebbets Field. I just wanted to be there and see it. It hurt. They had these big five-by-six-foot pictures in the rotunda and there was a good one of me diving through the air and tagging a runner. I asked Mr. O'Malley if I could have it. He said to pick it out and he would have it expressed to me.

The team, of course, was getting older. Campy had been hurt in the auto accident in 1957. That was worse than awful, and in 1959 Larry Sherry had kind of taken over as the main man in the bullpen, though I still pitched in quite a few ballgames. By this time I was thirty-three years old and could feel I was losing something. My curve was slowing up a little, getting lazy instead of having that sharp break. Some days the sinker was great, but other days it was also lazy. I'd get hurt when it wouldn't come in as low as it should. I guess you begin losing arm strength, paying the penalty for throwing so much over the years.

The trade to Detroit happened around mid-June of 1960. I first heard it as I was walking underneath the Coliseum through a tunnel going to the dressing room. I could hear Vin Scully, our announcer, saying it on an inside speaker. So it was being broadcast over the air before I was told. That made me angry. It wasn't because they traded me. They had a right to do that, most assuredly. But the way it was done showed me that loyalty didn't exist in many ways. I sure as hell felt they had gotten a lot out of me when they wanted me, and I deserved more than that.

It was really tough for me to say goodbye. God, I was leaving what I was born into in baseball. From the very start I had always been a Dodger. And that in itself was part of the whole makeup of that team. Most of us were not traded people. We didn't come from other teams. We were born and bred as Dodgers and we had their educational background of playing baseball. Today I'm in my sixties and I still feel that no one teaches baseball better than the Dodgers. Even now, they truly teach baseball.

I stayed with Detroit until just after the All-Star Game. Then the Pirates bought me, probably as pennant insurance. I felt I pitched well as a set-up man for Elroy Face and it was exciting. The World Series was another story. I had the flu. Hey, the day that little son-of-a-gun [Bobby Richardson of the Yanks] can hit a grand slam home run off me on my worst day, I'd have to be sick. No way I'd ever throw him a high, inside fastball. God, even to him I couldn't pitch that way.

In 1961 I was back with the Pirates and worked in fifty-six games. That year the club went into a "We're great and we're gonna be great again" thing, but it just didn't happen. That's not the way it goes. By then, I was ready to hang it up. The Pirates had released me and I went home, not thinking I'd be back. Then one day after the season I got a phone call from George Weiss. That was when the Mets were getting ready for their first year in the National League and he said we need you. They said they would pay me the same salary I had in '61.

When I got down there I went and talked to Casey, who I suppose was at the end of his career just as I was. He told me I could be a big help to the young pitchers, and that seemed to make sense. I roomed with Joe Ginsberg, another veteran about my age, and he, too, was told to work with the pitchers. What we didn't realize was that we were getting a snow job. I was taking on the pitchers and Joe had the pitchers and catchers, and neither of us was getting into the ballgames. When we asked Casey about it he said, you guys can do anything you want, but we've got to get these kids into the games.

Oh, boy. So what happens when the season starts and its cutdown time. Who do you think went? Joe and I. They cut us and gave us severance pay. I just thought it was a lousy thing to do. They should have told us to come down, set a price, and let us know we were going to be coaches and not players. In my case, I think they wanted as much of the old Dodgers contingent around as possible. They had Gil Hodges, Roger Craig, Charlie Neal, and Cookie Lavagetto as a coach. You know, bring in the old Dodger fans. Mrs. [Joan] Payson [the Mets' owner] was one of the nicest people you could meet, but she was under the influence of stronger baseball people.

Being with an expansion team like that takes your heart and puts it in your shoes. They couldn't play baseball, they really, really couldn't. The best pitcher they had there was Al Jackson. If he hadn't been with the Mets then he could have been even better than he was. But that was it for me. I went home.

I had gone into business with four other partners some years before. We had a manufacturing plant in Rhode Island and produced professional golfwear, rainsuits, and things like that. We subcontracted for companies such as Wilson and Etonic. Believe it or not, I was a designer. I learned the craft from one of my partners and actually enjoyed the work.

We stayed in the business until 1979 when, like many other businesses in the States, we found we couldn't keep up with foreign competition. Now, I'm a banker, of all things. I never, never thought I'd do that in my life. I've been a loan officer and a business development officer and have had several other positions within the company. I even got rid of my crewcut. My kids made me do that and I found I actually had hair.

So the transition from baseball wasn't difficult, probably because I already was involved in the manufacturing business when I retired. And, to tell the truth, the game had lost some of its excitement for me. It just wasn't what it used to be. Maybe because not much could top the Dodger teams of the 1950s. Even though 1960 was exciting, I never felt that Pirate team could have touched the old Dodgers talentwise, not by one iota. But I will say that Roberto Clemente was the greatest right fielder I ever saw.

I never had an urge to coach or manage, because doing that you're not governing your own life. Too easy to be fired. What I really love doing are the fantasy camps. I've done them with the Dodgers for about seven years now, and it's really enjoyable. Some of the participants come back year after year, yet they still don't know that much about the game—a lot less, in most cases, than they think they know.

Yet to see the guys from my generation out there, you can still see the pride they have in their profession and the smoothness with which they still move around on the field. Watching them play against the campers is like watching a thoroughbred against a mule. That pride, the pride of not wanting to be defeated. It never goes away. It's still there. And I guess it always will be.

BOB VEALE

◆ **MAJOR LEAGUE EXPERIENCE** ◆

Pittsburgh Pirates, 1962–1972
Boston Red Sox, 1972–1974

◆ **CURRENT STATUS** ◆

Retired after serving ten years as a coach
and pitching instructor for the Atlanta
Braves and New York Yankees.

Bob Veale pitched in an era of great hurlers. A six-foot-six left-hander with a blazing fastball, Veale often went up against pitchers like Sandy Koufax, Bob Gibson, Don Drysdale, Ferguson Jenkins, Juan Marichal, Steve Carlton, and Tom Seaver. That's pretty fast company. Yet Veale won 120 games and fanned more than seventeen hundred batters during his thirteen-year career.

A native of Birmingham, Alabama, Bob was a high school and college basketball star who once passed up a chance to play with the Harlem Globetrotters to pursue a baseball career. In his first season as a starter, in 1964, he led the National League with 250 strikeouts, and also topped the circuit with 124 walks.

He had a career high 276 whiffs in 1965 and said that he often had more trouble with the Punch and Judy hitters than some of the great sluggers who were in the league during the 1960s. Proof of the pudding is that in nearly two thousand major league innings, Bob Veale gave up only 91 home runs.

Sometimes plagued by control problems, Bob was also dogged by bad luck. In 1968, his record was a mediocre 13–14, yet his earned run average was a sparkling 2.05. Like most competitors, Bob hated coming out of a close game, and has often said that he would rather come away with a loss than a no-decision. And that's what pitching is all about.

Y ou've got to be dominant on the mound and you start by demanding respect. Every successful pitcher has to have a little meanness in him. Look at it this way. If you go someplace by yourself and you're afraid, there's no telling how fast you can run. But if you can conquer that fear and know exactly what you're dealing with, then you can be successful.

In many ways, baseball is a game of chance. The batter has a chance of getting hit with a pitch. The pitcher can be hit with a line drive. The baserunner has a chance to break an ankle. So there's always fear somewhere. A pitcher doesn't have to hit or maim anyone. But he has to demand respect. And every time I walked out to the mound I felt I had that respect.

If a hitter can come up there and leave the ground swinging, he can intimidate you and win overall. But if that same man comes up and you brush him back—I didn't say hit him, just brush him back—he's gonna think twice before he winds up like a helicopter and tries to take all the air out of your infield. A lot of people think they don't allow pitchers to come inside today. They don't allow hitting people, but they allow brushing back. That will always be part of the game.

When you see a guy hit in the head you know there's room for a warning. Or if a pitcher retaliates and hits someone, then there is definitely a warning. But there are also times when a warning can work in your favor. Who was warned more than [Don] Drysdale or [Bob] Gibson? But they kept throwing inside, getting their warnings, and winning.

Today, the game is different. The players are different. You have a lot of guys who cry every time somebody comes close to them. Then there are the guys who charge the mound. There's a lot of that today, too. But that's something a pitcher can't worry about. Let them charge the mound. Even when I was coaching I used to tell the young kids, if you come close to someone and they don't like it, let them run toward you. Take the brunt of it. I was teaching how to pitch and if that meant showing them how to back a hitter up, then I'd do that. As long as they learned how to pitch. Because every pitcher reaches the point when he's gonna be out there by himself. And I won't be around when he and his teammates have to handle the load.

When I pitched in the middle and late 1960s it seemed that the National League was loaded with great pitchers. There were guys like Koufax, Marichal, Gibson, Drysdale, Maloney, Jenkins, Perry, Bunning, Carlton, and Seaver. And you knew you'd have to work a little harder when you went up against one of those guys because you weren't gonna get many runs. I used to love to pitch against Sandy [Koufax] for that reason; it would be a tight game with very few runs. With Drysdale, you always knew something would happen sooner or later. He'd hit somebody and the game might end up 2–0 or 2–1. For some reason, we used to love to play the Dodgers and had a lot of luck against them. So I looked forward to those matchups.

Fergie Jenkins was another pitcher I enjoyed watching and pitching against. Fergie didn't throw that hard, but he had a lot of stuff on his ball and real good movement and control. I admired all of those guys and loved pitching against them. You always knew you'd be in a good game, a game that anyone might win at any particular time with just one or two key runs. So while there was more of a chance of a loss or maybe a no-decision, those were really the games you'd get up for.

I'll never forget one game we played with the Giants sometime around 1964 or 1965. I was pitching against [Juan] Marichal with about four stitches in my right foot. I hadn't told anyone that I was cut because I didn't want to miss a turn. Well, both of us had good stuff and the game was still scoreless going into the tenth inning. Suddenly the stitches in my foot came apart and the foot really began to bleed. Now this was really a great game and I didn't want to come out. But when I went back to the bench, our manager, Danny Murtaugh, noticed the blood coming out of the top of my shoe.

He said, "Veale, that's enough. What's wrong with your foot?" I didn't want him to know about the stitches because I knew he'd yank me, so I told him I probably broke a blood vessel. He still acted like he wanted me to come out, so one of my teammates, [Donn] Clendenon, I think, said let's finish this thing right now. And that same inning somebody belted one over the left-field fence and we won the game, 1–0. That was the kind of thing I really enjoyed, being up there and pitching under those conditions.

Of course, it didn't always turn out that way. I had more than my share of tough losses and no-decisions, games when I didn't get many runs or games when I came out before I thought I should. In fact, there were times when I felt if I had been pitching in the same circumstances as a Koufax or a Marichal that I would have had a few seasons where I won twenty or more. They usually didn't come out until they were ahead or the team was pushing for a run to win it. I used to wonder why I would win sixteen, seventeen, eighteen games, but not twenty. And I felt I wasn't always given enough of a chance to win. I could always throw a lot of innings, so it wasn't that I was getting tired.

Someone once mentioned to me that I gave up just ninety-one home runs in my career in almost two thousand innings of pitching. I guess that's a pretty good ratio. Maybe some of that was because I was a hard thrower with sometimes spotty control. So in that respect, my wildness might have been an advantage. If a hitter isn't sure if the ball is going to be over the plate or come at him he's not gonna dig in quite the same way. It's what I said before about the element of fear. I think some of the so-called home run hitters would be content just to make contact when I was pitching. Or maybe look for one they could hit out, but just try to make contact after that.

I'll give you a good example of what I mean. I wore glasses when I pitched. One night I was going against the Cardinals and I began having trouble with the glasses. They kept fogging up and I couldn't see right. Lou Brock was batting when this happened. Anyway, I couldn't seem to keep them from fogging, so I took them off and threw them into the dugout. Then I got ready to pitch without them.

I could see home plate all right. They were really more important for peripheral vision. But I guess Lou didn't know that, because he refused to get back in the box unless I put the glasses back. So I said, no, I didn't want the glasses. They kept fogging up. And Lou just wouldn't hit. He didn't want me throwing my fastball in his direction without the glasses. Finally, the umpire made me put them back on and then Lou finally got into the box.

Memories like that are fun. But my first recollections of baseball didn't even include the major leagues. I was born in Birmingham, Alabama, on October 28, 1935, and started playing primarily because of my father. As soon as my friends and I were old enough to know about the majors, we wanted to know why blacks weren't allowed to play. In fact, at one point it became almost a daily conversation. Why were we playing the game if we could never get a chance to go beyond the old Negro American League, which, incidentally, was a flourishing league back then?

I was educated in a Catholic school system, so I knew from the beginning that it wasn't right to exclude blacks from baseball. But we also knew there was a great deal that wasn't right about the entire social structure of the United States.

Still, I kept playing baseball. In fact, I played all the positions then, even caught without a mask or any other equipment. We just didn't have the stuff. The first professional players I watched were with the Birmingham Black Barons in the Negro League. I used to see guys like William Powell, Jimmy Newberry, Spoon Carter, and Piper Davis. I'm sure not many people remember them. But I used to watch and admire those guys.

Both the Black Barons and the Birmingham Barons, the white team, played at the same ballpark and since I worked there as a kid, I got to see both teams play. Of course, by the time I was about twelve years old, Jackie Robinson had come up with the Dodgers and things began to change.

I continued to play both baseball and basketball through high school, but at that time basketball might have been the better sport for me. We really didn't have much of a baseball program at the school. I was a six-six center on the basketball team and could have had a chance to play with the Harlem Globetrotters. But instead, I took a basketball scholarship to St. Benedict's College in Atchison, Kansas, and stayed there for three and a half years.

My father deserves credit for most of my early development as a pitcher. He played some Negro League baseball for a while, and also played in the industrial leagues around Birmingham. He was a manager for one of the plants and pitched for them as well. He was always more of a control pitcher than I was and had a good fastball, a curve, and a knuckleball, a hard knuckleball. That's one pitch I could never get the hang of. Back then my thing was just to throw hard, harder, and hardest. So I could always throw, but I don't think I really developed that much as a pitcher while I was in college.

I actually stopped playing ball for a while during my sophomore year. A real good friend of mine was throwing batting practice one day and he wasn't behind the screen. I hit one back through the box and the ball actually tore off the lower part of his ear. It really upset me and I didn't play at all for three or four months after that. But I started again and I learned later that I was being scouted for a good part of the time. The Cards and Pirates were looking at me. In fact, the Pirates had been watching me in high school.

The Cards were the first team to offer me a contract. They were actually after both Ray Sadecki and myself. Sadecki was about five years younger and maybe that's why they offered him about eighty thousand dollars and me only eighteen thousand dollars. I thought that was ridiculous and it proved out that way. But at the time it was the thing that turned me to the Pirates.

It must have been sometime during the spring of my last year at college, because the baseball season had already started. A Pirate scout came to the house and said the team was interested in signing me, but they wanted me to come to Chicago, where the ballclub was playing, and work out. This was in 1958, so I was already twenty-two years old at the time. By then I was pretty confident, because during the summer I had pitched batting practice for both the Birmingham Black Barons and the white Barons. And I threw the ball past a lot of their guys, including some ex and future big leaguers, guys like Gus Triandos, Jim Piersall, and Enos Slaughter. So if I could throw the ball past them, I knew damn well I could throw it past anyone else.

It might sound strange to sign a pro contract in your final semester at college. But I was lacking a few hours to graduate with my class anyway and I decided I wanted to make some money. I figured I could always go back and pick up the credits I needed. So I signed in the spring of '58 and began my minor league career. I started in Modesto, California, then moved on to Las Vegas, where the team played in a rodeo pasture.

From there I went to Wilson, North Carolina, in 1959, my first full year. I was a hard thrower with control problems then, and it was just something I had to work out. I've always felt that you can talk to someone until you're blue in the face, but this is something you have to work on yourself if you really want to overcome it. You've got to kind of balance the mental and physical chemistry within yourself and that can take time.

I know some people say that hard-throwing lefties take the longest time to develop. But I don't really believe that. I think it's the physical structure of the individual that has a lot to do with it, more so than just throwing. I could go out there and throw softly and hit just about anything. But I wasn't getting paid to throw softly, and to put forth the effort to make the ball invisible to the batter, that's where the problem and complications come in. You either overdo it or underdo it, if you know what I mean.

By 1961 I began getting itchy. I was with the Columbus Jets in Triple A and thought the ballclub would call me up. I had come up to Triple A the year before after throwing a no-hitter against the Raleigh Caps in 1959. Anyway, I was something like 12–5 at Columbus, but instead of calling me up they called Al McBean and made a relief pitcher out of him. Al had just a so-so record at Columbus, yet he did well in Pittsburgh and that kind of got to me.

I didn't hold it against Al, because he and I were good friends. But I felt I had pitched better than anyone in spring training, and that included veterans like Vern Law and Bob Friend. So when I didn't get called I began to feel somewhat bitter about it. Some of my other teammates, like Donn Clendenon, were also being called up. I was going on twenty-six at the time, but the years didn't bother me because I felt I could endure anything then because of my physical power. I was strong and could run all day. The thing that bothered me was not being allowed the opportunity I felt I so rightly deserved.

At one point I even told Joe Brown, the general manager, that I was gonna leave. He just said, "Well, Bob, next year you'll be here." But just before the team broke camp the next spring they sent me down again. I was finally called up at the end of the season and pitched in a handful of games, enough to mess up my rookie status. To me, though, it was another full year wasted and I was really ready to pack it in. I told Joe Brown to forget it. But my father told me there were a lot tougher things out there in life and if this is what I wanted I ought to stick with it. So I did.

The next year I finally got up there, but I pitched mostly long relief. At least I had made it, but my feeling was I should have been there a long time ago. In 1964 I became a starter, and that's when the pattern began, the one where I was taken out of maybe 75 percent of my games either with the score tied or with us one run up or one run down. So I didn't get to finish too many of my games [thirty-eight starts, fourteen complete games]. I won eighteen, but if I was allowed to stay in a little longer I could have easily won twenty.

I led the league in both strikeouts and walks that year [250, 124] and was essentially a fastball pitcher. I had a little curve, but the Pirates' philosophy was that the hardest ball to hit was a live fastball, so I was still mainly a thrower. The guy who really helped me was Harvey Haddix, who had come to the Pirates in 1959 and pitched the twelve-inning perfect game against Milwuakee that year, the one he lost in the thirteenth. Anyway, Harvey pointed out that even if you shot a ball out of a cannon, someone would be able to hit it. He told me I had to learn to move it around where I wanted it. I began to watch the way he worked the hitters and I think that helped. Up to that time I was just trying to excel with fastballs.

The funny part was that I often had trouble with the mediocre hitters, not the real good ones. I think that's because there's a tendency to let up a little with those guys. One reason might have been my control problems. Some days it would seem that my head was going one way, and my arm and butt the other way when I'd turn the ball loose. On those days when a weaker hitter came up, I didn't want to walk him, so I'd let up. Like

I said before, when you throw it softly you can put it anywhere. But these guys are just trying to make contact anyway, just hit it back up the middle. And these were the guys who sometimes hurt me.

About the only so-called big hitter that used to hurt me was Orlando Cepeda. He might have had three or four homers off me, but I handled most guys like that pretty well. Even my first full year as a starter. They were the guys who really brought all my energy out and it didn't make any difference if I hit them or not. You know, that little bit of meanness we talked about. So I never went out there worried about a guy's reputation.

I always worked hard at pitching. There's an old saying that you're no better than your environment and if a man is participating, working any job, if he can't learn something every day, well then he shouldn't be on that job. That's the way I always felt and I still feel that way today.

Yet the next five or six years the same situation seemed to prevail. It takes runs to win. A lot of times I never seemed to get them. Maybe they would take me out because they were afraid of late-inning walks in close games, I don't know. But there were times when the team seemed to always get a lot of runs for guys like Steve Blass and Bob Moose and when my turn came around we'd get only one or two. It was almost a matter of being what they call in baseball "snakebit."

The team was also up and down during those years in the middle 1960s even though they had some solid ballplayers, and there were times when I'd get discouraged about it. I'd rather come out with a win or a loss than come away with nothing. The worst feeling is to pitch a damn good game for seven or eight innings and come away with nothing. Maybe that's a selfish way of looking at things, but it's also a way of life in baseball. You get paid by what you win. The other stats don't mean too much. Try to go in there and negotiate a contract on an earned run average and see what it's gonna get you. You throw up the earned run average and they throw up the bases on balls. You throw up the strikeouts and they come back with the bases on balls. The name of the game is W and L's.

I think the 1968 season really illustrates what I'm talking about. I wound up with a 13–14 record, but an earned run average just over 2.00 [2.05]. That's kind of indicative of what transpired when I pitched, yet they look at the W and L's and ask what's wrong with you? What's wrong is that I didn't have the ability to pitch and be Babe Ruth at the same time. But what I had to say usually wasn't worth a damn.

Despite that, I never really wanted to leave Pittsburgh. You build up a relationship with an organization and feel that it means something. So I never asked to be traded or anything like that. I was already nearly thirty-three when the 1968 season ended and I think I had slowly changed my pitching style. I was throwing more breaking pitches then and my control was getting better. At the same time, I was beginning to lose a little something off my fastball. So it's kind of a balancing act you have to do.

That didn't really upset me, either. Even steel rails wear out and eventually have to be replaced. Life is like that. You can only do this for a certain number of years, and within those years you've got to learn to adjust. You've got to learn to change. I used to watch guys like Haddix and Law, the way they'd spot the ball around. They would try to cut the level and plane of the ball down, so they could keep it on the ground or get the hitter to pop it in the air. And you try to learn by watching guys like that.

I was a starting pitcher through 1970 and the next year they moved me to the bullpen. Not a single start. And I don't know why. Danny Murtaugh was still the manager then and they just said they were going to relegate me to the bullpen. I guess they felt I would better serve the team as a relief pitcher because of circumstances or my previous performance [10–15 in 1970, a 3.92 ERA]. But it wasn't easy for me to make the transition. A relief pitcher has to come in and throw strikes and I didn't always have real good control. I started as a long reliever, but when my bullpen appearances became fewer and fewer, I figured they were trying to tell me something.

Anyway, it began getting to the point where I didn't care anymore. I think that's because of the way I was being handled, with no consideration for my feelings. It was like they had put me in a dungeon and kept me there until they needed me. A lot of the games I got into were games that were already out of reach. I also had gained weight that year. I was up to about 275, 280 pounds. Someone even wrote that I looked like a beached whale. Nice stuff.

The weight didn't bother me, but in truth I wasn't as effective as I had been at 230. I guess I shouldn't complain because the team wound up in the World Series that year and they won it. But I only pitched two-thirds of an inning in the Series and that really took something away from it. I know I didn't enjoy it as much as the guys who participated. I was there, but when it was over it was almost like a forced reaction on my part. I was proud of the team and happy to share the money, but as far as the emotion was concerned, there just wasn't that much there for me.

By then I really wanted out, but I never asked, because I always figured when I finished playing with Pittsburgh that would be the end of it. The next year I was with the club only a short time and then they sent me to the minors, to Charlestown. In fact, they released me and told me I could go down and play myself back into shape.

Bill Virdon was in his first year as manager and he's the one who released me. I believe I was the first person he ever had to release and I could tell it was upsetting him. So I said, "Bill, I'll make it easy for you. I know what you're gonna say." He looked at me and said, "Bob, you're an A-one guy." And that was that. So I went and pitched pretty well at Charlestown. Then in September I was sold to the Red Sox.

The Red Sox said they were willing to take a chance. I pitched a few games for them at the end of the season, then they told me to get into good shape and they'd send me to their top farm team at Pawtucket. There I would be a pitcher-coach, helping out with the younger guys while still throwing myself. It worked out all right. I ended up in Boston for most of 1973 and pitched pretty well, this time in short relief.

It's funny how things work out. I know going back to the minors sounds pretty rough, but I felt better down there than I did the last couple of years with Pittsburgh, because at least I was pitching. And I still felt I had something to offer somebody. I just had to get myself into condition.

But I also enjoyed pitching in Boston. The people there know their sports. You can't bullshit them, so you've got to be ready to perform and when you perform they reward you. They'll let you know they appreciate what you're doing. I also liked the organization. A lot has been said about discriminatory practices in Boston, but they take good care of their people.

Like I said, I pitched mostly short relief. By this time I was more of a finesse pitcher, but I could still get up a good fastball, into the nineties. There was another National League veteran there, Bob Bolin, who had been with the Giants. He and I were both pretty effective, though I was sure we wouldn't really be remembered since we were both about at the end. I'd often be brought in to pitch to guys like Tony Oliva or Rod Carew, though lefties, and Bob would come in and throw against the righties. Pitching short relief you know you've got to get that one guy out, or those two guys out, because you won't be going back out for the next inning. So it's a whole different kind of thing.

In 1974 there were some problems on the club and I think they really decided to rebuild. That meant getting rid of the old guys. I didn't pitch much anyway and I was nearly thirty-nine years old. So I was pretty sure it was the end of the line. And when they released me at the end of the season I didn't bother to contact any other ballclubs, and none of them contacted me.

Leaving wasn't too difficult at the time. I think I was tired of going to the ballpark, especially the way things had deteriorated in Boston with the internal problems on the club and people bringing their problems into the clubhouse and onto the field. I told my wife it was time to get something else started, that maybe I would go into teaching.

It's funny. I was almost thirty-nine and I could still wind up and get one of two of them in the nineties. And when you can do that, you always think you've still got it. At least part of you does. But I went home and took a whole year off to kind of readjust. I guess my top salary was about the fifty-thousand-dollar mark, but during most of my peak years I was between thirty-five and fifty thousand dollars. Not real big money, certainly not by today's standards. But I had invested in some property in Birmingham and just hung out there trying to keep it up. I guess I was just sort of cooling out.

I had a cousin in Atlanta who had told me the Braves needed some coaches. So when I was ready I contacted Bill Lucas, the team's vice-president, and he offered me a minor league pitching instructor's job right on the spot. And I took it. I was more or less a roving instructor and did it for eight years, until about 1983.

It was something I really enjoyed, especially the closeness with the kids. You can't teach something if you don't know a person or some things about him. That makes it a lot easier, dealing with the individual personalities. I guess I found that the most interesting part of the job. And as I said before, my goal was to teach them to be fearless and dominant, and to demand respect. That, and the mechanics of pitching.

When I left the Braves I joined the Yankee organization for a year. I coached at Greensboro [North Carolina], but when the year was up they released me. I don't know why and I didn't call to ask. Then I went with a friend of mine up to Utica, New York, and coached with the Utica Blue Sox for a year. But that was in 1985, and that turned out to be the worst year of my entire life.

I lost my house when a guy we had helped broke in and burned me out. Everything was destroyed. That same year my mother, brother, and a cousin all died, also an uncle. It was really difficult for us to cope with all that. All my baseball mementos were destroyed, but like I told my wife, the things you cherished you'll always have in thought, and the material things can be replaced.

Since that year I've been relaxing and enjoying my pension, also doing what's necessary to keep our little property up. The pension is adequate, because I just got in under the wire. The only connection I've had with baseball is some participation in the Equitable old-timers' games.

Now I'm beginning to think I'd like to get back into coaching again. I think I'm pretty good with the kids and proved it during my eight years with the Braves. I always try to take a kid under my wing the same way I would want someone to take mine. Kids today have got to learn to concentrate on baseball. Their first year away from home they're going to find a lot of distractions, a lot of things that can mess up their lives.

If a kid wants to make baseball his livelihood, he's got to learn it as if he is going to school. He's got to make it everything, his whole life, because that's what it's all about. The game is built around the dollar sign now. A youngster today can make a lot of money. That's the biggest difference from when I played. But he still has to get there, and that takes the same kind of hard work and perseverance that it always took.

RAY BOONE

*Ray Boone had the unique experience of appearing in a World
Series after just six games in the major leagues. That happened in
1948, when the twenty-five-year-old Boone was part-time backup shortstop to Cleveland's playing manager, Lou Boudreau.*

*From there, however, Boone went on to become one of the fine
players of the early and middle 1950s, having several outstanding*

*seasons with both the Indians and Detroit Tigers. He drove home
more than 100 runs on two occasions, leading the American League
with 116 in 1955. He also hit twenty or more home runs for four
consecutive seasons between 1953 and 1956.*

*Born in San Diego, California, on July 27, 1923, Ray grew up
watching the Pacific Coast League, which paid its players so well
then that some preferred to remain there rather than go to the
majors. Signed out of Hoover High School by the Indians in 1942,
Ray was one of many players of his generation to lose several years
of his career to the service during World War II.*

*But he made up for it when he returned. In 1953 he belted four
grand slam home runs and finished his career with 151 round-
trippers. Originally a catcher, Ray ended up playing three different
infield positions. His son, Bob, started as an infielder, but has now
caught more ballgames than any receiver in baseball history, an
achievement that has made his father very proud.*

T he thing that still bothers me when I look back at my major
league career is that I didn't retire instead of going to Kansas
City, Milwaukee, and Boston, all in the space of one year between May of 1959 and May of 1960. As soon as Chicago said
they were gonna trade me to Kansas City, I should have packed
it in. But I was still making thirty thousand dollars. I wasn't about
to come home and make that kind of money.

Each time I was traded, I'd say all right, I might as well finish
the season. But all I was doing was being a pinch-hitter and filling
in, wherever they needed me. It was putting in time, not playing
a whole lot, and that was difficult. I think the toughest part was
not hitting with the starting lineup. Back then, the subs had to

come out and take batting practice early, before the regulars. I was used to being part of the starting lineup, and that bothered me.

But I knew I was going downhill. You start to lose something and it's compounded by not playing. In my case, I really stopped playing regularly in 1959. So when 1960 came around I was dead, because I rusted out in '59. When you get older, the skills disappear even faster if you don't play. That's the way it is with my son, Bob, now. He's over forty and he can't afford to sit. If he wants to keep playing he knows he has to keep active.

Bob began as a third baseman before he became a catcher. I went the other route. I was always a catcher until the Indians decided to make me an infielder. That's another regret, though there was no way to know it at the time. But if I had started as an infielder, it probably would have helped my hitting, because the transition was difficult. I enjoyed catching, don't get me wrong. And maybe if I had remained a catcher it would have been fine. But as it turned out, it was a waste of time.

I was signed as a catcher and caught at Sumter, South Carolina, and Wilkes-Barre, Pennsylvania, in 1946. The next year I was at Oklahoma City in the Texas League and catching again. But all year long we couldn't seem to find a shortstop. There must have been sixty-seven shortstops coming and going during the year. Finally, the last two weeks of the season when another shortstop failed to report, they asked me if I wanted to try it. So I played it for about a month right before the season ended.

In 1948, I went to spring training with the Indians. As always, I went down there with just my catcher's mitt. I didn't even own an infielder's mitt. Anyway, Lou Boudreau, who was the shortstop and the manager, said he had fairly good reports on my month at shortstop in Oklahoma City and asked me if I wanted to try it again. He said the organization was short on infielders.

It was something to think about. Cleveland had Jim Hegan catching then and Jim was a real good receiver. So I figured, why not, playing the infield might be another way to get to the majors. Boudreau was in his final years as a player, so I decided to take advantage of the opportunity. And Lou told me if I didn't like it I could jump back to catcher.

I had probably started catching when I was in the fourth or fifth grade, one of those deals when they asked who'll catch and I volunteered. From that point on, I was always the catcher, right through high school and American Legion, and again in the service. I never had a lot of speed, but I had a very good arm, so I felt catching might be the position for me. And as I said, I enjoyed it, and never really thought about giving it up.

The Indians had actually signed me back in 1942. I had been born and raised in San Diego and grew up with the Pacific Coast League. We were all San Diego Padres fans and got to see a lot of future big leaguers playing out there. I can remember watching Hank Greenberg, Rudy York, Joe DiMaggio, Ted Williams, and Bobby Doerr. So between the Padres and listening to recreations of big league games on the radio, I had the dream of being a big leaguer at a pretty early age.

In fact, Ted Williams was also from San Diego and I got to see him play in high school. He was the best hitter I ever saw, even then. He really used to pack the place because he was unreal to watch. If you saw him then you'd know why they called him the Splendid Splinter. He was really skinny, but boy could he hit.

The Coast League was always tough then. There were a lot of good ballplayers, some ex-major leaguers, and even some guys who refused to go to the majors. The pay there was so good they used to call it the pension league. In some cases, guys were making maybe eighteen thousand dollars to play on the Coast and were offered only twelve thousand to come to the majors. And they wouldn't go.

There weren't a whole lot of big league scouts on the West Coast in the early 1940s and I always felt that a number of real good players simply were not seen. But I guess because San Diego was a good baseball town they came there pretty often and the Indians finally offered me a contract with a five-hundred-dollar bonus. It was quite a bit of money back then. The funny thing was that shortly after I signed with Cleveland, the Red Sox came out of nowhere and offered me $2,500. Too late.

I went right from high school to Class C ball and was the highest-paid player on the Wausau, Wisconsin, team at two hundred dollars a month. When I finished the 1942 season with Wausau, I went into the Navy and played there. Good brand of ball. Bob Lemon played with me in the service. Bob was a third baseman–outfielder then and I was still a catcher. We used to play every weekend and sometimes draw nearly ten thousand people to the games. Most of them were recruits and to them this was great entertainment. I guess we played close to one hundred games a year.

It was when I got out of the service in '46 and returned to the Cleveland organization that I had to make the decision about converting to shortstop. Then in 1948, Lou Boudreau gave me a choice. He said I could return to the minors and play every day, or I could stay around as his backup. I said I'd stay, and I remember Hank Greenberg, who was the general manager then, asking me why I didn't want to go somewhere where I could play. "I can't believe you want to stay here like this," he said.

The reason, of course, was that it was the big leagues. But after about three weeks of sitting, I changed my mind. So I called Hank and told him I wanted out of there. "About time you wised up," he said, and sent me back to Oklahoma City.

It was a bit frightening being around the big leaguers at first. I remember being in camp the year before, in 1947. By the third day my legs were so sore that I was limping around the hotel. I looked the trainer up and the first thing he wanted to know was if I was with the ballclub. Then he told me to come back the next day. When I got there I looked in and saw Ken Keltner, Bob Feller, and Joe Gordon inside. Well, there was no way I was gonna walk in there with those guys and say I had sore legs. I passed that one up real quick.

Anyway, I went back to Oklahoma City in 1948, played shortstop, then came back in time to be eligible for the World Series.

We won the pennant that year by defeating the Red Sox in a one-game playoff. I got into only six games with five at-bats, but it was really a thrill to be part of that kind of pennant race. The guy who beat the Red Sox in the playoff to win it for us was Gene Bearden. Gene was a Navy veteran and I guess 1948 was also his rookie year. Anyway, he was great. He won twenty games for us, beat Boston in the playoff, and pitched very well in the World Series. He was a big reason we became World Champs. But after that it's kind of a sad story.

Gene was a knuckleball pitcher and he really baffled the hitters in 1948. But the next year they all began taking more pitches on him. They figured they had been swinging at balls the year before, not strikes. And sure enough, Gene began having a devil of a time throwing strikes. Everything was low, and it really hurt him. He stopped winning, but not because he didn't work. In that 1949 season, I never saw a guy work harder than Gene Bearden. He would throw on the sidelines, every day, trying to get his control back on the knuckleball. And the funny thing was, he really wasn't that wild. He was just missing, just missing all the time, enough for the pitch to be called a ball. And he never did get it back and was never the same pitcher again.

The 1948 Indians were a close-knit team, an awesome team in a lot of ways, with camaraderie and respect for one another. Bob Feller, who was still a star then, was a quiet man, but a guy who treated everyone great. I can remember standing in front of our hotel at spring training in 1947, and Bob drove up in his car and asked if I needed a lift to the ballpark. Things like that.

Being part of that team and then being in the World Series was a thrill, especially with the huge crowd of eighty-six thousand we got in Cleveland. That was awesome. We also had a big parade after we won and I was thrilled to death by that. Guys like Boudreau, Keltner, and Jim Hegan were all in the Series for the first time. Joe Gordon had been in a couple with the Yanks, but I think he might have been the only one.

There was a lot written about Bob Feller not winning a game, but he pitched great. He lost 1–0 to Johnny Sain, and that was on a disputed pickoff play at second with Phil Masi of the Braves. The ump called him safe and he later scored the game's only run. I remember Boudreau arguing that one so strenuously that I thought I was gonna get into the game. But he didn't get tossed out.

My only appearance was as a pinch-hitter. Warren Spahn struck me out, but I had some pretty good hacks at him because he threw me nothing but fastballs. I think that was the game where we got blown out, so he had a pretty good lead.

Another guy who gave us a shot in the arm that year was Satchel Paige. Satch was 6–1 as a rookie and, of course, he was already over forty years old. But from what I could tell, he was pretty happy with the way things went for him, even though he didn't get a chance in the majors sooner. He was already famous. I think more people had heard about Satchel Paige than maybe even Babe Ruth. So he was already a legend when he finally got to the majors. I used to see him pitch years earlier when he would barnstorm through San Diego.

He was easily as fast as Feller then, and he could throw all day. He had that slingshot kind of arm and you couldn't tell how he would throw the next pitch. He threw sidearm, underhand, and over the top. I hit a grand slam off him when he was with the Browns in 1953. He was a much more impressive pitcher in 1948. In fact, I got to warm him up a few times that year. I talked to a lot of old-timers who had hit against him years earlier and they said he was really awesome. But he helped us to the pennant and got into one game in the Series.

The next year I made the club and backed up Boudreau all year. I played in eighty-six games, then played a little over one hundred in 1950. In 1951 I finally became the regular. But when I really started seeing a lot of action at short in 1950, I had only played ninety-five big league games at the position. That really wasn't enough. What I could have used was a solid year playing short in Triple A. But I never even played Triple A. And I don't think I ever really had the hands for a shortstop. I could make some good plays, but Joe Gordon, our second baseman through

1950, was really the guy who kept me afloat in those first years. I eventually became a decent third baseman, but I was never really a shortstop.

When the Tigers made me a third baseman in 1953 it was like stealing. Night and day. To me, third base was an easier position by a two-to-one margin or better. And the transition was easy. As soon as I moved to third it was like saying hello to a new position. Nobody ever told me about this spot before.

I had actually begun splitting time with George Strickland at Cleveland in 1952. George came over from the Pirates and was a much better shortstop than I was. Of course, the Indians had Al Rosen at third so they weren't going to move me there. But I enjoyed my years in Cleveland. The World Series was a thrill in '48 and the team was always in contention after that. Of course, most of our time was spent chasing the Yankees.

That was some rivalry, very enjoyable. The Yanks always knew we were the team to beat and whenever we played there was some extra excitement. We'd pull into Grand Central Station at five o'clock in the morning and the press would be waiting for us to get off the train. And any time you came down to the lobby of the hotel the reporters would be all over the place. They didn't let you forget you were in town to play the Yanks.

There was always a great atmosphere at Yankee Stadium and the games were a battle. And let me tell you something. The Yankees then were *good*. They had an excellent ballclub. The thing that made the team then was the guys coming off the bench. I think they could have benched their entire starting nine and not lost too much with the second nine guys. Casey [Stengel] was the first manager to platoon extensively and it worked for him. When you can alternate a couple of guys like Hank Bauer and Gene Woodling, then you've got something good going.

They were a well-balanced ballclub and whenever they needed a shot in the arm they seemed to go out and get that big guy. I remember when they got Johnny Mize from the Giants. He really helped them a lot during those years. So really, our ballclub was outmanned. Except for our pitching. Our pitching staff was awesome. We just couldn't match them with our bench and maybe our bullpen. We chased them and fought them, never really fell down against them. But they just had a damned good ballclub.

I was probably making between five and seven thousand dollars in those early years, and when you think about it that wasn't bad. I remember having some friends who were teaching school then and they were making even less, maybe getting a couple of thousand for teaching. But we still worked in the off-season. Once the season ended you got home as fast as you could and started working the following Monday morning.

Anyway, I stayed with the Indians until June of 1953. That's when I was traded to Detroit, and that turned out to be my first big year at the plate. The trade wasn't a real surprise. They were using Strickland more at shortstop and the Tigers also wanted Steve Gromek, who had been a nineteen-game winner and also won one in the '48 Series. But I remember Hank Greenberg calling me in and saying, "Remember, I promised that I'd never trade you to a club I didn't like."

Then he told me he had traded me to Detroit, where he had played. He said Briggs Stadium was a great park to play in, and he also told me that the St. Louis Browns had been pressuring him to make a deal for me. I guess I dodged that one. That was one team I wouldn't have cared to play for then. But I liked Hank and felt he had been square with me. And I think he was always pulling for me to do well. I remember him saying, "Well, like all my trades I suppose you'll go over to Detroit and go crazy."

Of course, the Tigers moved me to third base immediately and I did go on to have a great year [twenty-six homers, 114 RBIs and a .296 batting average]. I think I became the eleventh player in baseball history to hit four grand slam homers in one year. I hit two before I left Cleveland and two more with Detroit.

The difference was that Detroit wasn't a winning team. The ballclub just couldn't compare with the Indians. In fact, when Cleveland finally won the pennant the next year, 1954, Al Lopez told both me and Steve Gromek that the only sad thing about winning was that we weren't there to share it. I thought that was a nice thing for him to say.

Playing for Fred Hutchinson at Detroit was another good experience. I always thought Fred was a grand person, God rest his soul. He was tough on the opposition, but never tough on his own players. I can remember him standing there when we were losing and yelling out, "It ain't always gonna be like this!" I think he knew we were overmatched, but you can't do it if you don't have the horses.

It wasn't long before the Tigers started to improve. Harvey Kuenn was a rookie in 1953 and had a great season. He was an outstanding hitter who could handle the bat with anyone. He'd make you laugh sometimes the way he could hit the ball. He was amazing. I've seen him hit the ball on a bounce or over his head. And I mean hit bullets. And you'd sit there wondering how the hell he hit the ball.

I also remember the first day Al Kaline joined the team. It was also in 1953 at old Shibe Park in Philadelphia. Al was just eighteen then and had a lot of advance publicity. So the press was there, and the photographers. And they were watching every move he made. He was a skinny kid then, skinny legs, and still a little on the weak side. We all gathered around when he took batting practice, and to tell the truth, he wasn't real impressive with the bat. Of course, it was his first day and the first day any of us had seen him.

Anyway, after that we went out for infield and I'm playing third. They hit the ball to Al in right and I got ready to take the throw. Well, he threw a rocket to third base, and that's what really opened everyone's eyes that first day. People were saying, "Look at the gun on that kid." He had a great arm. That's what stood out about him that first day. The year he led the league in hitting, in 1955, I led in RBIs with 116. That was a thrill, having the two of us leading the league like that. And Al really turned out to be a great player.

Even though I took the RBI title in '55 I always considered 1953 my best year. That's because I won so darned many games for the club that season. I wish they'd had that game-winning RBI stat around then, because I'd be curious how many I had. It was just that type of year.

Once I began to get a reputation as a top RBI man, I began to get more pitches thrown my way. But that was something you learned to expect. There were a number of pitchers around who were a little mean, but we had also gone to the helmet by then, and having it made you feel a little more secure. Before that they had the caps with the liners, but they weren't worth a nickel. The liner ran around the side of the cap, but was way up above the ears. So it protected the head, not the temple. And, of course, the first helmets didn't come over the ears, either.

What was called throwing at someone in those days was actually just brushing a guy back. Some pitchers did it more than others. Early Wynn was known for it. When I was at Cleveland, Early used to like throwing batting practice. He wanted to simulate game conditions and never used the screen. Well, he'd get madder 'n hell if someone hit the ball back up the middle. Even if you only did it once in a while, you'd better walk out of that cage right then and there. Because sure as hell the next pitch would come at you. And Early would stand there with a grin and say, "Oooops."

Allie Reynolds of the Yanks was another guy who wouldn't hesitate to brush you back, and neither would Virgil Trucks. Like I said, we all expected it. Early Wynn was a good man, but pitching was his business, his livelihood. Today you see so many players charging the mound as soon as the ball is in tight. That bothers me. In fact, you see a lot of hitters today who actually dive into pitches. They stride into the ball and then go down. And sometimes you'll see the catcher look around as if to say, that ball just missed being a strike, buddy.

I got into only one skirmish. It was with Tom Sturdivant of the Yanks, who didn't have a reputation for throwing at people. But we were beating the Yanks bad that day and at one point hit three consecutive homers off Sturdivant. It was at Briggs Stadium and Charlie Maxwell hit the third one, a real shot off the facing of the upper deck in right field. Well, I'm the next guy and I have a feeling about Sturdivant. But I wasn't too sure whether Sturdivant would throw at me or not. So when I got in there I kind of stayed loose. And he came at me. I didn't mind that so much, but he hit me in the helmet and that started it off. I went out there.

We ended up teammates at Kansas City years later and kind of laughed about the whole thing. That's how it was in those days. It happened and it was forgotten.

Charlie Maxwell, the guy I just mentioned, had a good career at Detroit. Charlie was the guy who always seemed to hit home runs on Sundays. I always felt I had a lot to do with Charlie getting his shot in the big leagues. He was with us one spring training, I think around 1956, and we had tried a lot of guys in left field, everyone but Charlie. One night I was lying in bed and thumbing through the press guide. I saw a picture of Charlie with his minor league record. It seemed like he hit a lot of home runs in the minors, but never really got the at-bats in the big leagues with the Red Sox.

So I told our manager, Bucky Harris, about it the next day. I explained why I felt Charlie should get a chance. It all worked out well. Charlie ended up with twenty-eight homers that year and made the All-Star team.

Bucky had replaced Fred Hutchinson as manager in 1955. They were like night and day. Hutch was always on the field a lot. Before the game he was all over, watching everything. Bucky was a grand person. But he'd always sit in the dugout. And he'd have only two meetings a year, one at the beginning to wish everyone good luck; and another at the end. Nothing in between. I remember him coming out on the field only twice during ballgames. Once it was for me. We were playing the Indians at Detroit and I had a tag play on Bobby Avila at third. I had to go up for the throw and I barely tagged his back as he went by me. I knew I touched him, but the umpire called him safe.

I told the ump I touched him whether he saw it or not and Bucky came out. He walked right past the ump and came over to me. "What happened?" he asked. I told him I touched Avila on the back. Then Bucky turned to the ump and told him he blew it. The umpire said he didn't, but Bucky simply said, "I know this man and he's not gonna lie to me. He said he touched him and that's all I want to hear." Then Bucky went right back to the dugout. End of argument.

In 1957, the Tigers moved me from third to first. Easy transition. But the reason they did it wasn't good. I was having trouble with my knees. The problem was calcium deposits, something that had bothered me even in my best days. Except for that one season [1951] in which I played 151 games, I was usually between 130 and 145 games each year. It was the calcium on my knees. It was a condition that couldn't be corrected by surgery, so from time to time I'd have to take a cortisone shot. Then it would take five or six days to clear the calcium out of there before I'd be ready to go again.

The funny part was that the only doctor who really knew how to take care of it was a Dr. Raska, who was the Washington Redskins' team physician. I guess the Washington Senators' trainer recommended him. He was the only one who knew just where to put that needle. So whenever the calcium problem would flare up, I'd have to fly to Washington from wherever I was to see Dr. Raska. Fortunately, the condition didn't threaten my career. But I think the hard fields and the wear and tear of playing made it a bit worse in those last years.

So my production fell off in '57 and the next year the Tigers traded me to the White Sox. I've got to admit it came as kind of a surprise. The team also threw in Bob Shaw, a kid with a real good arm. He ended up winning eighteen games for the Sox in '59. He was a decent pitcher who never got a chance in Detroit. But as far as I was concerned, the trade was handled well. They told me about it in the clubhouse while we were in New York. Then on the plane back to Detroit I had a long talk with John

McHale, the general manager. He thanked me for the years in Detroit, which was nice. I wasn't real happy about leaving, because I enjoyed playing there and I'll always remember that part of my career.

It was also the last time I played regularly. I was almost thirty-five then and like I said, in Chicago I was mainly a part-timer and pinch-hitter. And when they traded me to Kansas City the next year, well, that's probably when I should have quit. The funny part about it was that the Sox went on to win the pennant that year, and I ended up with Milwaukee, a team that lost the pennant in a playoff with the Dodgers. So I just missed twice getting back into the World Series.

Playing in Milwaukee gave me a chance to get a brief look at the National League and the difference was obvious. It was the black ballplayers. The National League just seemed to have almost all the good ones. They had players like Mays, Aaron, McCovey, Banks, Clemente, Cepeda, Frank Robinson, Pinson, right down the line. The National became the dominant league at that time because the blacks they signed were all so good. I can't tell you why the American League didn't sign as many good black players. Maybe it was because everything runs in cycles. But these guys were the difference and I could see it right away. They weren't just good; they were superstars.

I came back to the American League in May of 1960 when the Red Sox picked me up, and that's where it ended. The nice part was that I was able to finish my career as a teammate of Ted Williams. Ted was also in his final season. Like I said, I had seen Ted as far back as high school. In fact, we both went to Hoover High in San Diego, though I came along a few years after he did.

Ted, of course, had a great final year. He hit twenty-nine home runs and I remember him saying to me one day, it's awful to hit this many home runs and retire. I said, don't retire. And he said there were so many day games following night games then that it was awfully tough getting up for the day games. That's one of the things that took a toll on him.

I remember when he hit his five hundredth home run in Cleveland that year. He hit a high shot down the right field line and the umpire called it foul. Our first-base coach then was Rudy York, and Rudy started jumping up and down, arguing the call. Ted didn't say a word. He just came back, took his bat, and got set again. On the very next pitch he hit the same home run, same trajectory, same spot, and this time the umpire called it fair. It was really amazing. He said later it was the first time he hit two home runs in one at-bat. He thought the first one was fair, too, but he wouldn't argue.

When he hit a homer in his final at-bat it really wasn't a surprise. I had a feeling he would do it. Everything was just right. People were saying wouldn't it be great if he went out with a home run. And you just knew he would. Ted was that good a hitter.

I guess it would be nice if we could all go out like that. But I wasn't on a plateau with Williams and had resigned myself to the fact that that's the way it was. But I was proud of the fact that I had a solid career. During the time I played I never felt I had to take a back seat to anyone as far as doing my job with the ballclub. But it still would have been nice to play the last year of my career like Ted, announcing my retirement and then playing regularly right to the end.

Being in Boston for that final season turned out to be a break, because near the end of the year Mr. Yawkey called me upstairs and asked me what I wanted to do next year, if I was gonna play anymore. I said, no, I'm not playing. And he said, "Well, I want you to work for me, whatever you want to do." Then he picked up the phone and called downstairs to the minor league office and said, "I'm sending Ray Boone down. Hire him." Bang. Just like that.

That's how I became a scout. I started the very next year, right back home in San Diego, and I've been doing it ever since. I wanted to be near home, near my family, so I chose scouting over coaching or managing. I guess I was tired of traveling on the major league level.

So thanks to Mr. Yawkey, I got just what I wanted. He was really a down-to-earth kind of guy, proud of his players. You could never say anything bad about any of them. He'd even defend the worst player in the world. He was just a grand person. One time I had an ear infection and couldn't make the trip to New York with the ballclub. I was back at the hotel in Boston near the ballpark. Mr. Yawkey sent a cab over to bring me to his office at the ballpark so I could watch the ballgame with him. We spent about five hours together that day, and maybe that was one of the reasons he wanted me to work for him.

Being in scouting, I've watched a lot of ballplayers over the years, and I think there are some real good ballplayers around today. The biggest difference I notice is in the throwing arms. Players today just don't seem to throw as well as they did when I played. Maybe it's the Little Leagues. Kids play in fenced-in fields and have to make only short throws. On the playgrounds the ball would roll ten miles and you'd have to throw it as far as you could.

The other difference is in Triple A. There was one time when Triple A ball was excellent. But expansion took care of that. Take away those ten expansion teams and there would be another 250 ballplayers in Triple A.

But I have nothing against the players today making millions. In fact, I often defend them when I hear someone say that no ballplayer is worth that much. People don't blink when Paul Newman gets paid millions to make a movie, or Frank Sinatra to sing. Why not a ballplayer? It's like a lot of other professions. They money is just there. You know, you can sit in front of the TV and watch guys competing in a putting contest for fifty thousand dollars. I sometimes think the fans talk about it more than the ballplayers.

As for looking back over my career, two things still stand out. One was leading the league in RBIs in 1955. Kaline led the league in hitting and Mantle in home runs. There were just so many good hitters in the American League that year. The other thing was making the All-Star team in 1954, the year after the Indians sent me to Detroit. The game was at Cleveland and I hit a home run. A lot of people said the Indians shouldn't have traded me that day, and that kind of thing makes any ballplayer feel good.

BOB
BOYD

♦ **MAJOR LEAGUE EXPERIENCE** ♦
Chicago White Sox, 1951, 1953–1954
Baltimore Orioles, 1956–1960
Kansas City Athletics, 1961
Milwaukee Braves, 1961

♦ **CURRENT STATUS** ♦
Retired after twenty years with Dreamliner
Bus Company, Wichita, Kansas. Sets up
autograph shows with big league ballplayers in Wichita–Kansas City area.

*Bob Boyd was among the first handful of black ballplayers signed
into the major leagues in the years following Jackie Robinson's
1947 debut with the Dodgers. Born in Potts Camp, Mississippi,
on October 1, 1926, Bob grew up in an era when black youngsters
didn't even think about playing in the big leagues.*

But that didn't stop him from playing baseball. By 1947 he was good enough to make the Memphis Red Sox in the old Negro American League. Three years later he became the first black to sign with the Chicago White Sox organization. He really didn't see much playing time with the Sox, jumping back and forth between majors and minors until he was dealt to the Orioles in 1956.

In Baltimore, Bob Boyd finally had the chance to prove what he had known all along—that he was a major league hitter. He became the first Orioles regular to compile a .300 average for an entire season, and hit over .300 for three consecutive years as the Baltimore first baseman.

Known as "The Rope" for his hard line drives, Bob continued to play minor league ball, then semipro ball right into his forties. His only regret is that he didn't get an earlier start in the majors and that an ulcer might have prevented him from being a .300 lifetime hitter. He finished at .293.

W hen the White Sox first scouted me, I never even knew it. I was playing for the Memphis Red Sox in the Negro American League then. I started playing for them in 1947, the same year Jackie Robinson came up with the Dodgers. But even after Jackie signed, there was no great rush to sign other black players, just one or two here and there.

We already had one player signed from our team. Dan Bankhead, a pitcher, also went to the Dodgers and pitched in a few games in 1947, the same year Jackie started. But other than that, we never knew when we were being scouted. I found out later that a White Sox scout named John Donaldson had been looking at me. He was even riding on the team bus. But John never really introduced himself at first. So I didn't know who he was.

The Memphis Red Sox were owned by two brothers, black men and both rich. Dr. B. B. Martin was a successful dentist and his brother, W. S. Martin, actually owned a hospital. In fact, I ended up marrying one of his nurses. As I said, John Donaldson was watching me and we finally began talking about the White Sox. This was in 1949 and I really began to get the feeling that the Sox were interested. But I still had a contract with Memphis.

My pay when I started in the Negro League was just $175 a month. It wasn't much, but then again big leaguers didn't make that much then, either. Anyway, at this point the story gets a little strange. One night in the spring of 1950, the dentist, B. B. Martin, called to tell me he had just sold my contract to the White Sox. He wanted me to pack and come over right away so he could put me on a plane for the Sox minor league camp at Colorado Springs.

So out of the blue I'm on a plane at 12:30 A.M. headed for Colorado. I was surprised, but happy. I knew I was a good ballplayer and just wanted a chance. I thought this was it. The White Sox people welcomed me and I began working out with them. I was also the first black player signed by their organization. But that's not the end of the story.

I was at the Sox minor league camp for only a short time when they got a call from Memphis. It seems the other brother, W. S. Martin, wanted me back. He said I was supposed to be on his club and he hadn't agreed to sell my contract to the White Sox. So all of a sudden I wasn't sure what was gonna happen.

It turned out the two brothers had gotten into it over money. B. B. Martin had sold my contract to the White Sox for fifteen thousand dollars, and he intended to keep all the money for himself. Well, his brother wanted half of it and felt if he didn't get it, I should come back. So the battle wasn't over me as a ballplayer; it was over the money. And when the two brothers finally decided to split the money, they were more than happy to let me stay with the White Sox, and so was I.

Even though I started my career in Memphis, I was actually born in Mississippi, the town of Potts Camp, on October 1, 1926.

So I grew up in that era when blacks didn't play major league ball. Maybe that's why I never even thought about major league ball when I was growing up. In fact, I knew very little about it. I just started playing ball with my daddy and my brother. My daddy was a real good ballplayer and I guess I took after him, because as I got older, the only thing I knew how to do was play baseball.

I played right up to the time I went into the service in 1944, played there, and continued to play when I got out in 1946. A year later I just walked into the Memphis Red Sox camp and asked for a tryout. That's how I got with them. When they first signed me they sent me to a farm team club of theirs, then called me back about six months later.

The Negro League teams then were good, real good. I'd say they were close to the big leagues in ability. Not Double or Triple A, but the big leagues. Some of the guys I got to play against were Larry Doby, Monte Irvin, Willie Mays, Roy Campanella, Don Newcombe, Joe Black, and other guys who would make it to the majors. There were also many older players who were still real good, only they were already too old for the big league teams to give them a shot. But all these guys could play.

It's funny, but when Jackie first started with the Dodgers in 1947, we were all proud of him. But we didn't get real excited. A lot of us felt he might be the only one for a while and that it was gonna go very slowly. Maybe that was because there were a lot more players in the Negro Leagues who were nearly as good as Jackie but just couldn't get there.

I didn't know it then, but I'd wind up spending an awful lot of time in the minor leagues—before, during, and after my big league career. I was at Sacramento, Colorado Springs, Seattle, Charleston, Toronto, Houston, Oklahoma City, and San Antonio, among other places. So I kind of saw it all as far as the minor leagues were concerned.

Sacramento was one of my early stops in the minors. The Coast League was tough, with a lot of ex–major leaguers there. I remember playing against Chuck Connors, who became "The

Rifleman" on TV. Gene Baker was another friend of mine who played on the West Coast.

I was the first black player at Houston in the Texas League and I never had any real problems there. I guess you could say the only stuff we had to put up with in the minors was verbal. I remember being called "nigger" at Colorado Springs a few times, and the same thing at Houston and at Beaumont, Texas. But I could ignore that. I just kept on playing because I always wanted to get to the majors.

Actually, the incident that sticks out in my mind happened when I was already in the majors with the White Sox. We had spring training in California one year and then played some exhibition games in the South—in Alabama, Mississippi, Tennessee. Minnie Minoso and I were the only two black players on the team then and when we came into these Southern cities the ballclub assigned us bodyguards.

We couldn't stay at the team hotel then, so we would stay with a local black family, and these bodyguards would sleep on the front porch on chairs during the night. Then they would go with us to the ballpark and actually stay in the dugout during the games. We were barnstorming with the Cardinals and they had only had one black player then, if I remember. I don't know if the bodyguards helped or not, but there were no real problems.

Anyway, by 1951 I was really playing well and stories began appearing in the Chicago papers about me. Some of the sportswriters began saying that the ballclub ought to call me up. I still have copies of the papers. But they didn't make the move until the Coast League season ended. Then I got up for a few games. And while I was the first black player the Sox signed, I wasn't the first to play there. The team had traded for Minnie at the beginning of the season, so he was already there when I came up. Minnie was a great ballplayer and we were roomies.

I played in only a handful of games that year, but I felt I could make it. The problem was the Sox kept fooling around, sending me up and down. I was back in the minors in 1952 and hit well again. I think I always hit over .300 in the minors. Then in 1953 I got another shot, but a strange thing happened that set me back again.

One problem was the competition at first base. In 1951 and 1952 the club had Eddie Robinson at first. Eddie hit with some power and was usually good for between twenty and thirty home runs. Then in 1953 Eddie was gone, but the team brought in Ferris Fain to play first. He was coming off two straight American League batting championships, so the job was more or less his.

Because of Ferris, I wasn't playing much at first. But I did see some playing time when he was hurt for a while, and I didn't do badly. Then one day [Manager] Paul Richards decided to try me in the outfield. Minnie had been playing left, but they needed him to come in and play third for a few games. So I went out to left. You got to remember that I had always been a first baseman, ever since I started playing. One day I was out there against Cleveland and Jim Hegan hit one over third base. I ran over to field it and could see that Jim was trying for a double. So I wound up and threw to second base trying to get Hegan, who was one of the slowest men in baseball then.

Not only didn't I get him, but I actually broke my arm. I broke my arm throwing the baseball!

It was a bad break in more ways than one. I was hitting nearly .300 [.297] when I got hurt and felt as if I was on my way. Once my arm had healed, they sent me back to the minors to strengthen it up and the whole thing kind of messed up my season and maybe any chance I had to ever get any real playing time with the White Sox.

In 1954 I was only up for twenty-nine games, and when they sent me back to Houston again I almost didn't report. I told them I was going back to the Negro League. But I thought it over again and finally decided to try again. My wife and I got into the car, took our time, and drove to Houston. I remember being really tired from the drive when we arrived and not wanting to play that first night. But they gave me a uniform and told me to get in there. It took a couple of days, but then I starting hitting the way I always hit in the minors.

There were always good ballplayers in the Texas League. My first time there I played against guys like Ken Boyer, Don Blasingame, and Vinegar Bend Mizell. The second time I remember playing against Bill White, who was with Dallas. Good ballplayer. Good guy. There were also a number of other black players in the league by that time, but I can't remember all their names.

Looking back, I really feel that the early black ballplayers had to do a little better than the white players to make it to the majors. Now, of course, there is no difference. But back then they still picked black players carefully. If a guy was kind of rowdy and had an "I-don't-care" attitude, he never even got a chance. The White Sox kept me in the minors for the entire 1955 season and I began to wonder again if I'd ever get a real shot with them. Then in 1956 I ended up in Baltimore. Paul Richards had gone over there to manage and he wanted me. At least he knew what I could do.

I hit over .300 [.311] my first year in Baltimore, but only as a part-time player. Then in 1957, I became more or less their regular first baseman. I hit .318 that year [in 141 games] and finally showed what I could do if I had the chance. But I was already nearly thirty-one years old. So it really took a long time.

It was also in Baltimore that I got my nickname, The Rope. Luman Harris, who was Paul Richards's pitching coach, was the first guy who called me that. See, I never was a long ball hitter, but I could really hit line drives. So one day during spring training, Harris cut off a piece of rope and put it in his pocket. He was looking at me after I hit another liner and he pulled the rope out and held it in the air. "Rope" was all he said to me, and the nickname stuck. In fact, when I see some of the guys today they still laugh and call me "The Rope."

When I batted I rarely swung at strikes. I was always a bad ball hitter and usually hit pitches out of the strike zone. The best way for a pitcher to get me out was to throw the ball right down the middle. Ask anybody. I didn't care if it was inside, outside, on the ground, or over my head. I hit bad balls. And I don't really know why I didn't hit the ones down the middle. I did have to adjust somewhat once the pitchers realized this. But it's tough to convince a pitcher to keep throwing the ball down the middle. That goes against everything he's ever learned.

In those days I would use the whole field, hit the ball anywhere and mostly line drives. So they had to play me straightaway, no shifts, because they never knew where I was gonna hit it. I always tried to hit the ball between fielders because I could really fly back then. But I never stole many bases because Paul Richards used to tell me not to run. I think I could have, but he didn't believe in it and he was the one who would tell us when to try to steal.

When I hit over .300 [.309] for the third straight year in 1958, I got to admit that it bothered me all over again that I didn't get a real chance to show that kind of hitting earlier. I was nearly thirty-two by then, and the next year I began feeling lousy. I was still playing, but my average dropped off. I had developed an ulcer that would keep getting worse. By then, the Orioles had Jim Gentile and he took over as the regular first baseman in 1960. I got my average back over .300, but I pinch-hit a lot and didn't even get one hundred at-bats.

In a way, I couldn't blame Richards for making Gentile the first baseman. I was getting older and starting to slip. And big Jim had some kind of two or three years. He could really hit and he was a great guy. The one thing that was kind of funny back then was that Richards would often call on me to pinch-hit against a lefty. Yet he wouldn't start me against them. And I always felt I could hit anybody.

But I guess the handwriting was on the wall then. The Orioles traded me to Kansas City during the off-season. They traded me and three other players for Whitey Herzog and Russ Snyder. They needed Snyder to play the outfield and had Gentile to play first. So I became the odd man out. I really didn't know a thing

Tom Tresh as a Detroit Tiger and now.

Dale Long as a Washington Senator and now.

Mel Parnell as a Boston Red Sox player and now.

Jake Gibbs as a New York Yankee and now.

Al Smith as a Cleveland Indian and now.

Al Weis as a New York Met and now.

Clem Labine as a Brooklyn Dodger and now.

Bob Veale as a Pittsburgh Pirate and now.

Ray Boone as a Detroit Tiger and now.

Bob Boyd as a Milwaukee Brave and now.

Bob Hazle as a Milwaukee Brave and now.

Elroy Face as a Pittsburgh Pirate and now.

Roy Sievers as a Philadelphia Phillie and now.

Bill Bruton as a Milwaukee Brave and now.

Davey Williams as a New York Giant and now.

Dick Ellsworth as a Boston Red Sox player and now.

Ed Kranepool as a New York Met and now.

Bobby Thomson as a New York Giant and now.

Chuck Stobbs as a Minnesota Twin and now.

J. W. Porter as a Detroit Tiger and now.

Gary Peters as a Boston Red Sox player and now.

about the deal until it was all over. I thought I'd really get a chance there. Joe Gordon was the manager. He and I had played together at Sacramento in 1951, Joe at second and me at first.

As it turned out, I didn't play much at Kansas City, pinch-hitting again, mostly. Norm Siebern was their first baseman and he was having a good year. In June they sent me to Milwaukee, but it was the same thing there. Joe Adcock was on first and I wasn't gonna move him out. So again I was mostly a pinch-hitter, and when the season ended they assigned me to Louisville for 1962. Back to the minors again.

I didn't like it at Louisville and told them. I guess that was my ticket to Oklahoma City. By this time I was almost thirty-six and didn't think about getting back to the majors anymore. The ulcer was still bothering me and it seemed that no one could really help me with it. I went to hospitals in a number of cities, but it wasn't until I got to Witchita that they found it. It was hidden behind my liver and was about the size of a quarter. Once I had surgery I was fine, no more trouble. I remember the doctor saying you can eat anything you want, even horseshoes.

By that time I was back to playing semipro ball, but only after a few more years in the minors. From Oklahoma City I had gone to San Antonio in Double A. They cut me loose I think at the end of 1963 because they had young guys and I was making too much money. The Dallas ballclub contacted me and wanted me to join them, but by then I had had enough. I was tired of bouncing around and I told them I wanted to go home.

The only big league offer I had came from the Orioles. They wanted me to come to Florida and work with the young guys as a batting instructor. I thought about it, but I had been away from home for so long that I decided not to go. I wanted to spend more time with my wife and family. And at that time the ulcer was still bothering me.

I did do some scouting for the Orioles for a number of years. That's when I was in Wichita, but I didn't really miss the big leagues. My only regret about my career is that I didn't get a shot earlier. I was already in my mid-twenties when I signed and think I could have had a much longer career if I had signed earlier. And if that happened I'm sure I would have finished as a .300 lifetime hitter. [He finished at .293.] I might have anyway if the ulcer hadn't started bothering me and I didn't have to become a pinch-hitter.

Anyway, after I left the minors I ended up in Wichita, where I had the ulcer surgery. I also went to work for the Dreamliner Bus Company because they also had a semipro baseball team. It was a great situation. I played ball for the Dreamliners for five more years, making the all-star team each time. And I drove a bus during the week when we didn't play games.

It's funny, my top major league salary was $18,500, meal money for today's players. But I made more playing semipro ball, between my salary for driving and my pay for playing with the Dreamliners. I guess I played until about 1969 when I was already into my forties. There were a number of former big leaguers playing semipro ball then. Two I can think of offhand were Don Larsen and Bob Turley. But there were others, too.

I could still hit then, and even run pretty good because I never had a weight problem. I even remember some people asking me why I wasn't back in the majors. But I knew that was over.

When I look back now, I think it was a better game in my day. Of course, we didn't have the artificial turf. We played with holes in the ground and no carpet. Being the type of hitter I was, I wonder if they ever would have gotten me out if there was artificial turf when I played.

The best hitter I ever saw was Ted Williams. I played against the man and I know. Even when they began putting that shift on him he would still get the ball through there. I used to play almost a short right field when he was up. I remember one game when he hit a shot right down the line. The ball hit the first-base bag—the bags were held down by leather straps then—and it hit so hard that it broke the straps. The ball just died and stayed around first base, but the bag came flying out to where I was playing him in short right. So Ted got a single and I got the bag instead of the ball. I just laughed like hell at that one.

The three other greatest players I saw were Mickey Mantle, Willie Mays, and Hank Aaron. That's it. Mickey Mantle could just do everything. He not only ran to first faster than anyone when he first came up. But he ran hard, too, and if you were in his way you'd better move out of there and fast.

I can also recall when Brooks Robinson first came up with the Orioles. I could see right away that Brooks was gonna make it big. I told the Orioles there was no sense sending him back. Might as well just keep him here. He couldn't hit that well then, but he could sure field. They sent him down anyway, but once he came back he stayed a long time. Whenever I see Brooks today he always says, "Hey, Rope." They all still call me that.

Things definitely got better for black players during my time in the league. They got better every year. More players got a chance and it continued as all the clubs began to sign blacks. Once it got started it moved right along. There was just more opportunity.

I had both black and white friends in the game. I was close to Minnie my early years with the White Sox. At Baltimore I remained close with Brooks and Jim Gentile. I also stayed close to Virgil Trucks, who pitched with the White Sox while I was there. We both left, but whenever our teams met we would go out to dinner. Lou Kretlow was another good friend. I still keep in touch with a lot of the guys and see some of them when they come in here for autograph shows.

There were really never any problems with my teammates in the majors. Maybe there would be one or two guys who weren't nice, but you could tell. Strangely enough, one of the men who didn't like black players was Paul Richards. Yet in some ways he was the greatest man I ever played for and the smartest manager. He never broke his word and in that way, he was great. But he was prejudiced. He didn't like blacks. I was in enough team meetings where he would talk about the black players who were on the team coming in and he wouldn't say very nice things about them. Yet he wanted me playing for him when he went to the Orioles.

Another thing I remember about my early years in the majors is the pitching staffs of the Yankees and Indians. That's the reason those two clubs were usually one-two in the early and middle 1950s. They each had a big four. The Yanks had Reynolds, Raschi, Lopat, and Ford, while the Indians had Feller, Lemon, Wynn, and Garcia. Then Herb Score took Feller's place until he got hurt. Most of the other teams had maybe two tough pitchers, but against the Yanks and Indians you never got a break.

The toughest pitcher for me was a teammate of mine at Baltimore for a few years. I'm talking about Hoyt Wilhelm, who threw the knuckleball. I always hated the knuckleball, a real tough pitch for me to hit. I remember one time I was facing Wilhelm and he threw the knuckler with two strikes. I swung and missed . . . and the ball hit the toe of my right foot, my front foot. So it went in the books as a strikeout when I should have been hit by the pitch. But that was the knuckler. Like I said, I always hated it.

Once I began playing semipro ball in Wichita I decided to settle there. Even after I stopped playing, I continued to drive the Dreamliner buses and finally retired about four years ago after twenty years with the company. Since then, the only thing I do is organize autograph shows in the area.

People contact me to organize the show and I'll more or less fill their orders. After we get the players to come in I'll usually sit with them for an hour or so and sign some autographs as well. Most of the work is in the Wichita area, but I go to Oklahoma and Kansas City now and then to do the same thing. We agree on a price and I set the whole thing up for them.

There's also a minor league club here, the Wichita Wranglers, and I'll go out sometimes and talk to some of the young players. They know I had a pretty good career and they'll ask me about it. But very few of them seem to have a sense of the game's history, and they don't talk much about how it was for black players then. So I just tell them to try hard and believe in themselves, and they'll make it. But I wonder if they know what Jackie went through and some of the guys who followed him.

I still enjoy watching the game and see a lot of great ballplayers out there. They can make plenty of money today and whenever I see players from my day we talk about it. We really didn't make much back then, so it's good the guys today can make it. One thing I do feel should be changed is the pension for the older players. It really needs to be doubled for a lot of the guys and there are some people who are supposed to be working on that.

The game today is modernized in every way, the ballfields, clubhouse, uniforms, equipment. It's all different. Maybe that's one reason the game itself seemed tougher back when I played, a lot tougher than it is now.

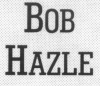

BOB HAZLE

♦ **MAJOR LEAGUE EXPERIENCE** ♦

Cincinnati Reds, 1955
Milwaukee Braves, 1957–1958
Detroit Tigers, 1958

♦ **CURRENT STATUS** ♦

Salesman for the Ben Arnold Company, a
wholesale distributor of wines and whis-
keys, in South Carolina.

*The way Bob Hazle greeted National League pitchers when the
Milwaukee Braves called him up in 1957, it's no wonder that he
acquired the nickname "Hurricane." Playing in just forty-one games
during the second half of the season, Hazle hacked away at a .403
clip, slammed seven homers and drove home twenty-seven runs
in just 134 at-bats. His was one of the most auspicious debuts in
National League history and it helped the Braves win the pennant
and World Series.*

Though the Woodruff, South Carolina, native had had a cup of coffee with the Reds two years earlier, he had been fighting to get out of the minors since 1950. Cincinnati had actually called him up in 1951, but he was derailed by a "Greetings" letter from Uncle Sam as he was about to pack his bags for the Bigs.

Injuries set him back at the beginning of 1958, and the Braves traded him to Detroit after just twenty games. After that, the lefty-swinging outfielder never again got a chance to play on a regular basis. He was out of the majors after the 1958 season, returned to the minors for two years, then called it quits at the age of twenty-nine.

Despite a big league career that spanned just 110 games, Bob Hazle goes into the books as a .310 lifetime hitter and a guy whose stroke was a sweet as anyone's during a three-month period in 1957. And in helping his team to beat the Yankees in the World Series, Hazle says he at least experienced the "ultimate" as a big league player.

I think the first time anyone called me "Hurricane" Hazle was in the winter of 1954. I had gone to Maracaibo in Venezuela to play winter ball. The owner of the team was a short, stubby fellow who couldn't really speak any English. I got there shortly after Hurricane Hazel had hit the coast, Myrtle Beach, and really ripped the place upside down.

So when this guy heard my name, he began making blowing sounds, like the wind, and asking if my name was Hurricane Hazle? That's the first time I was called that. The second time was in the second half of the 1957 season. And that's the time I prefer to remember. I saw both the good and bad sides of baseball during my short career, and 1957 had to be the good side. In fact, it was the ultimate. To get to the majors, then win the pennant, and finally beat the New York Yankees in the World Series, well needless to say, I was on cloud nine.

I'll never forget coming to Yankee Stadium for the first time. I mean, here I am, a little ol' boy from the little ol' town of Woodruff, South Carolina, and I'm in Yankee Stadium to play in the World Series, the same ballpark where Babe Ruth played, where DiMaggio played, and all the others. It was simply the ultimate.

We all went out to look at the ballpark after we got to town and it gave me chills just to be there. Naturally, being a ballplayer, I then went out to right field where I would be playing. That part was taking care of business. I looked at the wall and began throwing a ball off it in the corners and around, just to see the angles and how it might come off the wall. These are things a ballplayer does in any park he's seeing for the first time. But then to stop and look up again at that tremendous stadium. It was a thrill, no doubt about it.

The funny thing was that only six or so months earlier I was on the brink of quitting. My wife and I both agreed that I would play out the season in the minors, and if nothing happened that would be it. But then Bill Bruton hurt his knee and I was called up. In a way, it was just a matter of being in the right place at the right time. If Bruton hadn't been hurt, I doubt whether I ever would have seen the major leagues. But there were plenty of other times when I think I was in the wrong place at the wrong time.

I'm originally from Laurens, South Carolina. I was born there on December 9, 1930, but I grew up in Woodruff, which was only about seventeen miles away. I started playing baseball early, in the streets and cow pastures. Both my older brothers played, and I kind of tagged along behind them. In fact, they both signed professional contracts before I did, but neither made it to the majors. My older brother, Paul, signed with the Yankees and was with Lew Burdette in their farm system at one time, and my brother Joe signed with Brooklyn. Both Joe and Joe Landrum played college baseball at Clemson and took them to the playoffs one year. Then the two of them signed with the Dodgers. I think Joe Landrum got up for about a year or so.

So baseball was always in our family. We were all two years apart in age, so there wasn't that big a difference. It was kind of a standing joke at the high school that they never thought the Hazles would leave. We followed one after another and played all the sports. In high school, my favorite sport was football. There was a time when I'd rather hit a line than eat when I was hungry. I had a football scholarship offer from the University of Tennessee in 1949 and even attended spring workouts there. But at the same time, Pat Patterson was after me to sign with the Cincinnati Reds. So I had to make a choice.

Like I said, football was my favorite, but I played an awful lot of baseball as well. At one point I was playing high school ball, American Legion ball, and in the local mill leagues, all at the same time. There were rival textile mills all over the area and each one had a team. Good brand of ball. Each village had a team and a good field. Lou Brisse played there briefly and I remember them trying to get Max Lanier after he jumped to the Mexican League.

So while I didn't think much about the majors, I did have two brothers in professional ball. And coming from a small town, a baseball town, it's hard to say no when someone is offering you a chance. As much as I loved football, Pat Patterson kept talking money and we didn't have much back then. We were poor families. There was enough food, but few luxuries. Our mother made our clothes and we had a beat-up old car that all six of us would pile into. So when someone talked money, you listened. And I figured I could always go back to college in the winter. So that's what I decided to do.

It was a fairly good bonus, maybe six or eight thousand, but nothing like it is today. To me, a little country boy, that was a lot of money. The Reds started me off in the 1950 season playing at Columbia in the Sally League. So I was practically in my own backyard. My brother Joe was also in the league then and whenever we played against each other, the whole town of Woodruff would show up to see what happened to the Hazle boys. Joe stayed in the minors a couple more years, then quit and went back to college. He ended up a Little All-American fullback and was even offered a contract by the Chicago Bears. But he didn't sign. Went into coaching instead and ended up becoming a principal.

The Sally League back then was the bus league. We traveled to places like Jacksonville, Florida, and Columbus, Georgia. The bus would often break down or catch fire and we'd just pull into town in time for the game. We hardly had time to eat and when we did it was almost always at a Crystal Burger. They were fast-food joints in Georgia and Florida. We ate a lot of Crystal burgers in the Sally League.

In 1951 I was moved to Tulsa, Oklahoma, in Double A and I made the all-star team there. Then, right after the all-star break, I got a call from Cincinnati. They wanted me up. When I returned to my room to pack my clothes, I found something else waiting for me. It was a telegram to report somewhere else. This one was from Uncle Sam. Greetings. The Reds tried to get it put off until the end of the year, but the draft board wouldn't do it. So instead of going to the majors, I went into the army for part of 1951, all of 1952, and part of 1953.

I did get to play for both the regiment and post teams and we had a real good ballclub. I was lucky in that I was stationed at Fort Jackson, in Columbia, South Carolina. Right near home again. There were a lot of big leaguers in the service then. Our team had guys like Ed Bailey catching, Joe Cunningham playing first, Roger Craig and Vito Valentinetti pitching, guys like that. Like I said, a real good ballclub. And I remember playing against Willie Mays when he was at First Eustice. So service ball was pro all the way. But I had still missed a chance to go up with Cincinnati and when I came back some things started going a bit sour.

I came out in July of 1953 and the Reds sent me back to Tulsa to finish the season. The next year I went to spring training with the Reds and thought I had a good shot at sticking. But it didn't work out. They decided to send me to Indianapolis in Triple A. There was one problem. Indianapolis was in the Cleveland organization. It was the old loan system. I was still in the Cincinnati organization but playing for a Cleveland club. Naturally, Cleveland was going to play their guys, not someone on loan, and I sat the bench most of the time.

It was an excellent team, but I kept getting into it with the manager, Kirby Farrell—mainly about playing time. I contacted the Cincinnati people and told them I wanted out of there, but they said I had to stay. And at that point I almost decided to go home. But I didn't want to be a quitter and finished the season.

By the way, Herb Score was on that team in 1954 and Herb looked the best I had seen. He could throw, really make that ball jump. You could see he had all the makings of a fine big league pitcher.

But the reason I was so discouraged was that I was sitting. I had hit well at Columbia and Tulsa, around .300. But when you drift in and out of the lineup you just don't do much hitting. And that's why I got into it with Farrell. When you get down, especially in the minor leagues, it's hard to get back up. After the season, though, I decided to go to Venezuela to play winter ball. I went down there with Jim Frey, who later managed the Royals and Cubs, and learned a little bit more. Then in '55 they had me back in Double A, at Nashville, but at least it was in their own farm system this time.

If I remember, I hit .300 and led the league with twenty-nine home runs. I wasn't really a power hitter, but if someone put the ball in the right place I'd hit it out. And in September of that year I finally got called up and got my first taste of the majors. My first hit, believe it or not, was a single up the middle off Lew Burdette, and I felt good about it.

It's funny, I always had a lot of confidence without really being cocky. And I truly felt I would have been in the majors long before if the service hadn't gotten in the way. I was only in my second year and at Double A when they called me up that July, the same time I got my "Greetings" letter. So when I went to spring training with them in 1956 I really thought I would be with the team. And that's when they made the deal for George Crowe.

Corky Valentine and I went to Milwaukee for Crowe just before the season started. When the deal was made I really thought I'd get a shot to stick with the Braves, but they were already breaking camp and they sent me right to their Wichita farm team. I thought it was ridiculous, not to get even a look, but there wasn't anything I could do about it. If you recall, the Reds had a real power team in 1956. That was also Frank Robinson's rookie year. I had really felt I could have fit in somewhere with that team, but suddenly I was in the Milwaukee organization and again didn't know where I stood.

The Reds never gave me a reason for the trade. In those days a ballplayer was like a horse. Open his mouth, look at his teeth, check his legs, and say, "Trade him." But I went to Wichita and played under George Selkirk. I started hitting well and at one point in the season Paul Waner, the Hall of Famer who was the Braves' hitting instructor, came down to work with the Wichita players. Well, I watched him work with the other guys but he never said anything to me. Finally I asked him why and he said, "Bob, I haven't seen anything wrong with your hitting, and by the way, I have a feeling you're gonna be called up within two weeks."

Wouldn't you know a couple of days later I step on something in the outfield and hurt my knee. Bad. They flew me to Milwaukee and the doctor wanted to operate. I told them if they could tell me what was wrong then I'd let them cut on it. But if they just wanted to go in and take a look, then no deal. So I kind of hobbled through the rest of the season and I was really down, like the bottom had fallen out.

That was the winter I almost decided to quit. I was getting up in age and talked it over with my wife. I said I'd come back in '57, but if things didn't get any better it would be my last year. Then, I'd have to decide what I wanted to do.

One reason I didn't quit right then and there was that I wanted to play ball. I loved the game. And Ben Geraghty, the Wichita manager, had also shown faith in me. I really got off to a slow start in '57 and Ben could have sent me back to Double A. But he stuck with me and sent a younger guy with a higher average down. Then I started to hit. I think I got my average up close to .290 from about .220. And that's when [Braves center fielder Bill] Bruton hurt his knee and I got called up. It was Ben Geraghty who insisted they take me. I found out later that he told the Braves they'd be crazy not to call me because I was hot with the bat. So I finally went up in July of 1957.

The Braves had a great team and were in the midst of a pennant race, so it was a kind of weird feeling to suddenly be there. By that I mean it was a kind of nervous and jumpy feeling. You walk out onto the field and suddenly you're in the majors. It's all so different. It's the big leagues. You're even wondering how you're gonna be treated. As it turned out, the Braves were a helluva bunch of great guys and acted as though I had been there ten years. Bruton had been the center fielder, and what they did was move Hank Aaron to center and begin platooning me in right with Andy Pafko. My first time up was as a pinch-hitter and I was told to sacrifice. I did it, and when I got back to the bench they all said it's about time we got somebody who can move a runner over. That made me feel good.

My first time up as a starter I doubled to left. That's when I began to get my confidence and lose that nervous feeling. I was lucky. I got a hot start. I was four for four in one game and three for four in the next. That makes all the difference in the world. A slow start and you begin pressing, doing things wrong and putting more pressure on yourself. Then you begin making mistakes.

I had also promised myself that if I didn't make it in the majors, it wouldn't be because I didn't swing the bat. I wasn't going to stand up there and take too many pitches. In other words, I wasn't going to be called out on strikes. I was also a first-ball hitter. If a pitcher was going to stand out there and throw the first pitch down the middle I was going after it. Without swinging, you're on your way back to the bench. Fortunately, I stayed hot. After I was there a month I was still hitting around .500.

Even I knew I wasn't *that* kind of hitter, but I was enjoying it. I remember our catcher, Del Crandall, coming over once after I came back to the bench and just shaking his head. "I don't believe it," he said. "What is it? Can you show me tomorrow?" I just said, "Don't worry, Del. Water seeks its own level."

Another time we were playing the Cards and I walked. Stan Musial was playing first that day and when I reached the bag he began kind of rubbing up against me. When I looked at him, Stan just grinned and said, "Hey, I just want some of that hitting to rub off on me." That was something, a player like Musial telling me that. That was a thrill right there.

After a few weeks the pitchers began backing me off the plate more, and they were trying to find a pitch I didn't hit too well. A lot of them were going to off-speed stuff and pitching me outside. But I was hot and hitting everything. I was doing Yogi Berra–type hitting, connecting on pitches a foot over my head if I had to. So it didn't matter what they pitched me. We ended up winning the pennant and even though I cooled off a bit near the end, I still wound up hitting .403 in the time I was there.

The Braves that year were a loose and close-knit team. War- ren Spahn and Lew Burdette, they were the clowns. They'd always keep you loose on the bench. And guys like Eddie Mathews, Red Schoendienst and Del Crandall, all those players, they would come in after a game and be full of vim and vitality. And they were always pulling for one another. Hank Aaron was already a fine ballplayer by then, but a quiet guy who seemed to do everything at a slow pace. He never had too much to say then, and in that respect wasn't really a leader at that time. Spahn, Mathews, Schoendienst, Crandall, Burdette, they were the leaders.

Burdette and Spahn were also two great pitchers. Even in the seventh game of the Series that year, Lew acted like Lew always acted. Lew just didn't believe you could beat him. You had to show him. Give him the ball and he was as cocky as they come. He'd walk right out to that mound and just dare you to hit him. That's the way he played and he'd challenge you any time.

Spahn was also a competitor and to play behind him and watch him pitch to Crandall was something. I have never seen such artistry. He would just hit that mitt time after time, and do just what Crandall wanted him to do. He could set hitters up with changeups and sliders inside, then with two strikes bust that fastball over the middle. He was very good at it, and that motion he had just made him better. And like Burdette, he always believed he was going to beat you.

Warren even went to the minors and pitched at Tulsa after his major league career ended. He was in the mid-forties by then. But he loved the game and loved to pitch. I saw him at a reunion once and he said if the day ever comes when I can't talk to people and talk about baseball, that's the end of me. Take me out and shoot me.

But as I said before, the World Series was my ultimate thrill. I did cool off at the plate some. But I think that was because we had a few days before the Series started, and then the Yanks threw two lefties, [Whitey] Ford and [Bobby] Shantz, in the first two games. So Pafko played and I sat. By the time I got back in there I was kind of out of the groove. A couple of the games I did start, we fell behind early, and that makes you hit a little differently.

My only two hits came in the seventh and final game, but at least that's when it counted. I scored the first run, which turned out to be the winning run, so I felt I was a part of the victory. Funny part was that Warren was supposed to start, but he had the flu. So Lew went with just two days' rest. A few of the guys were coming down sick. I didn't feel particularly well, either, and two days later when I flew home, I was so sick with the flu that all I could do was go to bed. But we were World Champs!

Even though I knew I wasn't a .400 hitter I felt pretty good about myself for the next season. I knew Bill Bruton would be back, so I felt I might not be a starter. But I felt I would be on the team and hoped I could be the fourth outfielder. By this time I really felt I could play—play and hit. There was a problem in the off-season because the team wanted to give me only a twelve-hundred-dollar raise. Plus I didn't get a bonus I was promised. My World Series share was supposed to take care of that. But I told them I had earned that share and helped the team get there. It even reached a point where I told them if they didn't come up with a better offer I wouldn't play. I had asked some of my teammates what I could expect after the season I had, and the team didn't come close to it. We finally agreed, but maybe that whole thing led to what happened next.

During spring training I got hit in the head by Tom Morgan of the Tigers. He didn't mean it. Just one of those pitches that slipped. Then, at the beginning of the season I hurt my ankle sliding into second in Chicago. And that slows you down. But I felt I was starting to hit. We were in St. Louis for a three-game series. I drove in six runs in the first game, and we beat them bad again in the second when Frank Torre hit a home run. Then in the third game, we got off fast again and Frank hit another homer. I was up next and when Frank crossed the plate he said, "Be loose up there." I told him not to worry.

Larry Jackson was pitching. As he started to throw I began to step out of the batter's box, figuring the ball was coming at me. It was head high, all right, but it was behind me. And as I stepped back I couldn't change my momentum quick enough. I tried to throw up my hands, but the ball got me in the right ear. I was knocked cold and when I came to they were holding Eddie Mathews because Eddie was trying to go after Jackson.

Anyway, it put me in the hospital for a week or so and when I flew back to Milwaukee my equilibrium was still a little off. I finally joined the team in Cincinnati, played one game and went one for three with an RBI. The team was ready to head to San Francisco, our first trip to the West Coast. That's when Fred Haney just walked up to me on the bench and told me I had been sold to Detroit.

It came as a complete surprise and was a real blow. I'm telling you, it really got me. I couldn't believe that with the job I had done the year before they would sell me after just twenty games. I knew I couldn't live on the past, but I felt I deserved more of a shot. I never really knew why they did it. In fact, I still can't answer that question today.

Going to Detroit was a tough adjustment. The Tigers were loaded with outfielders and I couldn't figure out why they wanted me in the first place. They had Harvey Kuenn in center, Al Kaline in right, and Charlie Maxwell in left. Behind them were Gus Zernial, Johnny Groth, and Tito Francona. How many outfielders did they want? But Jack Tighe was the manager then and he told me he understood what I had gone through. He also told me that Kaline was sick and I was playing right field.

I went one for three and drove in a run. Then I played for about a week straight and was hitting over .300. Of course, when Kaline came back he played, but they began using me in left some with Charlie Maxwell. Then Jack Tighe was fired and Bill Norman took over. He took me right out of the lineup and I sat there until the end of the year.

They said they tried to move me, but no one wanted me. Maybe because I wasn't playing the word got out that I was hurt. I don't know. I do know that I wasn't any bench-sitter and that caused me to get the RA's. That was our language back then for the red ass. I wanted to play ball, but they kept saying they wanted to sell me. When nothing happened, they didn't even invite me to camp for 1959. Instead, they assigned me to Charleston in Triple A. That really made me mad, because they didn't even give me a shot in Florida.

I remember running into Bill Norman at Lakeland. He asked me how I was doing and told me to hang in there and have a good year. I said I was having a good year, but he never used me, never gave me another shot. Then I told him he wouldn't get past June as a manager, and sure enough, he got fired [after seventeen games].

But that didn't help me. I just didn't feel good. My confidence was shot. In the majors, you have it all built up inside you. But when you end up back in the minors there's the small ballparks again with no one coming out. It's very discouraging. And even though I was hitting well I just didn't feel I would ever get another chance. And as it turned out, I was right.

The next year they wanted to sell me to Bobby Avila, who had a team in Mexico City. But I told them I didn't speak Spanish too well. I refused to go. It just wasn't worth it anymore. Baseball back then wasn't baseball today. There just wasn't all that much money involved. So when I wouldn't go to Mexico, they got mad and sent me down to Birmingham in Double A. That's when I decided it was my last year. I'd go play at Birmingham, but I was just gonna enjoy myself. After that, I'd go home and decide what to do.

So I went to Birmingham and flat out didn't care. Then Fred Hatfield, a former major leaguer who was managing at Little Rock, asked if I wanted to come over and play for him. He said, "Bob, come finish the year with us and we'll have a lot of fun." That's what I did. And we had fun. It was an independent team and there were some offers to buy me. But I had gotten fed up. I said I would finish playing that summer and have a job by winter. And that's the way it went. I enjoyed the summer, hit well, but I had given up on the major leagues.

I'd be a liar if I said I wasn't mad. I had left baseball with a bad taste in my mouth. When I was in Triple A I felt I could still do it, but not once they sent me to Double A. Then I felt it was over. In the majors, you can always give that extra 20 percent. Your adrenaline gets going. But in the minors it's like the bottom falls out. So I felt it was time to quit and go to work. But I had never returned to college, so I had no degree and no job to return to. I was a jack of all trades, master of none.

And you know, it kept gnawing at me. It would have been one thing if I left the game knowing I couldn't really cut it, couldn't really play. But to leave the game knowing that you could still play. That's what hurt. There were times at night when I would just get to thinking about it and get angry all over again. I really had a hard time getting it out of my system, the knowledge that I couldn't play anymore. But I finally got rid of it.

Now, I don't hold any animosity. I'm even in the book as a .300 lifetime hitter in the majors and I enjoy looking at that. I did get quite a few reactions from other players. Most of them know what happens once you get a bad break. Looking back, maybe I should have tried to stay in baseball in another capacity. But I didn't, and no one ever called me. Of course, to me it would have been worth it only at the major league level.

When I left the game I looked up an old friend who was in the monument business, you know, tombstones and monuments. He was crazy about sports and used to drop by all the time to say hello. Anyway, I went to work for him as a salesman. I worked for him for a time then met a fellow who owned Coggins Granite Industry. He asked me if I'd like to come to work for him. I said, sure, if everything could be worked out. So he talked to my boss and we agreed I'd leave. He offered me a good job traveling five states—Georgia, Florida, Arkansas, Wisconsin, and New York.

I was still selling monuments, but now as wholesale granite. I'd call on dealers in all the states. I did that for ten years, then they wanted me to move my family to Georgia and I decided against it. So I left and went to work for a wholesale distributor of whiskey and wines. Spirits. I've been doing that ever since with two companies. Now I'm with the Ben Arnold Company in South Carolina. I have an area I cover and call on retail whiskey stores and wine shops.

I enjoy sales because I'd rather be outside than inside, and I've always enjoyed meeting people. Some recognize my name, but a lot don't know until somebody tells them. Then they get all over me, asking why I didn't tell them I played. But I always say I didn't want them to think I was big-headed. And then they've got questions, like why I retired so soon and what am I doing in the whiskey business because I should have a lot of money from baseball. After all, I played in the major leagues.

Of course, I don't blame today's players for getting all they can. No, blame the owners and general managers. There are guys today getting eight hundred thousand a year to hit .220 or .230. Meanwhile, the guys who made the game get very little in the way of pension. I'm not even talking for myself. I wasn't there five years, so I get nothing. I just wonder what an owner would have to pay Ted Williams today. Maybe give him the whole team.

I still go to a few reunions and get a lot of fan mail. Some of it is from youngsters whose fathers had told them about me. But it's nice that people remember. And some of them still build me up and make me feel as though I'm ten feet tall. I do enjoy those.

I've also done a few card shows and wouldn't mind doing more. But they usually want the big names. At our reunions, some players still remind me about what happened to me. Some of them still say I got a raw deal, but there were a lot of players who got the same thing. I'm not the only one. I've seen a lot of good ballplayers never get a shot.

Look at it this way. I'll always have 1957. There was the pennant race and then the World Series. Some players, even great ones, never get there. But I did. And we won it. And we beat the Yankees.

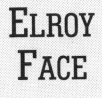

ELROY FACE

Pittsburgh Pirates, 1953, 1955–68
Detroit Tigers, 1968
Montreal Expos, 1969

Employed by State of Pennsylvania as a carpenter foreman at a state mental hospital in Bridgeville, Pennsylvania.

One of baseball's truly great relief pitchers, Elroy Face tied a record held by the great Walter Johnson by appearing in 802 games for the same team. He did that while racking up a bushelful of saves for the Pittsburgh Pirates from 1953 to 1968.

Possessor of a rubber arm that enabled him to pitch often and a forkball that allowed him to baffle National League hitters, the righthander from Stephentown, New York, once appeared in ninety-

three straight games without a loss. And from May of 1958 to September of 1959, he won twenty-two consecutive ballgames. Included in that streak was a marvelous season in 1959 when Face finished the year with an 18–1 mark.

A year later, he helped the Pirates to a World Series triumph by getting three saves in an epic battle between the Bucs and the New York Yankees, and he said he did it without his best stuff. A believer in keeping the ball down, even to low-ball hitters, Face said that if a pitcher got the ball in the right spot, the hitters wouldn't hit it.

Pitching in obscurity for a small high school in upstate New York, Face became a big leaguer almost by accident. But he made the most of his opportunity, his only regret being he wasn't born thirty years later. A trained carpenter, Elroy Face always returned to his trade in the off-season and again after his career ended. But even in his forties he showed he could still do the job out of the pen.

I never really had any intention of becoming a baseball player. In fact, I didn't even follow the game much after my high school years. So, in a sense, my major league career was almost an accident.

As far as I knew, I wasn't even scouted when I played in high school. I went to Averill Park High in Stephentown, New York, where I was born and raised. There were no Little Leagues in town back then and I didn't really start playing ball until I was about fifteen or sixteen. I was always small for my age, so when I did get on a team before that I usually didn't get to play. My early baseball experience was limited to just some sandlot games with my friends.

When I went out for the Averill Park team I played shortstop and pitched. My second year there we won the championship for the first time ever. I think I had an 8–1 record and threw pretty well. But when I was eighteen I left high school and joined the army. It was 1946 and the war was over, but a friend of mine and myself figured if we didn't sign up we'd be drafted. So we signed up.

As I said, at that point I had absolutely no thought about becoming a professional ballplayer. We had our own team over in Guam and we played against other companies, but I didn't play on any of the so-called service teams. I pitched and won a couple of games. Then I came home and got a job as a mechanic, since I had been a mechanic in the service. At the same time, I joined a town team that played other teams in the Stephentown area. This was in 1948.

Again I was pitching and playing the infield and I put together a pretty good streak. I struck out eighteen in one game and nineteen the next. And I guess that's when the word started to get out. Fred Mathews, who was a bird dog from the Philly organization and based in White Plains, read an article about my strikeout streak and he came to the garage where I worked to see me.

I still didn't think much about it, but then he asked me to get some guys together after work and go up to the ballfield so he could take a look at me. So I rounded up the guys, did some running, hitting, throwing, and fielding. That was the week before Labor Day. He stopped by a week later, on Labor Day, when he was on his way back from vacation. We were playing another local team and after the seventh inning he called me over to his car and had me sign a contract with the Phillies. And until that day I hadn't really thought about becoming a major league player.

Once I signed the contract everything changed. At the time I signed, my brother and I had joined a labor union and were making $70 a week. We also had a chance of getting better jobs in Albany, but I gave it all up to go to the minor leagues for $140 a month.

My first year in the minors was 1949. And even though I had been signed, I was told right away that my chances might not be that good because I was small and twenty-one years old. I must have weighed about 150 pounds then and was three or four years older than most of the kids starting out in the low minors. To many baseball people, that was already two strikes against me.

I had two good years at Bradford, Pennsylvania, in Class C, going 14–2 and 18–5, but in the winter of 1950 the Phils left me unprotected and Mr. Rickey drafted me into the Dodger organization. In those days, they had to move you up at least one class to protect you, and why they left me eligible was both a mystery and a surprise. But I went to Pueblo in 1951, where I think I had a 23–9 record with a sixth-place club, then moved on to Fort Worth in Double A for 1952 and led the league in earned run average, strictly as a starting pitcher.

That winter, the Dodgers put me on their Montreal roster. Since they could lose only two ballplayers in the draft, they would load up one roster with guys they wanted to protect, knowing they couldn't lose more than two. Well, Mr. Rickey had moved on to Pittsburgh right after he drafted me for the Dodgers two years earlier, and in early 1953, he made me the number-one pick off the Montreal roster. That's how I found my way to the Pirates.

Even though I knew the Dodgers had a great team then, it didn't bother me to leave. Because I also knew they were loaded with pitchers, guys like Preacher Roe, Don Newcombe, Karl Spooner, Clem Labine. So there wasn't much chance of breaking in there. The Pirates, on the other hand, were rebuilding, and I looked at the move as an opportunity to get to the big leagues more quickly.

As it turned out, I was right. Even though I was still a two-pitch pitcher then, fastball and curve, I did as well as any of the other pitchers they had that spring, and I was added to the roster before the 1953 season began.

There were a couple of other things the minor leagues did for me. For one thing, my experience there made the transition to the big leagues easier. There were no surprises because I had played with so many former major leaguers in the minors.

For example, in my first start in the Texas League, I pitched against Johnny Vander Meer, who had thrown two straight no-hitters for the Reds back in 1938. Johnny was finishing up down in Tulsa and I beat him, 2–1. There were a lot of other guys down there who had been up before. One I remember was Al Gionfriddo, who had made that great catch off DiMaggio in the 1947 World Series. So I heard quite a bit about the majors before I got there.

Something else happened in the minors that really affected me, really changed my philosophy of pitching. I was a pretty aggressive pitcher back then. Like a lot of other guys, I was trying to get to the big leagues any way I could. And if that meant throwing at hitters, I'd do it. In fact, when I was playing at Pueblo in 1951, the Wichita team was hitting me pretty good and I wanted to put a stop to it. So I went out there and hit four straight guys intentionally and forced a run home. George Schultz was the Wichita manager then and he was coaching third base. After I hit the fourth guy he started for the mound and had to be restrained.

But there was another incident that really cured me of that. I almost hit a guy square in the face one day. The only thing that saved him was that he threw his hand in front of his face and the ball hit his hand. I found out later that he was married and had a couple of kids. And I said to myself, what if I had hit him and injured him for the rest of his life? What would his family have thought? If that had happened, I would have had it on my mind the rest of my life. After that, I never tried to hit anyone intentionally ever again.

Anyway, I joined a Pirate team in 1953 that didn't have much going for it. The team finished last [with a 50–104 record] and it seemed a lot of the guys were small like myself, 150 to 160 pounds. I started thirteen games that year, relieved in twenty-eight, and finished with a 6–8 record. But right after the season ended, Mr. Rickey told me he was sending me back to the minors to work on an off-speed pitch. He didn't feel the fastball and curve were enough.

So I spent the 1954 season at Fort Worth. But before I got there I already knew the pitch I wanted to work on. It was the forkball, and I had seen Joe Page throw it in spring training with the Pirates that year. Page had some great years with the Yankees and was trying for a comeback with Pittsburgh. He wasn't there very long, but long enough for me to watch him throw. I think he was the only one using the pitch then, but because I was just a kid and he had those great years with the Yanks, I was hesitant to talk to him about it. I just decided to work on it by myself.

There's very little rotation on the forkball. In some ways, it's like a knuckler, but it doesn't dance the way the knuckler does. It just goes in and the bottom drops out. So it's an off-speed pitch with a good, hard motion and I basically taught myself how to throw it.

I returned to the Pirates in '55, figuring I'd be a starting pitcher. But I pitched both ways again that year, though I had more relief appearances than starts. Then in 1956 Bobby Bragan took over the club and he's the guy who really made me a relief pitcher. Bobby had managed me at Fort Worth in '54 and knew I had an arm that reacted quick and clean. I could throw often. So he began using me more in relief. I made my last start in St. Louis in 1957. Danny Murtaugh took over the team the second half of the year and he kept me in the pen. I had been fairly successful as a starting pitcher, so I guess the main reason they made me a reliever was the way my arm bounced back.

I really enjoyed the challenge of relieving, coming in with a couple of guys on and no outs. In fact, I'd rather pitch in that situation than start an inning with no one on base. And it worked out well because I never really had an arm problem until late in my career when my arm sort of wore out.

Another advantage I had as a reliever was that I was always able to throw strikes. Control was one of my strengths, that and keeping the ball low. I'd try to keep the ball down on everybody, even on a low-ball hitter like Duke Snider. I felt that it was best to stay with my strength. If I come up to his weakness, I'm also weakening my strength. So it didn't matter who the hitter was; I'd always pitch the same way. And nine times out of ten if the ball is where it is supposed to be, it's hit on the ground. I always felt I got into trouble when I got the ball up.

During this period the team was beginning to get a lot of good, young ballplayers, guys like Dick Groat, Bill Mazeroski, Roberto Clemente, Bill Virdon, Vern Law, and others. But it took a while for them to get experience and to get to know one another. Plus the league was extremely competitive in the mid and late 1950s. The Dodgers, Braves, Giants, Cards, and Reds were all tough. Because there were only eight teams, there were good ball-players—a lot of good ballplayers—on each team. And any team was capable of knocking you off.

But the Pirates were getting better. Then in 1959 I had a year a lot of people still remember. I won my first seventeen games and finished at 18–1. In fact, I had won my last five decisions in 1958, so that was twenty-two straight wins. And I think I pitched in ninety-three straight ballgames without losing. But I had good luck and a lot of support. Without that luck, there were a number of times I could have lost during the streak. I know there were maybe six or eight games when I came in with the score tied and gave up a run. But we'd always get the run back and then win. There were even times when I came in with a two-run lead, let the other team tie it, only to have us win it again. Any kind of a streak like that takes some luck.

I was throwing well that year and had plenty of confidence. But I always had confidence, even when I started in the minors. It carried right through. In fact, when I was forty-two I still felt I could get someone out. But the streak in 1959 was special, no doubt about it. My first loss came in September, in the first game of a doubleheader in Los Angeles when the Dodgers were still playing at the Coliseum

The game was tied and Maury Wills led off with a base hit. Junior Gilliam then hit a ball that bounced over Clemente's head in right for a double. Then Charlie Neal got a broken-bat hit between third and short to get the run home. So the streak ended with a broken-bat single. See what I mean by luck?

Anyway, I remember coming into the clubhouse after the game and there were about a dozen writers at my locker waiting for me. Someone asked how I felt now that I had lost my first game. I told them that now I would have the chance to start another streak. They just looked at me and all walked away. I don't know what they expected me to say.

Maybe the strangest thing that happened during the streak, though, was the stories that I was letting teams tie up games so that I could get the win. Hank Foiles was my roommate that year and once those stories began getting around, we'd play along with them. After I'd win a game we'd come back in the clubhouse and he'd start saying things like, "Thataboy, roomie, it happened just the way we planned it." That always got us a few stares.

Something else happened in 1959 that I'll never forget. That was the twelve-inning perfect game Harvey Haddix pitched against the Braves . . . and lost in the thirteenth. It was one of the few games when I didn't go to the bullpen. I used to always go down to the pen around the fifth or sixth inning, but because he was pitching a no-hitter none of us moved. We just stayed and enjoyed it.

When the game remained scoreless into the middle innings there was a lot of talk on our bench, guys telling each other to come on, to get Harvey a run. But it never happened. At first, I don't think Harvey even realized he was pitching a perfect game. But he had confidence in the team and I think he felt we'd score. With all the hits we got it always looked like we'd get a run. We had the opportunities, but Burdette kept shutting us down. I remember around the seventh inning Bob Skinner hit a ball to right that looked like it was gone. But the wind held it up and Andy Pafko caught it against the fence.

Around the tenth inning I think it started to get to Harvey. We wouldn't score, and we all knew that we had to try to get them out again. Then in the thirteenth the perfect game ended when Don Hoak made a throwing error at third. Don was a competitor and knew errors were part of the game and he didn't talk about it much. But I know he apologized to Harvey afterward. The Braves won two hitters later when Joe Adcock hit what looked like a three-run homer. Hank Aaron had gotten on behind Felix Mantilla, who was safe on the error, and when Aaron saw Mantilla cross the plate he figured the game was over and cut across the infield to the dugout. So when Adcock circled the bases he was ruled out for passing Aaron and it went into the books as a 1–0 game.

I remember the next day Virdon and Groat were coming down the elevator in the hotel and a fan asked them if they were at the game the night before. They said yes, but didn't say they were ballplayers. The fan remarked that it was one of the best games he had seen all year. Heck, it was one of the best games ever pitched in the history of baseball.

In fact, Harvey didn't even go to bed that night. He just walked the streets until sometime in the morning. It was really a tough game for him to lose, and I guess that's really an understatement.

I think I got a $5,000 or $10,000 raise after 1959. I had been making in the twenties for the past couple of years, and eventually got up to about $42,500. I might have been the highest-paid player on the team for a time, though Clemente was beginning to make his way to $100,000. But the Pirates never paid that well and for that reason were never going to go out and try to get established ballplayers. They preferred to develop them within their own system. Surprisingly, not that many guys complained about the money. Bill Mazeroski, for one, would never argue about money. He'd get a contract from the team each year, sign and return it.

Maz, of course, became the World Series hero in 1960 when he hit the home run off Ralph Terry in the ninth inning of the seventh game. Even though we finally won it, 1960 was something of an odd year. What happened, simply, was that everyone had a good year at the same time. We had added guys like Don Hoak, Smokey Burgess, Haddix, and Vinegar Bend Mizell during the previous couple of years and those four ballplayers really made a difference in the team. The next year we were expected to win it and finished sixth. That year it just didn't seem to work out because some guys just didn't put that much into it.

Our team was up and down during that period and I guess a lot of the guys felt we should have been better than we were. That's why I say 1960 was the exception. In other years, maybe three or four key guys would have good years, but others would have off years. And while we had some well-established front-line players, I think the team always had too many fringe players.

But 1960 was definitely a highlight for me. Just to take part in the World Series made it a highlight. It's like a football player being in the Super Bowl. The funny thing was that I don't think my stuff was good throughout the entire Series. I had three saves, but in the last game I gave up five or six runs. It kind of caught up with me. Berra hit a home run and [Clete] Boyer got a double with the bases loaded. I was really tired from the long season and was throwing more sliders. In fact, I hardly used the forkball at all. But I guess I was smart enough to jam them and they were popping them up. I also think I was able to use the late-afternoon fall shadows at Yankee Stadium to my advantage. But, as I said, in the seventh game they caught up to me, but Mazeroski bailed us all out.

The funny part was that I had developed the slider only a couple of years before. I worked on it from about 1956, but no matter what I did I just couldn't get the ball to slide. Then one day in the bullpen it just came. It must have been in 1959 or '60. Anyway, I used it in a game that same day and struck a guy out with the bases loaded. And, again, it was something I did on my own. At first I didn't think I really needed it because my forkball made my other pitches. But maybe it helped later in my career, the last three or four years or so.

When you're the team's top relief pitcher you can't beg off just because you don't have your best stuff, especially in the World Series. You more or less go with the stuff you have. I didn't even tell anyone I was tired in the Series, just tried to throw better pitches. But I remember everything being off, even my control.

By the middle 1960s I was well into my thirties, but I still felt pretty good. Being the kind of pitcher I was, I don't think being into those middle years bothered me. And at that time I didn't think about the end getting near or about retiring. I used to go home in the off-season and work as a carpenter. I figured that hammering and sawing would keep my arm in shape and strong. So that's the only kind of working out I did in the off-season.

I was sold to the Detroit Tigers at the end of August in 1968. That's an interesting story because the Pirates were aware of something that I was not. I don't even know how the whole deal came about, but one day one of the ushers at the ballpark told me he just heard I had been sold to Detroit. Said he heard it up at the Athletic Club, which was in the ballpark, and I didn't know what to think. Then Larry Shepard, who was the manager in '68, called me in just before the game and told me I was starting.

That struck me right away, because I had gone some five hundred ballgames without a start. So I knew there had to be a reason. I told him I wouldn't start, and when he asked me why, I simply said I had gone five hundred games without starting and wasn't about to break that string. So he say, okay, he'd start Steve Blass instead.

Blass started the game but when the second batter came up Shepard called time and told me to warm up. Sure enough, he brought me in and put Blass in left field. Carl Taylor, who had a bad leg anyway, started in left and came out. I pitched to one batter when Shepherd came out again and pulled me. He then brought Blass back in from left to finish the game. And when he got back to the dugout he told me to go see Joe Brown, the general manager. Then I knew it was true. They had sold me to Detroit, and they wanted me in that one more game because it enabled me to tie Walter Johnson's record of 802 appearances by a pitcher with one ballclub. So even though they had made the deal they wanted to give me a chance to tie the record. And that's why Larry Shepard wanted me to start.

I wasn't with the Tigers long. They wanted me because they had a chance to win the pennant, which they did. But the funny thing was that after I got there, they got thirteen straight complete games from their starters. So in the month I was there I only pitched in two games, a total of one inning. And I missed being eligible for the World Series by one day. I went back there the next spring, but was released before we broke camp.

Even though I was forty-one by then, I was still able to throw and felt I could help somebody. But no one called and I didn't contact anyone. In April I was in New York talking to a friend about a possible business venture. That's where Gene Mauch reached me and said he wanted to look at me. He was managing the Expos then and after I worked out, he signed me to a contract. I pitched in forty-four games for them from the middle of April to the middle of August. Then I got released. They were going nowhere and wanted to bring up young players.

The next year I wasn't sure what to do. I had signed a contract to pitch for the Hawaii team in the Pacific Coast League, and shortly after that I went in on a bar and restaurant deal in Pittsburgh with a friend. So I didn't report to spring training. Instead, I pitched batting practice for the Pirates for about ten or twenty dollars a day. While I was doing that, Roberto Clemente told me he wanted me to come down and play winter ball in Puerto Rico with him. But Hawaii had suspended me when I didn't report to spring training, so I called to see if they would lift the suspension. Instead, they asked me again to come pitch for them. So I reported in July and finished the season with them. I still pitched well on occasion. In the game that clinched the pennant for Hawaii I struck out Leon Wagner, who was playing for Portland, to end it. Chuck Tanner was our manager then, and he said winning that game was one of his biggest thrills in baseball.

But Clemente never did contact me when the season ended. I had already been playing ball for twenty-two years and figured the time had come. So that was it. I still enjoyed the game at forty-two, but I knew it couldn't go on forever. I had sold my interest in the bar when I went to Hawaii, but I never worried about what I was going to do. I was a professional carpenter and knew I could get a job. That's what I did. Since 1979 I've been working for the State of Pennsylvania. I'm currently a carpenter foreman at one of their state mental hospitals, but I hope to be retiring in another year or so. We recently bought a motor home and when I retire we plan to do a lot of traveling. That's when I'll look up a lot of the guys I played with.

Because I always knew what I would do after baseball the transition wasn't difficult. In fact, I never even tried to get back into baseball because after twenty-two years I was tired of the traveling. I never had any thought of staying in the game as a coach or anything else.

But I've had plenty of time to look back at the game and see the way it's changed. Back when I played each team had one stopper. The Cards had Lindy McDaniel, for instance, the Giants had Hoyt Wilhelm. That was the guy who always got the ball come the eighth or ninth inning. It didn't matter which batters were coming up or whether they were left- or righthanded. Today there are more relievers, kids who are groomed for the job in the minors. So each team has three or four guys, set-up men, closers, righty and lefty specialists.

I do think that today's players are better athletes, at least better physically. They are better conditioned, do things like working with weights in the winter, and are bigger and stronger. But as far as desire, well, I think there was more desire on the part of the guys back when I played. Today's players are in it strictly for the money.

The Pirates back when I played were a close-knit group, even when they were losing. We did a lot of things together, ate and went out together after the games. We'd also sit around the clubhouse for an hour or two afterward, talking about the game and about baseball in general. Today, everyone is gone within twenty minutes. I heard that from John Hallihand, who has been the Pirates' clubhouse man for about forty years. So he should know.

And for those reasons, I think if you took a team of guys from my time, guys like Mays, Aaron, Musial, Williams, and Mantle, and put them in a game against the best players today, they would still beat them, even enough today's players have a physical advantage. Funny thing, though. I never had trouble with the free swingers, guys like Mays and Aaron. I had more trouble with contact hitters like Richie Ashburn, Matty Alou, Solly Hemus, or a guy like Walt Moryn when he was with the Cubs. Moryn would never swing at a bad pitch. He made you come to him. Aaron hit a home run off me in 1969 when I was pitching for Montreal. It was the only one he ever hit. And I remember pitching against big Joe Adcock, another big swinger. I faced him eleven times and struck him out each time.

Knowing you could handle the big hitters was always a good feeling. I remember Hank Aaron once did an interview with Steve Blass before a Pirates game and he was talking about the old Pirates-Braves rivalry. He said when Face came in, it was over. And Stan Musial put me in his book as the best relief pitcher he faced. But I always said, get it in the right spot and they won't hit it well.

Today I do some card shows locally and get at least fifty or sixty letters a month requesting autographs. Some are from kids, and some from older guys who want to give the cards to their kids. But when I look back at my career, the one thing I always say is that I should have been born thirty years later. I'd be rich now. That's the one thing that bothers the players from my time. We don't hold anything against today's players for getting the big salaries. It's the pensions, the pensions we're not getting, but could get if they'd let go of some of it. A twenty-year man now at the age of sixty-five will get $90,000 a year for the rest of his life. They're making millions now, so what will they even need the $90,000 for? A lot of us are just scraping to make a living and they're giving us $600 or $700 a month pension.

Yet we're the ones who set it up for them and paid into it. They don't have to pay anything. I had to start taking my pension when I was forty-five, so my guarantee is just $450 a month. That's all I get for fifteen years in the majors. A fifteen-year man today will get about forty to fifty grand when he retires. Maybe, someday.

Blass, who now broadcasts the Pirates' games, often does interviews to have ready when there are rain delays. I spoke with him recently and we were talking about one of the fantasy camps that the Pirates run in Florida each spring. Blass was down there. So were Nelson Briles, Jim Rooker, Mazeroski, and other guys who played in the fifties and sixties. The guys at the fantasy camp were mostly in their thirties. A lot of them were jocks, guys who had played high school baseball. Yet at the camp they couldn't compete with the former big leaguers, most of whom were in their fifties. Blass or Rooker would ask them where they wanted the ball, then throw it there. And these guys would either miss it or foul it off. They weren't good enough to handle the ex–big leaguers, who were much older. Blass's producer, who was also down there, said he had more respect than ever for major league players after he saw that.

But like I said, we could really play the game.

ROY
SIEVERS

♦ **MAJOR LEAGUE EXPERIENCE** ♦

St. Louis Browns, 1949–1953
Washington Senators, 1954–1959
Chicago White Sox, 1960–1961
Philadelphia Phillies, 1962–1964
Washington Senators, 1964–1965

♦ **CURRENT STATUS** ♦

Retired and living in St. Louis, Missouri.

In 1949, Roy Sievers become the first ever American League Rookie of the Year. Playing for the old St. Louis Browns, the six–one 195-pounder hit 16 home runs, had 91 RBIs and a .306 batting average. Not bad for a kid who had signed for nothing more than a pair of new shoes in 1945.

A shoulder injury slowed him for several seasons, but after being traded to the Washington Senators in 1954, Sievers went

*on to become one of the top sluggers in the American League.
In 1957, he was the American League's home run and RBI king,
with 42 and 114 respectively. And the guys he beat out were a
couple of pretty fair ballplayers—Ted Williams and Mickey Mantle.*

*Born in St. Louis on November 18, 1926, Sievers hung around
old Sportsman's Park as a kid, watching both the Cardinals and
Browns perform and idolizing such old-time players as Joe "Ducky"
Medwick.*

*Sievers remained a respected slugger, even after being traded
to the Phillies in 1962. When his career ended he had hit 318
home runs and driven in more than 1,000 runs. Always a keen
observer of hitting, Sievers loved watching the great hitters of
his time, and still enjoys talking about them today.*

T he main thing I tried to do as a hitter was not have too many
bad days in a row. I thought if I could get three hits in every ten
at bats, thirty hits in one hundred at-bats, that's a .300 average.
And I also tried not to strike out too much. But it didn't always
work out that way. Hitting is a matter of split-second timing and
it's not easy, especially when you consider some of the great
pitchers I faced in my career.

It seemed that in the late 1940s and all through the 1950s
almost every team had four good starters. The relief pitching
wasn't as great as it is today, and most of the starters went nine
innings. They wanted to go the distance. But that didn't make
hitting them any easier.

When you went into Cleveland you faced [Bob] Lemon, [Early]
Wynn, [Bob] Feller, and [Mike] Garcia. In New York it was
[Allie] Reynolds, [Vic] Raschi, [Ed] Lopat, and [Whitey] Ford.
You never got a rest. In Detroit you faced [Virgil] Trucks,

[Dizzy] Trout, and [Hal] Newhouser, three more guys who could really throw. So it was a daily battle, you against him, hitter against pitcher.

The key to being a good hitter is to hit the pitcher's mistake when he throws it. If you don't do that you're gonna go oh for four. Because the old saying is true; good pitching will stop good hitting. That was evident all over again in the 1988 World Series between the Dodgers and Oakland. The Dodgers' pitching just shut the A's down, although I thought a couple of guys on the A's were overswinging.

There was also a definite difference hitting in the two leagues when I played, and from what I understand the same differences exist today. The big difference is the strike zone. When I first came into the American League in 1949 the strike zone was the letters down to the knees. Then when I went to the National League in 1962, the strike zone became the belt down to midshin, between the ankles and the knees. From what I've been told, it's always been that way, and it looks like it still is. In the National you couldn't wait. You had to swing the bat.

But I think the hitter has the advantage today, simply because the pitchers aren't allowed to throw at them in any way. And that takes the edge from the pitcher. He loses a trump card if he can't go inside or knock a hitter down. Back in my day if the guy in front of me hit a home run, I went down. It was automatic. You expected it. But it wasn't that bad. And any kind of hitter should be able to get out of the way of the ball unless a real hard thrower lets loose with one that tails in on him. It's just instinct. You may only have a split second, but you know what the hell is going on and you know that ball is coming at you.

Looking back at my own career, I really have no regrets. And that's because I've always felt that sports is a great way to make a living. But I did spend a good part of my career with two second-division teams, both of which don't even exist anymore.

I grew up in St. Louis right around the old ballpark—Sportsman's Park. When I was young I joined the old Browns' Knot

Hole Gang, and they issued free passes for the kids to get into the park. Because both the Browns and Cardinals played there, I got to watch both the American and National Leagues and see all the big stars from both leagues.

One of my early favorites was Joe Medwick when he played for the Cardinals. A few years later I couldn't wait to see Joe DiMaggio and Ted Williams come to town. That was one of the thrills I had when I made it to the big leagues, to be able to play against some of the great players I had seen as a kid.

There were a heckuva lot of good ballplayers in north St. Louis, and we used to play on the sandlots from early in the morning right up to suppertime. When I was a little older I began playing Legion ball. Yogi Berra had been on the same team before me and so were a lot of the kids who became my teammates at Beaumont High School. Bobby Hofman played for our team, and Earl Weaver was a freshman when I graduated. But with all the baseball I played, it wasn't until my last couple of years at Beaumont that I thought about playing professionally.

Because the high school was only a couple of blocks from the ballpark, both the Cardinals and Browns looked at me during that time. In fact, Walter Shannon, my Legion coach, was also a Cardinal scout and he came out to the house almost every day for a year trying to convince me to sign with them. But back then the Cardinals were keeping guys down in the minors for seven or eight years until they felt they were really established as ballplayers.

My father had always been an American League rooter and when I asked him for his advice he said I'd have a better chance getting to the majors with the Browns than with the Cards. As it turned out, I signed with the Browns and my mother said I should have called Mr. Shannon to at least see what the Cards' deal was. We never did that. But after I signed, Mr. Shannon said the Cards were ready to give me five thousand. I said why didn't you tell me that in the first place. All the Browns gave me was a pair of shoes. That was it. Really.

I signed with the Browns right after I graduated high school in 1945, but then I went into the service for two years. I always said that Hitler heard I was coming over so he surrendered. I ended up an MP stationed in Kentucky and I played ball for two years with the service team. But that helped, because I played with some former major leaguers who still knew how to play the game.

After my discharge in February of 1947 I joined the Browns and was sent to play Class C ball in Hannibal, Missouri. I had a good year and in '48 played everywhere from Double A to B ball in Springfield, Missouri, where I hit nineteen home runs. But my totals for the entire season were thirty-four home runs, 141 RBIs and a .317 batting average. And the next year I made the Browns. So maybe it was worth taking the shoes instead of the five thousand after all.

The Browns were a kind of unusual organization back then. The team was always near the bottom of the league, so I figured I had a good chance to make it with them. But they also got rid of a lot of good ballplayers because they needed the money to survive. Still, I felt if I made it to the big leagues with the Browns and had some good years there, I would stay awhile.

I had a good spring, made the team, and then struck out my first two at-bats and figured I was gone again. But my third time up I pinch-hit a double and drove in a couple of runs. After the game my manager, Zack Taylor, told me I was going to start both games of a doubleheader the next day. Fortunately, I got hot with the bat, had six or seven hits, and the other left fielder didn't play anymore. I had the job for the rest of the season, and it turned out to be a good one.

But until I won the regular job and started to produce, it was tough just being on my own ballclub. For some reason, rookies weren't treated very well back then. For instance, we had to come out real early just to get batting practice. We never got to hit with the regulars, the veterans. And half the time the pitchers wouldn't throw to us so we had to get someone else, maybe the batboy or another guy who wasn't playing, to go out and throw early.

To this day I don't know why it was that way. I always figured, hell, we're teammates, why don't we all pitch in and do this together? But about half the veterans wouldn't even speak to us. And I gathered it was the same way with some of the other teams then. Maybe a lot of the older guys were afraid of losing their jobs. I don't know. But the big guys just didn't talk to the little guys. Finally, around the middle of the season it began loosening up a bit. I was hitting pretty well by then and I guess they finally figured that this kid was going to fit in.

As it turned out, I ended up in a three-way race for Rookie of the Year with Gus Zernial and Johnny Groth. It was the first year they had the award, so when I won it was kind of extra special. I wound up with sixteen homers, ninety-one RBIs, and a .306 batting average. And I thought, man, I'm on my way to a great career. This is it. The Browns, of course, were in their usual spot, and I had already begun to think what it would be like to play with a first-division team. But then I ran into a couple of tough years.

In 1950, I guess I was the victim of what they call the sophomore jinx. Part of the problem was that the Browns tried to change my stance. For some reason they wanted me to hit to right field more. Well, the whole thing screwed up my swing and I lost my stride and ended up hitting .238. After that, I said I was going back to my own way of hitting and I never let anyone change me again.

Then the following year I dove for a ball in the outfield and dislocated my shoulder. I tried to come back about a month later, but the arm wasn't responding. So I went through the whole year kind of completely lost, played in just thirty-one games, and when the shoulder came out the first day of spring training in 1952, I decided to have an operation. The funny part was that the injury didn't bother me hitting, only throwing, but they didn't have the DH back then.

Because of the shoulder I only played in eleven games in '52 and I began to think that my career might be over. Believe me, it was a sick feeling. I had had such a great rookie year and even weathered the second year all right. But after the shoulder I was really down. And there was no one on the team that I could really talk to about it. It was my wife who encouraged me to work hard and to make up my mind to come back.

It finally came back, but it took time. I did construction work in St. Louis during the off-season for two or three years and always worked to build up the shoulder. The Browns had made me a first baseman in 1953 to make the throwing easier and I got into ninety-two games. Then the team moved to Baltimore for the 1954 season with a completely new organization taking over. Jimmy Dykes was the manager and he got a letter from someone in St. Louis stating I couldn't throw. But it apparently was the main reason they decided to get rid of me.

So I was traded to Washington for Gil Coan and still not sure what was in store for me. But Bucky Harris, the Washington manager, put my fears to rest. He told me I was his left fielder and I shouldn't worry about my throwing. The shortstop would always be there to take a cutoff throw and he felt my arm would get better. The big thing was they wanted my bat in the lineup.

Bucky was true to his word. I played every day and my shoulder got stronger. I had twenty-four homers and 102 RBIs in 1954, but my average was just .232. I'm told that's the lowest average of any player ever driving in one hundred runs. I think part of it was that I was really just getting into the flow of the game again and adjusting to playing every day. I didn't hit that good, but I guess it was good enough to drive in the 102 runs. But the next three years were better, and looking back, I really had some great seasons in Washington.

The only problem was that the team didn't win enough ballgames. The pitchers would often go good until the fifth, sixth, or seventh inning and then, bang, something would happen. We just didn't have that kind of pitching, a staff that could hold them. Plus as a team, we didn't drive in enough runs. It takes everybody working together to produce a winning team. Still, we had some good ballplayers, guys like Pete Runnels, Mickey Vernon, Eddie Yost, Jim Busby, Johnny Pesky, Bob Porterfield, Mickey McDermott, Chuck Stobbs, and Camilo Pascual.

But the team was really like any second-division ballclub. You just went out and did your job and hoped you could beat someone. For some reason, we played better against the first-division ballclubs. I think we wanted to beat them more than the other second-division teams.

Overall, I guess, a team like ours had a lack of depth, a pitching staff not going as well as it should, and some guys not hitting in certain situations. And we didn't have a bullpen. It was the same with the Browns. You'd have one or two fairly good starters and if they couldn't do it you'd lose.

After a while, you begin to feel that something will always go wrong. What's gonna happen next, you'd ask yourself. And the good clubs usually capitalized on the mistakes you made. The Yankees were famous for that. So once you made a mistake or an error, it usually opened the gates and, bang, another loss.

Then in 1957, I had my best season. I started well and when things kept getting better, I figured I was really going to have a good year. I could just feel it within myself. And when I won some ballgames with late-inning homers, it gave me that little extra drive. But that wasn't really the big thing. The big thing was that I was battling for the home run title. And the two guys I was battling were named Ted Williams and Mickey Mantle. That inspired me even more. Williams was my idol when I was younger and Mantle was already a superstar, having won the triple crown the year before. And here I was, battling both of them.

It was still close when we went into Baltimore late in the season. I hit three home runs there and it put me in the lead. One was a grand slam off Ray Moore. After that I stayed ahead. And I was definitely motivated going up against those two guys. I wanted to beat them. I wanted to beat them badly.

As it turned out, I won the home run title with forty-two and the RBI crown with 114. I also hit .301, but Ted took the batting title with an incredible .388 average. Years later, I saw him at a card show and said, "Ted, you deprived me of my triple crown." When he asked what I meant, I reminded him that I hit .301 in 1957 and he only beat me out by eighty-seven points. He got a big laugh out of that.

But it wasn't so funny when I talked contract with Calvin Griffith after the season. That's when he said that if the team finished last with me, they could also finish last without me. He was willing to give me a raise, but not the raise I had anticipated getting. I think I was making about sixteen or seventeen thousand then and I knew Mantle and those guys were making a lot more. I figured if they could make it by hitting homers, I should, too. I wanted a 100 percent raise, and after a big battle, I think I got about 80 percent.

To show you how Calvin was, the next year I came back with thirty-nine homers and 108 RBIs, hit .295, and he wanted to cut me ten thousand. Said I didn't win a title. I just said, "Calvin, you gotta be kidding." I ended up with a small raise, but not the one I thought I deserved.

By 1959 the team had a lot of power. [Harmon] Killebrew had forty-two homers that year, Bob Allison and Jim Lemon could also hit the long ball. But the pitching wasn't that good and the team was still way down in the standings. Plus I was hurt a good part of the year and had an off season. I still felt I would stay in Washington, but in the off-season I was traded to the White Sox for Don Mincher, Earl Battey, and $150,000. So I finally got my wish to play for a first-division team and Calvin got the money he needed to save him for the year.

The White Sox were coming off a pennant in 1959 and had a strong team. Al Smith, Minnie Minoso, and Jim Landis were set in the outfield, and Ted Kluszewski was the first baseman. I wasn't playing at the beginning of the season and it ticked me off. Even Nellie Fox said to me, "How can they play that big Kluszewski over there when we have you?" Well, about a month into the season Kluszewski wasn't going well and I got my shot. Klu didn't play again and I went on to have two great years with the White Sox.

It didn't take long to see the difference between a first- and a second-division team. The guys knew how to play and liked to win. In fact, I always said we should have won it again in 1960, but our pitching fell off a bit. Still, we had a two-and-a-half-game lead going into August, but after losing a tough game in Baltimore, we just sort of went backward. But the players really wanted to win.

Let's face it, everybody hates to lose. We hated to lose as a second-division ballclub. When you win, it makes it easier to play and the things on the field go a little easier. Then after the 1961 season, I think Al Lopez wanted the Sox to go back to more speed and defense. That's when I was traded to the Phillies for John Buzhardt and Charley Smith. I was thirty-five years old before the 1962 season began and I think as every ballplayer gets older, he begins to think this could be his last year. So he tries to keep himself in fairly good shape and hopes he has a good enough year to survive.

The trade really surprised me. I didn't do badly with the Phils until '64, when they almost won the pennant. The team really had some fine ballplayers, like Johnny Callison, Tony Taylor, Clay Dalrymple, and in '64, Richie Allen. I tell you, I never saw a guy work harder in my life to learn how to play third base. He would take extra ground balls every day and was really a gifted athlete, a very strong hitter.

But in '64 I had a pulled calf muscle that kept me out a month. Then after a few days, I hurt it again. With a chance to win, the Phils needed another righthanded hitter and in July I was sold back to Washington. I finished the season there, then twelve games into '65 I was released.

Gil Hodges was the manager there and he called me in one day and told me this was the toughest job he had as a manager. "I've got to release you," he said. "I want to play the younger kids and I've talked to the general manager about it. I've got to have a younger body in there than you."

I just looked at him and said, "Gil, I was hitting pretty good." And he said, "I know." But that didn't change anything. I was gone. I still felt in excellent shape and didn't think I was ready for the scrap heap. So I called Al Lopez in Chicago and asked him if he needed a righthanded hitter. I went to Comiskey Park and worked out with the team for three or four days. Then I talked with the general manager, Ed Short. He asked me about my leg and then said the team was willing to sign me for two weeks.

Two weeks! I said, "Ed, you've seen me play for seventeen and a half years. How could you want to look at me for two weeks?" I couldn't believe he wouldn't sign me for the remainder of the year. I think they were afraid I would get hurt again and they'd have to pay me for the whole season. I just said to him, "You'll go out and sign a kid for a hundred-thousand-dollar bonus and yet you won't sign me for twenty thousand. I can't believe it." Then I went to St. Louis and worked out with the Cardinals.

Their manager, Red Schoendienst, said he had never seen me hit the ball as well, but when it came time to talk contract, they told me they didn't need a righthanded hitter. And at the time their righthanded hitters on the bench were Dal Maxvill, Carl Warwick, and Bob Uecker! That's who they decided to go with. I came home that night and told my wife it was time to quit.

I don't think any ballplayer in my day prepared for retirement until it was time. I never made the big money. I think thirty-four-thousand was my top salary. But I figured if I could stay in the majors as a coach for another three or four years I'd have twenty years in and it would help my pension. I knew Bill DeWitt in Cincinnati from his days with the Browns and he hired me to be a coach with the Reds. It lasted just a year. The manager, Dave Bristol, fired me because he wanted to bring his own people in. There was a lot of politics back then.

After that, I managed for two years at Williamsport, Pennsylvania, for the Mets, but this time I was fired by Whitey Herzog, who was their farm director then. The only reason I was given was that they wanted to make a change, but again I think he wanted to bring his own buddies in. The same thing happened with Oakland. I managed their A team in Burlington, Iowa, for two years and was fired from there. I tried a couple more teams and was told there were no spots available. It was time to go home and stay there.

That wasn't easy, either. Everybody was asking, "What happened, Roy?" And I'd just say I had a bad leg the year before and that's why some clubs didn't want to take a chance on me. What else could I say? I guess it's hard to admit it's over.

After that I went to work for the Yellow Freight Company in St. Louis and stayed with them until 1986. Now I'm home and living on my pension. It's not what I'd like it to be, but . . .

There is an effort to get more money for guys who played during my time, especially for the widows of those of us who have died. Early Wynn is really involved with it, but it's gonna take the young guys playing today to vote on it. So who knows. People sometimes ask me what I'd be making if I played today. I tell them probably a million dollars, but you can't let yourself think about that too much.

Still, I've got some great memories. I often think about some of the good hitters I saw. I always enjoyed Mantle because he was so good from both sides of the plate. If he had had good legs there's no telling what he might have done. George Kell was another great hitter, and I always loved to watch Yogi. He was supposed to be a bad-ball hitter but, hell, he could hit everything.

Harvey Kuenn was another hitter I loved to watch because he always got the good part of the bat on the ball. And when I was in the National League I saw Musial, another really great hitter, as was Kenny Boyer of the Cards. But every club had one or two guys who were fairly good hitters and I always loved to watch them hit.

Now I go to some card shows and old-timers' games. I saw DiMaggio at a card show pretty recently and told him it was an honor to play against him. He said, "Don't give me that honor stuff. You were a good ballplayer and always gave the Yankees fits." That made me feel good.

And I still get a thrill pulling on the uniform and trying to perform in old-timers' games. But I think my biggest thrill is going back to Yankee Stadium with sixty-thousand people in the stands. They introduce Whitey Ford and the people give him a standing ovation. Then they bring Yogi out, then Mantle, and they get standing ovations. And finally they bring out the big guy, DiMaggio, and he always brings the house down. And I just stand there on the foul line getting goosebumps.

I also take part in some golf tournaments with the Baseball Alumni Association. They put on ten or twelve a year with half the money raised going to charity and the other half back into the association. It's great seeing guys you may not have seen for twenty or twenty-five years. We had fun, were together all the time, and have a helluva lot to talk about.

From time to time I even think about getting back into the game. I went to the last two World Series that were played in St. Louis and made some inquiries. But they want young guys who can throw batting practice. I even asked about being a hitting instructor in the minors. I said I can still talk hitting and show kids how to swing the bat. But it was no again. And for the same reason. They just want younger people.

BILL
BRUTON

♦ **MAJOR LEAGUE EXPERIENCE** ♦

Milwaukee Braves, 1953–1960
Detroit Tigers, 1961–1964

♦ **CURRENT STATUS** ♦

Retired after twenty-three years' service with
the Chrysler Corporation in Detroit,
Michigan.

*When Bill Bruton was signed by Boston Braves' scout John Ogden
in 1949, he was already twenty-four years old. But on Ogden's
advice, he told the team he was just twenty, keeping the secret
throughout his twelve-year big league career. So while most official
baseball publications list his birth date as December 22, 1929, in
reality he was born on that date in 1925.*

*But that didn't stop the fleet center fielder from becoming one
of the finest defensive outfielders of his day. Bruton also led the*

National League in stolen bases in each of his first three seasons in the league, but unlike many of today's fleet baserunners, he never stole for the sake of numbers, only when he could help his team.

Out with a knee injury when the Braves won the World Series in 1957, he rebounded the following year to bat .412 against the New York Yankees in the 1958 fall classic. A year later he became just one of two players in baseball history to hit two bases-loaded triples in the same game.

Traded to the Detroit Tigers in 1961, Bill Bruton finished his career in fine style, hitting a solid .277 in his final season, 1964, when he was nearly thirty-nine years old. Always looking to the future, Bruton planned for his retirement and made an easy transition to nonbaseball life, working for the next twenty-three years for the Chrysler Corporation.

I had twelve good years in the majors and for that I've always felt I was very blessed. After all, I was on two pennant winners, played in the World Series, and my teams were in contention most of the other years. But I always knew I could only stay in the game for so long as a player. For that reason, I looked at baseball as a way to open another door for me once my playing days were over. And I thought that way from the very first day I put on a major league uniform.

At the time I retired in 1964 about the only thing they might have offered me as a black player was a scouting job, and I wasn't interested in that. There were no coaching jobs open to blacks then, no minor league managing jobs. And unlike a lot of other players, I always thought about a second career. I knew plenty of guys who didn't think about it until the day came when they couldn't play anymore. Then they couldn't deal with it.

With football and basketball, many of the players had at least some college education. But the majority of baseball players back in my time were signed right out of high school. So they had very little formal education, very little training for anything else.

Because of this, an awful lot of the players back then wanted to remain in baseball. But there just weren't enough jobs. Again, maybe it was because they never thought about life outside the game. The prevailing attitude seemed to be, "We'll worry about it when the time comes." Maybe it would have really helped if there was someone to talk with the players then about their postplaying plans. But there was no one.

I started thinking about the future as soon as I joined the Braves in 1953. That was the first year the team was in Milwaukee, and that winter I went to work for the Miller Brewing Company, worked there for four years. They had a sports promotion program and we traveled throughout the state, and to places like Cleveland, Denver, and Salt Lake City, doing promotional work. What I had in mind, ultimately, was a Miller High Life distributorship. In fact, that might have materialized, but in 1955 the president of the company, Fred Miller, was killed in a plane crash. After that it kind of fizzled, because I had the relationship with him.

So when I was traded to Detroit in 1961 I began to think about it all over again. That's when I contacted the Chrysler Corporation for the first time. I went to work for them following the 1963 season to learn how to sell automobiles. I did it because they were a large company and I wanted to learn the retail end of the business and eventually own a dealership. The program they offered me as a veteran player who was beginning to think of retirement was pretty good, and that winter I worked at a dealership selling automobiles.

As it turned out, I spent twenty-three years with Chrysler before retiring in January of 1988. I had a variety of positions in the company, but my last one was as a kind of troubleshooter for one of the top executives. I worked in customer-owner relations and dealt with people who wanted to talk to the chairman or president or vice-president about a car problem. I also worked in advertising and sales promotion, and even had a dealership for a couple of years. So I did a lot of things and it worked out well. And because I had the commitment of a job from Chrysler even before I retired, it made the transition an easy one. I was lucky.

Maybe I was lucky at the beginning, too. I was signed by a scout named John Ogden back in 1949. I was twenty-four years old then, and Ogden told me right away that was too old. He suggested I take a few years off my age, and he told everyone I was twenty. So my birthday in most publications is listed as December 22, 1929. But I was actually born in 1925.

Ogden felt I would get a longer look if they thought I was twenty back then. He was probably right, because a twenty-four-year-old who still needed seasoning would probably have been considered more of a risk.

I was born in Panola, Alabama, but my parents moved to Birmingham when I was about six or seven. That's where I grew up. While I played all the sports as a kid, almost all of it was on the sandlots. There was really no organized baseball for kids back then. We also never thought about the big leagues then, because we all knew that black players weren't allowed to play. But we knew about the Negro Leagues, and we'd watch the games every summer. That was *the* professional league as far as we were concerned.

Of course, we had heard about guys like Babe Ruth and Lou Gehrig, but we had our own heroes, players like Judy Johnson, Josh Gibson, Satchel Paige. We saw some of them play and they were the ones we emulated. In fact, Judy Johnson ended up being my father-in-law. He was inducted into the Hall of Fame in 1975, but I never saw him play.

After I graduated from high school I went into the service and played ball there. When I came out I continued to play, this time in the Wilmington, Delaware, area. But I still didn't know what I wanted to do and was trying to decide whether I should go back to school or just continue to work at a factory job I had at that time. That's when I got the opportunity to play semiprofessional ball, again in the Wilmington area.

Then in 1949 I had the chance to go to spring training with the Philadelphia Stars of the Negro League, but I was released before the season started. They said I'd never be a ballplayer. I found out later that the real reason was that there was some animosity between the manager of the team and my father-in-law. Anyway, a guy had seen me work out whose brother managed a barnstorming team from International Falls, Minnesota, and he said the team needed an outfielder. So I joined them and we traveled around through Iowa, North and South Dakota, Ontario, Canada, and other places. They were also an all-black team and they had some fine ballplayers.

In fact, I'd say that seven or eight of them might have made it to the majors if they'd been given the chance when they were younger. Most of them had never thought about the majors. But when more teams began signing young black players after Jackie Robinson joined the Dodgers, then I think some of those older guys began to feel even worse that it was too late for them and they would never get at least a crack at the big leagues.

But it was lucky for me that I had joined the team, because one of the scouts who worked with John Ogden saw me play and that's how I was invited to the Braves' minor league training camp the next year, 1950. I was assigned to the Eau Claire [Wisconsin] Bears in the Northern League to begin my minor league career.

Like a lot of the other ballplayers back then, I needed my time in the minors. Up to then, I had had only informal training in the game. In fact, I always felt I could have done even better my first year with the Braves if I had still another year in the minors. I went to spring training with the Braves for the first time in '52, stayed with them all spring, played in the preseason series against the Red Sox, then was assigned to the Milwaukee Brewers, who were a Triple A American Association team back then.

There still weren't too many black players in organized ball then, and I did run into a few problems in the minors. I remember being assigned to a team in Hagerstown, Maryland, in 1951, but apparently they weren't ready to integrate, so instead I was sent to Denver. But that was the only time that happened.

Anyway, being in the big league camp in 1952 was a real thrill. I also gained a great deal of experience, and the next year I went down there with a heckuva lot of determination and I made the team. Not only did I make it, but I became the starting center fielder. Of course, they all thought I was twenty-three, but I was really twenty-seven.

That was also the year the team moved from Boston to Milwaukee. The move didn't bother me at all. In fact, it was almost like going home, because I had enjoyed my stay there with the Brewers. The players weren't told about the move until spring training, but most of the veterans didn't seem to mind. Boston had always been a Red Sox town. You know, twenty-five hundred letters is a big pile of letters; but twenty-five hundred people in the stands is not an awful lot of people.

I wasn't the only black on the team then. They had both George Crowe and Jim Pendleton in 1953, and Henry Aaron joined us the next year. I guess by that time everyone knew that blacks were in the league to stay so there were no problems. The only thing we'd run into once in a while was a housing situation. St. Louis and Cincinnati were probably the last towns to integrate their hotels. So we stayed at black hotels, which were more than adequate.

We actually opened in Cincinnati that year and I had a pretty good opening day. Then we returned to Milwaukee for the first home opener ever in County Stadium, and I was fortunate enough to hit the game-winning homer off Gerry Staley of the Cardinals. The whole thing—winning the starting job and then hitting the game-winning homer—was such a grand, wonderful feeling that I really don't think I have the words in my vocabulary to adequately express it. It was a real thrill.

The Braves had a combination of both older and younger players that year and were a solid team. There were guys like Joe Adcock, Johnny Logan, Eddie Mathews, and Del Crandall there. They would all play a big role in the pennant-winning teams of the late fifties. And we already had the core of the pitching staff with Warren Spahn, Lew Burdette, and Bob Buhl. But we also had vets like Sid Gordon, Andy Pafko, Max Surkont, Sibby Sisti, and Walker Cooper. And as I said, Henry Aaron was a year away.

As a rookie, the toughest thing for me was to familiarize myself with all the ballparks in the league. Back then, all the old parks had different configurations. They put them right in the cities where they had available space. It wasn't like it is now, with the parks on the outskirts of town and all having just about the same dimensions.

But I really enjoyed all the old parks. Crosley Field in Cincinnati had that incline or terrace in place of a warning track just before the outfield wall. I remember on opening day there in 1953 they had such a big crowd that the fans were all sitting right on that little rise in the outfield. A couple of times I had to go back there and kind of lean into them to catch fly balls that could have been doubles. I guess I was fortunate not to step on anybody. But the fans out there were good. They didn't get in your way and they let you make the play. I always liked playing there, as well as at places like Forbes Field [Pittsburgh], Ebbets Field [Brooklyn], and the Polo Grounds [New York].

I led the league in stolen bases my first three seasons in the majors. After that I dropped off a bit. One reason was the knee injury I suffered in 1957, but another was a managerial change. Charlie Grimm was the manager when I got there in '53. And Charlie said, "You've been through the minor leagues and you know how to play this game. If you get on base and get a good jump, then go ahead. You know when to run and when not to run."

So he left it up to me. He knew I'd only try to steal if it meant something to the team. My object was to get into scoring position. Depending on the circumstances I might try it with one or two outs. I'd never run if there were no outs. I never ran just for the sake of stealing a base or to get my numbers up. And this was the kind of thing that was taught in the minor leagues.

People sometimes ask me if I could have stolen eighty or one hundred bases a year the way guys like Rickey Henderson and Vince Coleman do today. I always tell them that I didn't learn to play the game that way. When I played there just weren't that many opportunities to steal, especially when you hit at the top of the lineup. The object then was to have the third and fourth hitters swing the bat. So if you were on base and were thrown out stealing, you'd be taking the bat out of their hands. If you had home run hitters on the ballclub you used them.

I think it started changing when Maury Wills began hanging up those big numbers on the bases. Sure, there were times when everybody in the ballpark—including the pitcher and catcher—knew I was gonna run. It didn't matter. I still ran. And I studied the pitchers and used a number of different slides. For these reasons I guess if I was turned loose like the guys today, yes, I could have put those kinds of numbers up.

But instead, my numbers went down. Fred Haney took over the team in the middle of the 1956 season and he had a different philosophy about running. With Haney it was run only when he said so. Charlie Grimm more or less let us play the game.

But I guess by the same token you can't argue with success. We were second when I joined the team in 1953, third in 1954, then second again in 1955. So we were close. After Haney took over in 1956 we finished second by a game, then won it the next two years, and lost in a playoff in 1959. But I think the team was ready for that. It's too bad, because just before Charlie Grimm was released we couldn't seem to do anything right. But by then we knew we had a good team.

I think the biggest single factor in our winning it in 1957 was getting Red Schoendienst to play second base. We had had some problems at second in the previous years and Red was an experienced player. He just took over at second and took charge in the infield. It may sound strange, but one player can really do that for a team. Plus the shortstop–second baseman combination is very important to a team. A double play can get a team out of a lot of real jams.

But like I said, the team was really solid by then. We had Henry Aaron since 1954, and he was coming into his own. There was never a question about his hitting ability. The first day he came to camp he hit one out of the ballpark. But he had come through the minors as an infielder and needed work in the outfield. It really took two or three years for him to feel comfortable out there. He and I were roommates and would often talk baseball and talk about defense. So I was probably able to help him that way, though he never directly asked for it.

I think it took Hank longer to get the recognition he deserved because of where we played. Mays and Mantle, for instance, both played in New York with all those newspapers and reporters. In Milwaukee we had two papers, so I think the location had a lot to do with it. And in the big cities, they dwelled on their own stars. Mays, Mantle, and Snider in New York, Ernie Banks in Chicago, that kind of thing.

When we finally won the pennant in 1957 I wasn't there to be part of it. I hurt my knee in Pittsburgh right after the All-Star break. Felix Mantilla was playing short that day in place of Johnny Logan and we both went after one of those little bloopers, a Texas Leaguer. Since neither of us knew whether we'd reach it or not we didn't call it and we collided. We both wound up with injured legs, but mine was worse, a torn ligament in my right knee. I tried some therapy on it, but it didn't work and I needed surgery.

There were no guarantees the surgery would be successful, so I thought about my career ending right then. But I also knew I couldn't play ball on it the way it was, so we went ahead. I think I could have accepted it if the operation failed, but fortunately it worked out pretty well and I came back early in the 1958 season.

As I said, I missed the victory over the Yankees in the World Series in '57. I didn't even go and had kind of an empty feeling about it. But I figured that was the way the cookie crumbled and I just couldn't do anything about it. It would have been even worse if I had gotten injured off the field. I think the thing that hurt the most was missing the experience of playing in the World Series, but later on I was proud to wear that World Series ring, even though I wasn't there.

Of course, the next year we were back in the Series again, and this time they beat us in seven. But it was still a thrill to play. I can remember having butterflies during the opening ceremonies at Yankee Stadium. But once we began playing it was just like another game to me. And when I think back to those days I'm still not sure who had the better team. We were seven and seven in two Series and maybe could have settled it if we played them again.

We had a very confident group of guys then. During those years in the middle and late fifties we always felt that if we could beat the Dodgers and the Giants for the pennant, then we could beat the Yanks in the World Series. Of course we didn't play them again. People have often said that with a few breaks here or there we could have won four or five pennants. Maybe. But you can't point to one or two games and say that's what lost it for us. It doesn't work that way.

I remember a close ballgame against the Cards toward the end of the 1956 season. Eddie Mathews let one go through his legs at third that cost us the game. After it was over he was crying, because he thought he might have cost us the pennant. And I'm sure he felt bad when we finished one game back. But like I said, you can't point to one game and say it lost the pennant. Because there are so many others you might have won if this or that happened. But Eddie was a competitor and he took it hard.

I've always said that Eddie Mathews could have broken Ruth's home run record if he hadn't played in County Stadium. It wasn't that right field was that deep, but the air was stagnant and some days you really had to powder the ball to get it out of there. I can't tell you how many times one of us thought we had hit one out only to see the outfielder come in a couple of steps and catch it. So you knew there had to be heavy air out there.

But Eddie was a strong hitter. He'd have hit a lot more if he played in Tiger Stadium in Detroit, or even in Sportsman's Park in St. Louis or Ebbets Field in Brooklyn. Yet even with the dead air, Eddie and Hank formed quite a home run combination for quite a few years.

Johnny Logan, our shortstop, was a steady infielder who wasn't going to be spectacular, but who would be in there fighting and scrapping every day. He was a fiery player. Del Crandall was a pretty good receiver who worked hard to improve his throwing, hit well enough, and could handle Spahn and Burdette and our other pitchers. Joe Adcock was one of the best guess hitters I knew. And when he guessed right, that pitch was going a long way. Add Aaron and Schoendienst, as well as our pitching staff, and we had a real solid team.

Spahn and Burdette were the leaders of our pitching staff and a couple of really great guys. Burdette was a low-ball pitcher who tried to make them hit it on the ground. Spahn was a high-ball pitcher so the outfielders stayed busy when he was on the mound. His big thing was to keep them from getting too much wood on the ball and hitting it out. So they were two different type pitchers and as a center fielder I had to play the hitters differently when each of them pitched. Standing in center field I could see whether the ball was inside, outside, or down the middle and I'd move accordingly.

Of course, being an outfielder I much preferred playing behind the one who kept me busy, and that was Spahn. You always knew there would be a lot of fly-ball outs. A lot of pitchers can't pitch high, but Spahn's ball had a tendency to rise and for a hitter to catch it just right was pretty tough. So the hitter would get a piece of the ball, but it wouldn't be enough. Every once in a while one would get away from him and go down the middle of the plate. He hated himself for that because he always said the plate was only seventeen inches wide and he wanted the two inches outside and the two inches inside. The umpire could have the rest.

The big talk with Burdette was that he threw a spitter. He used all that talk to his advantage. They were giving him pitches he didn't have and he'd go through all those gyrations just to make it look better. But I don't think too many pitchers really threw the spitter back then. Maybe the most prominent one I knew was Preacher Roe. I do remember this young kid coming up one year—can't even remember his name—but he didn't know what he was doing. One day he loaded it up so bad that it was actually flying, and you could see the spit jumping off the ball. The umpire said hold it right there and told him no more of that.

But Spahn and Burdette could really pitch. So could Bob Buhl, a solid pitcher you don't often hear much about. And we had Gene Conley, who played basketball for the Celtics in the winter. He helped us on the mound, too, as did our stopper, Don McMahon, who was always tough out of the pen. So we had a good staff.

I eventually made a complete recovery from the knee injury, played in the World Series of '58, and then had a couple more good years. In 1960 I had a .286 average with twelve home runs, led the league with 112 runs scored . . . and I was traded to Detroit in the off-season. I was out hunting with Henry Aaron and another guy, and when we got back we heard about the trade. The Braves needed a second baseman and had their eye on Frank Bolling and the Tigers wanted a center fielder so they could move Al Kaline back to right. So the trade was made.

It wasn't really tough for me to change teams. The way I saw it you didn't leave friends, you made new friends. Friendships would always be there and the way I looked at it, there were only sixteen companies back then that could give me the work I liked to do. So to me it didn't make any difference which club it was. That's a personal feeling. When I was with the Braves I did everything I could to help make them better. When I went to the Tigers I had the same philosophy. My attitude toward the game remained the same. I had no regrets and the transition was easy.

My first year in Detroit was 1961 and I wound up with career highs of seventeen home runs and sixty-three RBIs. That was the year Roger Maris had sixty-one homers and everyone else was hitting them as well. But to me, that year marked the end of a very great era. In fact, I have always thought that the baseball played during the 1950s was the best baseball ever played. I mean, the all-around game. There were just sixteen teams, eight in each league, and back then the eighth-place club could knock you off any time. It was just that somebody had to finish last. I realize that's saying a lot, but I really feel the game in the 1950s was the best the country has ever seen, and I'll tell you why.

It seemed as if every club had three or four solid starting pitchers. Just look at the New York teams. The Yanks had Reynolds, Raschi, Lopat, and then Ford. The Dodgers had Newcombe, Roe, Erskine, Clem Labine, Joe Black, Billy Loes. The Giants had Maglie, Hearn, Jansen, and Antonelli. Pitching staffs like that were manager's dreams. And it almost seemed as if it was that way everywhere.

But it started to change in 1961. That's when the American League expanded by adding two new teams, and the National followed in 1962. With just two new teams you could see there were players in the big leagues who just weren't ready, and more pitchers who weren't as sharp. With expansion, they were forced up before they were really ready. Remember, each of the established teams had to give up players, and that meant they had to bring up youngsters to fill their rosters. It really began to make a difference.

In fact, you see the same thing today. And that's the only thing about the salaries they're paying today that bothers me. You see journeymen players making a million dollars, or $750,000 a year, and you know that somehow that cost is going to be passed down to the fans. And I don't think the public should be paying the high ticket prices just to see minor league baseball. That's really how I feel. Many players in the majors today should still be in the minor leagues.

The Tiger team I joined in '61 was a good one. They had the type of pitching staff I was talking about with Jim Bunning, Frank Lary, Don Mossi, Paul Foytack, and Phil Regan. And with players like Al Kaline, Norm Cash, and Rocky Colavito, they could hit. They won 101 games and finished second to the Yankees.

I hit second at Detroit instead of leadoff and I liked it. Jake Wood was the leadoff man and we both had good speed, so they got very few double plays on us. At Milwaukee, Johnny Logan hit behind me and he wasn't very fast. Batting second with Wood leading off made it a little easier for me.

Both of the teams I played on had their share of fun guys who kept everyone else loose. With the Braves it was Spahn, Burdette, and Eddie Mathews. The Tigers had Kaline and Cash, Hank Aguirre, and Frank Lary. They always got something going. Lary, of course, was known as The Yankee Killer. We all got up a little bit more for the Yanks, but they seemed to feel the pressure when Lary was gonna pitch. Sometimes it seemed that all he had to do was throw his glove out there and they were beat. It's hard to explain something like that, how one pitcher can dominate a team, especially a good team, so consistently. Whether it was his delivery, his motion, or the stuff he had on the ball I never knew. But he sure could beat them.

I played with the Tigers through the 1964 season. I had been feeling my age for a few years, especially in doubleheaders. You start to feel tired in the sixth inning or so of the second game. And that was something that had never happened before. I think a player's peak years are when he's about twenty-eight or twenty-nine. After that he begins to slip a little. And let me tell you, he's the first to know it. A lot of players don't want to admit it, but they know it.

The thing that really clinched it was when Charlie Dressen took over the team in the middle of the 1963 season. He began platooning me almost immediately and continued it into 1964. He felt a lefthanded hitter couldn't hit a lefthanded pitcher. I can see platooning a guy against certain pitchers who give him trouble, but not just because a guy's a lefty. In fact, there were some righthanded pitchers I would have liked to have been platooned against.

But in May of 1964 I made up my mind to quit. I told the Tigers in August and that was it. I felt I could have played a couple of more years, but I would have been platooned and I didn't want to sit around and waste my time. I had four children and it was time to get on to something else. Everyone has to give it up sometime, and I didn't want to hang around until someone pulled the uniform off me.

Like a lot of players, the thing I missed most was spring training, and I felt a little strange the following spring. But I had made up my mind. I didn't want to subject myself to calling teams, looking for another season here or there, and going through that whole scene. My only connection with baseball since I quit is my work as chairman for an exhibition game the Tigers play with the Reds every year, with the proceeds going to amateur baseball. I've been general chairman of the event since 1974. The two teams schedule the date, and then we organize the game as far as all the amateur leagues are concerned.

I've also gone to a few old-timers' games, but I'm really not interested in playing. Since I've retired from Chrysler my wife and I do a lot of traveling. We'll go away for four or six weeks, then come home for a while, then go again. And about the only way I might become involved with baseball would be to help a group of young people. I just wouldn't want anything that was confining. Not now.

But as I said, I have no real regrets about my career, how it went, or how it ended. In fact, I've always believed in what the great Satchel Paige used to say. "Don't look back, something might be gaining on you."

DAVEY WILLIAMS

♦ **MAJOR LEAGUE EXPERIENCE** ♦

New York Giants, 1949–1955

♦ **CURRENT STATUS** ♦

Expediter in a Dallas, Texas, contract shop.

Davey Williams played major league baseball for the New York Giants during a glamourous era, the early 1950s, when the three New York teams were the talk of the town. A scrappy second baseman, he took part in both the 1951 and 1954 World Series and was the cutoff man when Willie Mays made his fantastic catch in the 1954 fall classic.

Though hampered by a bad back that eventually shortened his career, Williams played with and against many of the great and colorful players of the day. He has vivid memories of Leo Durocher, Jackie Robinson, Roy Campanella, Eddie Stanky, and the incomparable Mays.

A native of Dallas, Davey Williams was born on November 2, 1927, and played high school ball with the likes of football stars Bobby Layne and Doak Walker. He did this despite being the smallest kid on the block.

The bad back kept him from reaching his full potential as a major leaguer, but the gritty Williams played when many players would have sat. And despite his condition, he never shied away from a tough spot or potentially painful collision on the diamond. He remembers those, as well.

I received a letter a while back from a fan who asked me a question that I'd been waiting nearly thirty-five years for someone to ask. He wanted to know who Mays threw the ball to after he made his great catch in the 1954 World Series. I'll tell you what. If they had kept the camera on I would have been on TV more than Johnny Carson. Because Willie threw the ball to me!

It was a great catch, all right, especially considering the time and place he picked to make it. But I saw Willie make much better plays than that one. In fact, I knew he had Wertz's shot all the way because I noticed him slow down just a little and adjust as he was running. Well, maybe not all the way, but I thought he'd catch it.

I remember another play he made at the Polo Grounds. We were playing the Dodgers and he went to his left to catch a line drive in right-center field. After he caught the ball, he made a complete turn away from home plate, but came out of it throwing and fired a strike to third base to nail Carl Furillo sliding in. In my mind, that play sticks out even more than the one he made in the World Series.

Willie, of course, was the greatest I ever saw. He could just do everything. I first saw him when we were both at Minneapolis in the spring of 1951. Tom Heath was our manager there and he told me about a kid who was gonna play center field who I wouldn't believe.

Well, the first time we're taking batting practice in Jacksonville that spring, Willie got in the cage and started taking his licks. Suddenly he fouled one right off his foot and dropped down in the batting cage and started rolling over and over and over. We only had about ten minutes for batting practice for everybody and I finally told him that if he wanted to roll around to do it outside the batting cage so the rest of us could take our licks.

Later I started thinking how saying that was a good way for me to get sent all the way back to Trenton. Here I was talking to Willie that way and he was the whole franchise. Only I didn't know it then. I was just a young kid myself.

As it turned out, Willie was called up to the Giants in May, and I came up that July. Leo [Durocher] made him the starting center fielder right away, but I was stuck playing behind Eddie Stanky at second. The funny part was that I had a great spring and thought I might beat Stanky out then. But I remember one day hearing Tom Sheehan, who was our chief scout, tell Leo: "You better get Williams the hell outta here and quit playing him. Otherwise, you're gonna have a hard time telling the sportswriters why you're sending him out. The little sonofabitch is playing great. You better get rid of him now."

So he did. Leo still wanted to go with Stanky. He had his favorites and when he made up his mind it was hard to budge him. I had even been up briefly in '49 and Leo said I looked good. But he had already worked out the trade for [Alvin] Dark and Stanky and they played every day in 1950. Stanky was an old pro, but he was through by then. He couldn't go five feet to either side and I could out-field him any way you fixed it, and cover twice as much ground. In fact, by the end of the 1951 season he had already locked up the manager's job at St. Louis.

But I wasn't gonna be a hardnose about it. I felt I was the better ballplayer, but I wouldn't show my dissatisfaction or create any disharmony on the ballclub. So I kept it to myself, especially in view of what was happening on the field.

The funny part was when I came up in '51 Eddie wasn't playing well and Leo put me in the lineup. I played real well up in Philadelphia and then we came back to the Polo Grounds to face Philly again in a doubleheader. Leo came up to me before the first game and said that Stanky would play the opener, and I'd play the nightcap. Well, I was surprised he was taking me out, because I had been playing well, but I figured I'd be right back in there in game two. So we go out there and win the first game and then Leo comes into the clubhouse, stands in the middle of everyone, and says, "We're not changing a winner. Same lineup!"

Would you believe we won sixteen in a row! Same lineup. And the routine was that Stanky would play seven innings and then I would go out and holler, "Caddy, mister," and play the last two. But by then we were in one of the greatest pennant races ever and I wasn't about to rock the boat.

I was always the smallest kid on the block when I was growing up in Dallas. But that didn't stop me from playing all the sports. I guess my father was my main influence. He was an old minor leaguer who didn't get very far, but he was interested in seeing his son get to play. Plus I grew up in an area where the kids were really sports minded. There were organized teams all over the city. We had age group tournaments and the winners would go over to play teams from Fort Worth. I remember playing with and against guys like Bobby Layne and Doak Walker.

Dallas had a team in the Texas League then, a Double A ballclub, and I used to work at the park as an usher or whatever, anything to get in free and watch the games. Playing in the big leagues might have been in the back of my mind then, but the important thing for me was just to be able to play every day.

Probably the biggest thing that happened to me back then was being selected to play in the Esquire All-American Game back in

1945. *Esquire* magazine started a thing where they picked kids from different states to form a pair of all-star teams, East against West. And they took us to New York and we played the game in the Polo Grounds. Believe it or not, the managers of the two teams were Ty Cobb and Babe Ruth.

Cobb managed our team and seemed to enjoy it. But a lot of it was like a publicity routine. There was a picture of Cobb and me down in a simulated crouch. He was supposed to be showing me how to field a ground ball. But it was a joke because we were in such a squatted position that if you tried to really play that way it would be ridiculous.

But one thing happened there that I'll never forget. In the first inning of the game I walked and on a double-play grounder slid hard into second. The shortstop came down on me and his spike nearly tore the nail off one of my fingers. When I ran into the dugout I hid my hand because I didn't come all the way to New York to leave the game in the first inning. So I went into the corner and tore the rest of the nail off, then put a piece of tape around it. And I played eight innings.

The next morning I was with the sportswriter who brought me to New York, Louis Cox, and Ty Cobb approached us in the lobby of the New Yorker Hotel. He wanted to see my hand. So I took off the tape and showed him. Then a couple of months later I got a letter from him and he said you don't know how you endeared yourself to me, that you didn't let anybody see you were hurt and that your determination and desire to play are what the game is all about. I still have the letter and have always cherished it as well as cherishing the memory of that particular situation.

I went to Sunset High School in Dallas where we always had a really good baseball team. We won the state championship my senior year and five or six scouts were at the game. I talked to both the Cubs and the Tigers. They were the most serious. But I also spoke with the Atlanta Crackers, and that's the way I decided to go.

The war was still on and I wanted to enlist and get it over with. Atlanta was an independent ballclub then, and if I played well for them, they would have the opportunity to sell me to any of sixteen big league clubs. So I went into the service for fourteen months, went to airborne school and played ball. I came out in 1946 and joined the Crackers for spring training in Gainesville, Florida, in 1947.

In those days, an independent club like Atlanta had working agreements with other clubs and could actually send you down. So I spent 1947 with Waycross [Georgia] in Class C and 1948 with Pensacola [Florida] in Class B ball. And at the end of the '48 season the Giants bought my contract for sixty-five thousand dollars and two players. Part of the deal was that I'd play for Atlanta again in 1949, which is what I did until the Giants brought me up at the tail end of the year.

Then in 1950 I was with the Giants' Triple A team in Minneapolis and the following year I met Mays and we both ended up with the big club in that great pennant race. But before we started gaining on the Dodgers in August, I think even Durocher had given up. I remember playing one day in Chicago when he had [Sal] Maglie coaching third and [Larry] Jansen coaching first. And Leo was sitting down at the end of the dugout with his sleeves rolled up getting a suntan. We're maybe thirteen, fourteen, or fifteen games out and Leo is already at the beach. The reason I think he had quit then was that nonsense of having two of his starting pitchers coaching on the bases.

But even when we really started closing the gap I don't think any of us thought we would ever catch them, at least not until we got down to three or four games behind. Then we all saw the opportunity was there. And I guess there isn't a baseball fan who doesn't know what happened after that.

I'll never forget the final playoff game. We had won the first and then they took the second. In the third and final game we're losing, 4–1, in the ninth and I remember Jackie Robinson running out to the mound and shaking hands with [Don] Newcombe. It was like he was already congratulating him. In fact, Newcombe had been pitching so well that it was inconceivable that we were gonna jump on him.

I was sitting in the dugout with Jack Lohrke, who was a utility player for us. In fact, there's a story about him. He was on a minor league club in Seattle that was involved in a bus wreck that killed about fifteen players. Jack had missed the bus for some reason and after that everyone always called him Lucky Jack Lohrke.

Anyway, when Robinson went out and shook Newcombe's hand, Lohrke turned to me and said, "Know what, piss on the fire and I'll call the dogs. I think the hunt's over." I'll always remember those words. But we did rally and Thomson hit the homer to win it. Complete pandemonium. Bobby couldn't have told you his name when he jumped on top of home plate. In the clubhouse everybody was just screaming and yelling.

Being in the World Series that year was a pleasure, even though I didn't participate to the point where I really felt I was playing. I pinch-hit against Ed Lopat when the score was about 13–1. I could have hit the ball to Yonkers and it wouldn't have helped much. We lost in six games. Maybe we were a little too satisfied by what we had accomplished against the Dodgers. The rivalry with the Yanks just wasn't intense.

I guess it was the following year when I became the regular second baseman that I fully realized how intense the rivalry with the Dodgers was. It was a tough, tough routine. I led off most of the time when I started and we had a situation where the guy who led off on both clubs knew that the first pitch was gonna knock him on his ass. Or the first pitch would be behind him. That's how we started off most of the ballgames.

But you accepted that as part of the game. And in turn you'd do things like trying to bunt and run over the pitcher. Or knock the hell out of the double-play guy, whoever you could get to first. I remember Durocher giving Maglie the Dodger lineup card and Sal would go down it something like this:

"Billy Cox is leading off. I'm gonna knock him down and then pitch him low and inside. Reese is hitting second. I'm gonna knock him down and pitch him high and tight. Robinson's hitting third. I'm gonna knock him down and then pitch him low and away. Campanella's next. I'm gonna knock him down and pitch him inside." That's the way Maglie went down the lineup cards back then. Not with every team, but especially with the Dodgers. And when Stanky got down to St. Louis we had a little rivalry with him, because he and Leo kind of fashioned themselves after each other.

In fact, it was our rivalry with the Dodgers that led to the incident with Jackie Robinson. It happened in 1955. I always had a bad back and would miss time because of it every now and then. Gil Hodges, one of the finest fellows I ever knew, ran over me on a double play in 1952 and hurt my back real bad. But I had an arthritic spinal condition, and each time I got knocked down it hurt.

Anyway, we were playing the Dodgers again in '55 and Maglie was on the mound again. He knocked Robinson down a number of times until I guess Jack was looking for the guy in the gray suit and I happened to be the first one he found. He bunted the ball toward first, hoping to get a chance to run over Maglie. But Sal didn't field the ball. And Whitey [Lockman] was standing there like me, just waiting for the fight to start. Finally, Whitey realized he had to field the ball and I realized I had to cover first. But when I got there so did Jack. Only I had come to a complete stop and he was running wide open. He just ran right between my legs, right through the middle.

Later, I guess he told Howard Cosell I was the only guy he ever hurt on purpose. And I never did anything to him. I remember wanting to get up and fight him, even though I felt I would get knocked down again because he was probably a little tougher than I was. But I wasn't able to get up because he had done such a good job. And I couldn't lift my arm for about ten days.

Of course, Alvin got him back the next inning, running into him at third while stretching a double. And Jack dropped the ball.

Then the first time I came up after the injury it was to pinch-hit against the Dodgers. Erskine was on the mound and his first pitch knocked me down. I said, "God damn. I can't believe this shit." I could still barely lift my arm and I got knocked down. But that's just the way we played.

I really don't have any right to say anything about Jackie Robinson. He was a great player and a great competitor, and he took all the guff that anybody could possibly take. But the thing I think about from time to time was that after having taken all that and showing what a great player he was, at the end of his career he had to turn it around and try to get even with everybody. He had handled it so well for so long, and then at the very end to turn it around and see how many people he could hurt and spit on. That was something I was sorry to see him do.

Campy was just the opposite. Roy and I were always great buddies. That time I came up against Erskine after my injury, Roy said, "Aren't you gonna speak to me today?" So I said, "Hi, Roy, how are you?" And then on the first pitch Erskine knocked me down.

I think I always knew that my back problems were going to shorten my career, but I've got a lot of memories packed into those few years in the middle fifties. For example, our 1952 team finished just four and a half games behind the Dodgers. And we did it with Mays in the service. Monte Irvin, another great ballplayer who wore the ball out the last month of 1951, broke his ankle in spring training. Both Maglie and Larry Jansen went home with bad backs. Yet I think we had a 13–9 advantage over the Dodgers that year. They beat up on the second-division teams— the Reds, the Pirates, and Braves. So we really had a heckuva season.

In '54, with Mays back, we got it going all over again. The electricity was in the air. Dusty Rhodes had a great year pinch-hitting, but so did Bobby Hofman, who roomed with Dusty. It was a year where we would win games we really shouldn't have won, but you have to do that to win a pennant. Then in the

Series, everyone thought the Indians would beat us. They had won 111 games and had that great pitching.

But there's something many people don't know. We went into that Series really confident. In fact, there really wasn't a question in our minds that we'd win. The reason was that we had beaten them all spring. We trained with them and saw them all the time. So we really had our confidence. Then Willie made the catch in the first game and Rhodes hit the homer to win it in the tenth. I think it was over right there.

I also remember spring training in 1955. We were in California and Leo always had a lot of his Hollywood friends around. He was married to Laraine Day then and knew a lot of movie stars. Jeff Chandler always worked out with us, and people like Groucho Marx, Robert Wagner, Dean Martin and Jerry Lewis, and Ricardo Montalban would drop by. Before we headed back to New York, Leo and Laraine always had a big party. Bobby Hofman, Rhodes, and about five or six of us bought a trophy and decided to give it to the Scrubini of the Year.

A scrubini or scrub was a second-string or utility player with the team. But in '55 we gave it to Jeff Chandler, and Jerry Lewis got all pissed about it. He was really disappointed that he wasn't named Scrubini of the Year.

I can remember all kinds of big stars at Leo's parties, guys like Gary Cooper, Humphrey Bogart, William Holden, and Glenn Ford. They had their wives there, too. We were all in awe of them. Someone once said that they probably looked up to us as ballplayers, but I didn't catch anyone gawking at me like I was gawking at them.

My problem was that my back was getting worse and I started trying some crazy things. Robin Roberts told me to see this guy at one of the hotels in St. Louis. Some kind of masseur. This guy put me in the shower and shot me in the back with a hose. And the water pressure was really high. Later, when I got onto the rubbing table our trainer, a beautiful guy named Frank Bowman, saw that my back was still discolored from that hose and asked me what I had done. I told him and he said, "You dummy."

Another time in St. Louis I went with Maglie, Wilhelm, and Jansen to see this guy who was supposed to be some kind of chiropractor. He put me in one of these chairs where you could turn these cranks. They split your legs apart and put your arms and back in some kind of weird position. The guy was really hurting me and wouldn't let me out of the chair until I threatened to stomp on him if he didn't.

So I was doing a lot of those things and taking codeine pills. But I couldn't even sleep through the night in a bed. I'd always end up in a chair. Then in August I slid into home plate in Milwaukee and couldn't get up. I had to roll over on all fours and the next day Leo told me I was going to the Mayo Clinic. I guess he was sick of looking at me all the time, rolling over and not being able to get up. So I went to the Mayo Clinic and they told me I had an arthritic condition and if I kept playing, there was a possibility I'd be crippled for life. And since I was already at the point where I wasn't happy with my performance, to stay on would just be stealing time. I thought it was time to try something else.

So I called Leo from the Mayo Clinic and told him I was through. And it hit the afternoon papers the next day. My top salary then was about twenty-nine thousand dollars. If I had some of the numbers they have today, I might have refused to go to the Mayo Clinic at all. But I don't think guys today would have even played some of the times I was in there. They seem to be always protecting themselves. It's like they're not willing to jeopardize their careers.

I went home for the remainder of 1955, then returned to the Giants in '56 as a coach. Leo had also left at the end of '55, so I coached for two years under Bill Rigney. I'd be a liar if I said I didn't miss playing. I was twenty-eight or twenty-nine years old and felt I could be playing at least another few years. But I also knew I couldn't do it anymore, not at a level that would satisfy me.

Then after '57, Rigney decided to change his entire coaching staff. The team was going to San Francisco and Tommy Henrich,

Bucky Walters, and myself were not invited to go. That's when I got an opportunity to manage the Dallas ballclub in the Texas League. So I took that job and it lasted only half a season. The team had an owner who didn't know anything about baseball and a general manager who would say one thing to me and another thing to him. In fact, I think part of the reason I was hired was that I was a local boy who had had some success.

After that, I called one friend in baseball and tried to get a coaching job in the Cleveland organization. But he had nothing to offer me and really couldn't help. That's when I said the heck with it. I had a wife and three kids and it was time to stop the gypsy life. I decided to find something else.

I did a number of things after leaving baseball, including retiring twice, each time for six years. Maybe I shouldn't call it retiring. You've got to have money to do that. Let's just say I quit working. My wife and I spent six years playing and having a good time. Then I went back to work for eight years as a criminal investigator for Dallas County before stopping again for six years. This time, my wife and I fished and went to the horse races. I'm delighted that I did it because I lost my wife four years ago from an aneurysm. At least we had those years together, just a great time twice. A lot of people don't have the opportunity we had.

My job in between retirements might raise a few eyebrows. While I was classified a criminal investigator, my partner and I actually worked lunacy warrants. When somebody locked themselves in the house and was going to kill their entire family or anybody who walked up on the front porch, they called the two dumbbells to get him out. And believe me, you've got to be a dummy to do that.

I once had a guy stick a .22 rifle in my stomach as I opened the door. I managed to get the rifle away from him, but as he turned he pulled a pistol from his pocket and I had to wrestle him for that. It was ridiculous work. I also carried a gun, but I only took it out once.

And it was depressing. You were constantly involved with people whose lives were going downhill. The atmosphere of the whole day was a complete downer, and that's probably why I retired again.

After my wife died, a friend of mine asked me to come to work for him. Now I'm an expediter in a contract shop, and we do a lot of work for the government, and for companies like McDonnell Douglas and Bell Helicopter.

I still keep in touch with some of my old teammates, call guys on the phone and see some of them at old-timers' games. The card shows I don't go for. Maybe I have the wrong attitude. There were four old-timers in Dallas recently, all signing autographs. Lou Brock went for seven dollars, Frank Robinson for eight, and the two other guys for twelve and fifteen. I just don't believe in that. In our day we signed because it was a pleasure and part of the game. We did it to satisfy some little ol' kid who might have been a hero worshiper or something. To sign your name for money just turns me off.

Looking back, I never missed the road trips or being away from home. But I'll always miss the competition and camaraderie. And I always felt I would have liked to have played a few more years and done a little better than I did. And maybe help a ballclub have the kind of success the Giants had in 1954. But if nothing else, perhaps a few more people will know that I was the guy Mays threw the ball to after that great catch, when the camera went off a split-second too soon.

DICK ELLSWORTH

♦ **MAJOR LEAGUE EXPERIENCE** ♦

Chicago Cubs, 1958, 1960–1966
Philadelphia Phillies, 1967
Boston Red Sox, 1968–1969
Cleveland Indians, 1969–1970
Milwaukee Brewers, 1970–1971

♦ **CURRENT STATUS** ♦

One of the principal owners of Pearson
Realty in Fresno, California, a real estate
company specializing in commercial and
agricultural brokerage.

*Just five days after graduating from high school, Dick Ellsworth
pitched a four-hit shutout for the Cubs over the Chicago White
Sox in an annual exhibition game between the two teams. He was
just a few months past his eighteenth birthday and had had a high*

school career that saw him compile more than one hundred victories against just a handful of defeats.

Pitching mostly for second-division teams, Ellsworth experienced both the good and bad sides of the game, having seasons of twenty wins as well as twenty losses during his thirteen-year career. An observant and analytical player, he was able to see the good and the bad in the several organizations for which he played.

Though he wonders to this day what his record might have been had he played with a winner, Ellsworth knew there was life after baseball right from his first full season in the majors. He began planning for his future year by year, knowing it wouldn't be easy for a player who signed just two days out of high school.

While he has had a very successful second career in real estate, the former hard-throwing lefthander feels that baseball, as well as other professional sports, should help its athletes prepare for the future, especially those who have little formal education and who will not reach superstar status within their sport.

A lot of ballplayers in the big leagues when I played just weren't prepared for the real world. Leaving baseball is always a major adjustment, even if you feel you have come to terms with it and know it's time to go home. Because when you get home the fear sets in that all of a sudden you haven't got anybody to take care of you anymore.

It may sound strange, but as a major league baseball player you never even touch your luggage—and I'm going back twenty years—never even have to make a decision for yourself if you don't want to. You've got a manager to tell you when to hit and run; you've got a catcher to tell you what to throw; and you've got a traveling secretary to hand you an itinerary.

So even though you're in the public spotlight and subject to the press and media in general, you really lead a sheltered life. And when you finally come home all of a sudden you've got all the decisions in the world that you've got to make. That's perhaps the one thing that disappointed me about professional athletics. There is nothing to prepare the athlete for the real world. And in my own mind to this day, I feel that is a responsibility that professional clubs shun and there really ought to be something done about it. I believe the owners should take it upon themselves to help prepare these young people for the real world, because in all the major sports the majority of ballplayers are out of the game before their thirtieth birthday.

Take my own case. I signed a professional contract just two days out of high school. I had no formal education whatsoever. I never had a tie around my neck before. I never had a sportcoat on my body before. The most important thing to me as an eighteen-year-old was whether I had a pair of spikes that fit and a glove that was in decent shape. But in that sense, baseball probably afforded me the opportunity to grow up in a much better economic situation than if I had not been in the game. For that, I'll be forever grateful.

But by the same token, had I not taken advantage of what free time I had to learn something about the real world, I might have had a big problem when I retired. I knew an awful lot of ballplayers who didn't do this.

The time is certainly there. Baseball is virtually an everyday activity for eight months of the year. But each of those days, even during spring training, involves maybe six or seven hours. So here is a group of young people, full of energy, who sit around hotel lobbies wiling away the excess time. As I said, the time is there if the players are willing to take advantage of it.

I was fortunate enough to see this early on, and from the time I was twenty years old until the time I left baseball, I worked every winter but one. And because of that, I always felt there was life after baseball. I also felt strong enough about my own abilities and

confident that I would get involved in something else, be successful at it, and be able to provide for my family. But that still doesn't
mean leaving the game was easy. And as I said, the element of
fear is always there.

In some ways, the getting there was the easy part. I was born
in Wyoming, but my family moved to the Fresno area of California
when I was three years old. I started playing baseball competi-
tively when I was about eleven or twelve. I remember being a
little overwhelmed by Little League and just playing in local park
and recreation leagues for a year or two. Then I became involved
with the Babe Ruth League at about age thirteen and took off
from there.

I was always a pitcher and as far back as I can remember had a
strong arm. As a kid I always had a pocketful of rocks or
something of throwing size. My targets were telephone poles or
some other object I'd pick out. But I remember throwing being
almost a kind of obsession with me.

Growing up as a pitcher, I had three things going for me. I was
always a little bigger than most of the other kids, threw the ball a
little harder and, surprisingly, at an early age was able to throw
strikes. I think it was this combination that made me begin to
think about pitching in the big leagues.

In California, we had an incredibly long season. It began in
early January and went right through August. High school ball
would start in late February or early March, but we'd start
practice games even before that and would play Fresno State's
freshman team. We'd also play Stanford's freshmen, and the
University of California's first-year players. After the high school
season ended we'd go right into Legion baseball, then back to the
park and rec leagues. So it was four or five games a week right
through August. To give you an idea of the number of games we
played, I think my three-year pitching record in high school was
something like 105–5. That's a lot of ballgames.

As I said, by the time I was in high school I was definitely
thinking about the majors. I first became aware of scouts looking

at me when I was a sophomore, but my coach later told me he was getting inquiries about me when I was still in the ninth grade. So by the time I was a senior there was no doubt in my mind that I could play minor league baseball and there were a lot of scouts talking to me by then. And virtually all of them told me what I wanted to hear—that I was a definite major league prospect.

There was no draft back then, so a player could more or less sort out the offers he had. But I already was leaning toward the Cubs. Both my parents and I had established a good relationship with their scout, Lee Handley. He had impressed upon us the fact that the Cubs at that point and also in the foreseeable future were in dire need of lefthanded pitchers. I also knew they were extremely competitive in the bonus process and for those reasons they seemed to offer the best opportunity. So I signed . . . and fast. I graduated from Fresno High on a Wednesday, signed on Friday afternoon, and was on a plane for Chicago on Saturday. This was in 1958. I received a sizable bonus, so at that time things couldn't have been better.

I reached Chicago that Saturday and on Monday night the Cubs were scheduled to play the White Sox in their annual crosstown game at Comiskey Park. The Cubs decided to showcase me a little. Mr. Wrigley [Cubs' owner Phil] had heard I had pretty good credentials for a kid and they figured they could evaluate me a little by letting me pitch a few innings against the White Sox. As it turned out I kept getting guys out and was still fresh, so they kept me in and I completed the game and threw a shutout. We won it, 1–0.

It was a strange feeling. In fact, I didn't really know how to feel. Just being in Chicago was scary to me, kind of intimidating. I had gotten off the airplane and they checked me into a hotel, gave me the key to the room, shook my hand, and said goodbye. They told me to show up at Wrigley Field the next morning. And when I got there all the guys seemed to be about twice my age then. It all happened too fast. Then I throw a four-hit shutout at the White Sox. Like I said, it was a strange feeling.

But I think the adrenaline was pumping to the point where I used up so much energy just trying to function that I didn't go beyond myself and didn't overthrow. I was probably so worn out from all the nerves and everything else that all I did was throw strikes. I kept the ball down, did all the things a pitcher is supposed to do. I don't think I walked a single batter. Funny thing was that I stayed with the ballclub long enough to start one regular-season game. And that night I did everything a pitcher shouldn't do. I overthrew, tried to prove I could throw the ball nine hundred miles an hour, and started walking people. I came out after two and one-third innings and left the bases loaded. The reliever who came in promptly gave up a grand slam to cement my welcome in the big leagues.

There was also a lot of hazing by the veteran players then. The Cubs had a number of prominent guys at the tail end of their careers, players like Alvin Dark and Bobby Thomson, and they had also had a superstar in Ernie Banks, who was at the peak of his career. I can't remember what the Chicago papers said about it then, but my bonus was considerably more than most of the guys were getting in annual salary. So I'm sure there was some bitterness and I heard about it. Of course, once I shut out the White Sox they all got a big laugh. They thought it was funny that some kid just out of high school could do that to the White Sox.

But after my second outing I was sent down to Fort Worth, which was a Double A team then, and I finished the '58 season there. The next year I was at Fort Worth, only the team had been elevated to Triple A in the American Association. The main thing I really had to learn in the minors was to recognize the fact that hitters actually came to the plate with bats and they also got paid to do what I was getting paid to do. I think I struggled with the fact that there was more to baseball, more to pitching than just throwing the ball over the plate and challenging hitters. In some ways, that was hard to accept at first, because I had had so much success in high school.

As far as the technical part of pitching, nobody tried to change me at all. I was compelled to learn from my own mistakes. I was sent down again at the beginning of the 1960 season, then recalled about the first week in May. The Cubs were not a very good team that year [60–94] and I finished the year at 7–13. I felt right away when I was recalled that I was good enough to be there, though I was still in the learning process. Lou Boudreau had taken the club over from Charlie Grimm the day after I pitched my first game, and he and his coaches told me all year long that I was there to stay, that I belonged and I should just keep doing what I was doing. Again, it was part of the learning process and I'd continue to get the ball every fourth day.

I had about a .500 record the next year [10–11] and then in 1962 had a 9–20 season. That year we were part of a scheme that was supposed to revolutionize major league baseball. Instead of a single manager, the Cubs had a revolving coaching staff, with each coach taking a turn at running the ballclub. It was like the Abbott and Costello "Who's on First?" routine. Everybody had his own philosophy, there was a new coach every month, and nobody really knew what was going on.

It was my third year in the majors and I pitched a few good ballgames, but I also pitched a lot of bad ballgames. Looking back, I can say that I was responsible for the twenty-loss season because I did some things that caused me to lose games. I'm not talking only about hanging breaking balls or making bad pitches. But other things, like throwing changeups when you're ahead on the count, little things that caused my own downfall. And we were a bad ballclub.

Then two things happened that meant a lot to me. In 1962 the team acquired Bob Buhl from the Braves. It became apparent to me immediately that this pitcher knew more about how to get hitters out than anybody on our staff. Pitching, to him, was a science. Then between '62 and '63, the team got Larry Jackson from the St. Louis Cardinals. I remembered Larry from the time I was twelve years old when he was setting all kinds of California

League records. He was also a fine pitcher. So I made up my mind to tag along with these two guys and pick their brains. I knew I was better than what I had shown.

Both Buhl and Jackson told me there were just a few basic things I needed to pay attention to in terms of approaching hitters and the overall philosophy of pitching. In those days, starting pitchers prided themselves on how many innings they pitched and how many games they could complete. It was really hammered home to me that you weren't worth your salt at all unless you completed a lot of ballgames and pitched a lot of innings. And that spring I got to the point where I believed I was a good pitcher. By the time we broke camp I didn't think there was anybody in baseball who could beat me. Buhl and Jackson had helped me learn to throw a slider. We also had a pitching coach then named Fred Martin who worked with me on a changeup. Before that my changeup was just a waste pitch, and I was essentially a two-pitch pitcher, but I left spring training that year confident that I could throw any one of four pitches and get them over. The result was a 22–10 season.

We were a loose ballclub that year. Jackson [14–18] and Buhl [11–14] didn't have the won-lost record I had, but they both pitched well. Bob Kennedy was the one and only manager and for the first time since I had come there people actually thought we could win ballgames.

Yet the next two years things didn't really improve. My record wasn't as good [14–18 and 14–15], but both years I got off well only to end up struggling in the second half because of tendinitis in my elbow. And looking back, I really don't think I did anything constructive to take care of it. I didn't want the doctors' help and I was just vain enough to think I could continue to get the ball every fourth day to justify my existence there. I also wanted to be a great pitcher and it turned out to work against me because of the way I struggled in the second half of both years. I'm even frustrated to this day when I look back on that because those really were the best years, physically, of my baseball life. I should have known better and not have been so hard-headed.

Then in 1966 I had my worst year at 8–22. But by that time we had a pretty sorry ballclub, I felt. The Cubs had talent, there was no doubt about that. They had players like Banks, Santo, Williams, Kessinger, Beckert, and Randy Hundley. Yet I had been there for seven years by then and finally realized that all the raw talent never got help from the organization in terms of making them better ballplayers. The guys who did go on to be great players— Banks, Santo, Williams—did it by themselves. The Cubs were just not an organization that contributed to anyone's development. I think history will prove that correct. We just didn't play good baseball.

Despite my record I think I pitched well enough in 1965 to have a winning season. I'll take the blame for losing twenty games in 1962, but in 1966 Dick Ellsworth didn't lose twenty-two ballgames. The Chicago Cubs lost twenty-two ballgames. I can't remember how many one-run ballgames I lost in the late innings because we coughed it up. There were a lot of breakdowns on the field and it wasn't any one individual. It was the organization. Leo Durocher had taken over the team the previous winter and he was still trying to get to know the players. I don't blame Leo, either. There just hadn't been any discipline on the ballclub all those years and there hadn't been much teaching. It wasn't run like a successful organization. The Cubs were night and day as opposed to the Dodgers, or the Cardinals, or the Yankees.

Losing, I feel, breeds losing. That made it even tougher on Durocher, who came from a winning background. He kept giving me the ball every fourth day and reinforced on many occasions that I deserved to pitch, that I was pitching better than the record indicated. But he was very frustrated.

After the season, the team sent me to the instructional league in Arizona. I think they wanted me to get back to a positive mental attitude as well as to work a little on the breaking ball. I came home in November and felt much better. Then in December I learned I was traded to the Phils for Ray Culp. And it was a shock.

I had been with the Cubs for seven years and I was still only twenty-six. But I guess Durocher felt he had to make changes. He could have blindfolded himself and thrown darts at names to decide who stayed and who went. The trade itself was handled well. John Holland, the general manager, called and told me. And he thanked me for my time there. So that wasn't a problem. The problem was Philadelphia. I spent my most miserable year in baseball there. I was absolutely shocked, for lack of a better term, by the treatment I received.

To them I was an outsider. I mean, here I joined a club that for the past several years hadn't done anything, but it quickly became apparent to me that there were cliques in baseball and I was an outsider. I was not someone from within the organization so I just really didn't fit. The only people who fit were the organization people, in terms of the players and their relationships. But I don't think that was as important as the relationship I had with Gene Mauch, who was the manager. That, too, was very disappointing.

From the day I got there in spring training it became apparent to me that I was at best going to be a spot starter. I just didn't fit into Gene Mauch's plans. There seemed to be an immediate rub between us. I don't think he was comfortable around me because I'm a fairly straightforward person and somewhat intelligent, and I just really wouldn't put up with the bullshit. I held Mauch accountable for the things that happened and I don't think he was ever comfortable with that.

I also felt that Mauch, throughout his career, overmanaged, and got nervous before anyone else. As a result, he made moves and changes before they should have been made. And as an athlete, it was awfully hard to believe in yourself or have any self-confidence playing for him because he never really gave you an opportunity to prove anything. It got to a point where I finally told him I would quit baseball before playing for him again. I also said he had taken whatever fun there was out of the game. He thanked me for my honesty and I urged him to speak to the front office about moving me. And I meant it. I would have quit, because I had never been so miserable in my life.

That's when I was traded to the Red Sox, and it was a 180-degree swing. They were a team in trouble even though they had been to the World Series the year before. Jim Lonborg, their top pitcher, had been injured in a skiing accident and they needed pitching. So they gave me the ball, and when I got somebody out, they gave it to me again. Dick Williams [the manager] was the sole decision maker on the field and Darrell Johnson, the pitching coach, told me I was going to pitch. They got me back to the point where I believed in myself and felt I had a role to perform. To this day I believe I would have won twenty games that year [he finished at 16–7] if I hadn't caught the mumps from my son and missed about five weeks of the middle of the season.

The Red Sox, too, were a close ballclub, and even though I had success there, I still felt somewhat like an outsider. When you grow up in an organization with other guys, come to the big leagues together, and literally live together for seven or eight months of the year, there's a camaraderie that's kind of special. But when you come in on a trade there is always something to prove, and even when you've earned your stripes or the right to be on that club, there is still not the closeness that there is from within the organization. There was respect at Boston, however, and the players were all business on the field. Plus the fans were very rabid and showed a lot of emotion at the ballpark. In addition, the team paid well, so it was a very positive time in my baseball life.

Unfortunately, it didn't last long. Early in the 1969 season I was traded to Cleveland. Again, I really couldn't believe it. The Indians were in Boston at the time of the trade and I just had to switch clubhouses. Alvin Dark was the manager there and he had just gotten Ken Harrelson from the Red Sox for Sonny Siebert, Joe Azcue, and Vicente Romo and said he wanted a lefthanded starting pitcher to complete the deal. The Red Sox never gave me a reason why they dealt me, none whatsoever. By this time,

I was realizing how much of a business baseball really was, and the whole thing was beginning to sour me a little on the game.

Things didn't work out at Cleveland, either. After being told I was a very important part of the trade and that I was going to pitch a lot of baseball for the Indians, I was relegated to spot starting and little else. It soon became apparent that I was not on a good ballclub and that I was going to see only limited action there. What made it worse was that I hadn't really wanted to leave Boston. I thought I had found a home there, especially after the year I had, and to this day I don't know why they traded me.

It never really got better at Cleveland. Alvin Dark was a lot like Gene Mauch in that he got nervous and had to make changes just for the sake of the changes. When I was sold to Milwaukee in August of 1970, I knew the handwriting was on the wall.

I was only thirty years old, but there were several factors to consider. For one thing, physically I wasn't the ballplayer I was at twenty-two or twenty-three. I had been pitching since I was twelve and had thrown a lot of innings. In addition, I hadn't found any positive reinforcement from anyone in baseball after I left Boston. Even now, with my work in the real estate field, I've found that if you treat people respectfully, pat them on the back, and demonstrate that you believe in them you'll get a lot more out of them than if you ignore them or throw negative vibes at them all the time.

In Milwaukee it became a matter of shall I see how long I can stay or shall I go home now. I pitched a lot of short relief, one or two batters, because they knew I could throw strikes. But now, after all these years, they were telling me I couldn't get right-handed batters out, and I pitched only against lefties. Well, probably 98 percent of the hitters I got in my life were righties. Now all of a sudden I'm not good enough to get them out. So it had reached the point where I didn't look forward to going to the ballpark every day.

The Brewers released me sometime around early July in 1971. I had come to the park that day with my eleven-year-old son:

That's when the manager, Dave Bristol, told me about it. It was awfully final, to be thirty-one years old and playing in a world where ego is so important. Then, all of a sudden, it's like somebody with a chainsaw has just cut your ego down. But I got over the initial shock of being told to pack my bags and then I didn't have any trouble accepting the fact that my career was over. At that point I just wanted to get home and get on with my life. I never contacted another team about a job.

Looking back, you can't change the things that happened and I've never been one to think like that. It was disappointing that I was never involved with a winner. Because of that, I don't think I'll ever know whether the stats I finished with were the best they could have been. I wonder how I would have done pitching for Boston for three or four years when they were winning, or maybe pitching for the Cardinals or Dodgers, teams that always won. But I made my own decision to sign with the Cubs and for seven years they treated me respectfully, they really did, so I can't look back and blame anybody for not giving me an opportunity. I had that, but I also have the disappointments. On the other hand, baseball gave me a chance to meet a lot of interesting people, both on and off the field, as well as to travel to all corners of the country. And, of course, there are a lot of memories.

I can remember facing the likes of Stan Musial and Red Schoendienst of the Cards when I was just a twenty-year-old kid. They were guys I had heard play on the radio while I was growing up. I was both thrilled and awed to be playing against them. I remember when Musial was retiring and making his last trip around the league. I asked him to pose for a picture with me in the outfield during batting practice, and he did. He also told me I was the only pitcher who ever struck him out four consecutive times. It was just a thrill to hear that from a player of his magnitude. The player who maybe gave me the most trouble at the plate was Willie Mays. Willie could have been on his deathbed and I think he would have grabbed a bat if he had the chance to hit against me. I had a hard time getting him out, and even when I did, it seemed he hit the ball hard.

As a pitcher, it's also important to have a catcher who pays attention to you and who understands your style of pitching. It's almost like a security blanket. Dick Bertell with the Cubs was like that. He was a great pitcher's catcher. So was Elston Howard, who I met at Boston. I only pitched to Ellie for one year, but it was a pleasure. I told him I needed his help because I didn't know the strike zone, the American League hitters, the umpires, the parks. It was all new. He simply said he knew I had good control and that I would have to have confidence in him. The first time around the league at least he said he would tell me what to do and hoped I would do it without question. He said if you do that I'll catch a lot of winners and you'll get off to a good start. And he was right. When he called for a curve I didn't question it. When he wanted a fastball to a spot I tried to put it there. He proved to me right away that he knew the league and the hitters, and he made it very comfortable for me all year long. So a catcher is important.

I still enjoy watching some of the older pitchers who are still in the league today. I don't know if the economics of the game changed, but it seemed in my day they were faster to turn away from you when you hit thirty. Now they seem to keep giving the older guys the ball. Look at Tommy John. Of course, he's a rare exception, as was Warren Spahn before him. Tommy is doing the same thing he did fifteen years ago and the hitters are still going back to the dugout, throwing their helmets and breaking their bats and screaming at him to go get a real job. Yet he keeps getting people out.

The greatest pitcher I ever saw was Sandy Koufax. He not only had the greatest stuff, but he had a lot of class and always pitched like a winner. I never saw anybody as consistent as Sandy during the 1960s. He was the most awesome. But there were plenty of other good ones, guys like Bob Buhl, Larry Jackson, Jim Bunning, Bob Gibson, Spahn, and a lot of guys I'm leaving out.

I do think the game has changed today. I was at a Cubs' old-timers' game a few years ago and this young relief pitcher came into the clubhouse and began looking at himself in a full-length mirror. He wasn't happy with the way his uniform fit and began chewing out the clubhouse man until he got another uniform. Then he did a few pirouettes in front of the mirror and was satisfied that he looked good enough to perform. In my day the guys were just happy to have a uniform. But I couldn't believe the clubhouse that day. During the game a lot of the players were in the clubhouse, watching on TV, joking, and smoking cigarettes instead of being part of the game. I don't blame the players. A kid will get away with whatever he's allowed to get away with. The fault, as far as I'm concerned, is with management.

As I said earlier, I always felt I'd be able to earn a living outside baseball. My top salary was in the forty-five- to fifty-thousand dollar range for four or five years, and I knew it would take work to get back up there outside the game. But I've always been an analytical type person and willing to learn. Because of my off-season work I had my real estate license three years before I got out of baseball. I had acquired that as a result of buying some property as an investment and wanting to learn the language and economics of real estate.

I eventually became fascinated with the business and went to work with an old-line company, Pearson Realty, in Fresno. About ten years ago I was offered the opportunity to buy into the business and now I'm one of the principal owners of the company. We specialize in commercial and agricultural brokerage.

There are really no connections with baseball except that my son, Steve, is a pitcher in the Red Sox organization. He hasn't had an easy road, with serious arm surgery a couple of years ago. But he's still trying. Steve's a big, six-eight righthander and hoping to get a shot with the Sox in 1989. But I have basically stayed away from advising him on his career. We both feel it's best that way. He's intelligent, goal-oriented, and much his own man. So I don't worry about him

Otherwise, it's just an occasional old-timers' game when I have the time. Of course, I think back on my career often. As I said, there are a lot of memories, some good, some not so good. I remember losing a no-hitter against the Dodgers back in 1965. There were two outs in the eighth inning when Al Ferrara wrapped one around the foul pole in left for a home run. I tried to throw a pitch inside, but it wasn't quite inside enough. The batter before him was safe on an error, so the homer made it a 2–1 game. Don't let any pitcher ever tell you he isn't upset losing a no-hitter.

I really thought I was going to do it. I always pitched well in L.A. and I felt really good that day. The pitch to Ferrara was the only marginal pitch I threw. After I got the third out of the inning I came off the field and my teammates tried to console me. I just brushed right past all of them, walked up to the clubhouse, undressed, and jumped into the shower. I knew it was over with. We were on the road and we were now losing. I didn't even talk to anybody, just went inside and walked into the shower.

Ed Kranepool

♦ **MAJOR LEAGUE EXPERIENCE** ♦

New York Mets, 1962–1979

♦ **CURRENT STATUS** ♦

Part owner of Madison Triborough Group,
manufacturers of point-of-purchase dis-
plays in Jamaica, New York.

*Born in New York City on November 8, 1944, Ed Kranepool first
attracted attention from the baseball world when he broke many
of the hitting records set by Hall of Famer Hank Greenberg at
James Monroe High School in the Bronx. Signed right out of
Monroe, Kranepool came to the big leagues at age seventeen,
seeing limited action with the New York Mets in 1962, the first
year of the franchise's existence.*

*A year later he was back to stay and would remain with the
Mets throughout his eighteen-year-career. Though he never*

achieved the kind of stardom that some predicted for him, Kranepool became a solid pro and a superb pinch-hitter who batted a sizzling .396 coming off the bench during a five-year stretch from 1974–1978.

Kranepool's tenure spanned several eras in Mets history. He was there at the beginning, playing alongside such legendary veterans as Gil Hodges, Richie Ashburn, and Duke Snider on a club piloted by Casey Stengel. And he contributed to the Miracle Mets of 1969, the World Champions, and the pennant-winning aggregation of 1973.

Undaunted by the way his career ended, Kranepool almost made the biggest hit of his career. He tried to buy the ballclub. When that failed, he turned to the business world, where he has been a hard-working success ever since.

Nobody takes care of you when you leave the game. You make your own way in business and you do your own thing. Nobody ever called me from the club and offered me anything. Even if they had, there's a question of whether I would have done it or not. And that's really besides the point.

But I had a very sad parting of the ways with the Mets. To be honest about it, I went out on a pretty low note, spending my final five years or so with a last place club. During that period, the team management had changed. Lorinda de Roulet had taken the club over from her mother, Joan Payson, who was a very fine woman. And when I tried to get a two-year contract to play a couple of more years, she just wouldn't negotiate with me. She sided with the general manager, Joe McDonald. That was near the end of the 1979 season. And in those last couple of months I knew I wasn't going to be with the ballclub anymore.

I really felt very sad about it, having played seventeen or eighteen years for a family and suddenly being treated like a piece of furniture. So in that sense, I have no good memories of Lorinda de Roulet, not after the way she treated me after all that time.

Of course, I knew that many players were treated the same way. That's why I don't blame guys for holding out and getting whatever they can. I was only thirty-four at the time and felt I could still play. But I hadn't seen much action in 1979, and it was frustrating being on a bad ballclub and watching mediocrity. By the same token, I didn't want to be traded, didn't want to leave New York. It just wouldn't have paid.

Back in those days the thinking of the owners was different. They figured a thirty-four-year-old man was ready to be pensioned off. Now they got guys with long-term contracts, so they stick with them. But because of the way it was back then, I just felt that to go to another city for a year or two wouldn't pay. In fact, I could even have gone to Japan, but that was something else I never seriously considered. The lifestyle over there would be terrible for me, and I just flat out wouldn't leave my family.

Believe it or not, I even tried putting a group together to buy the team because I knew it was going up for sale. But the Doubleday group offered a richer deal and they got it. About the only other thing that would have interested me was becoming general manager, but I had no relationship with the new owners and Fred Wilpon was very upfront with me. He told me he was bringing Frank Cashen in as his GM. So that was it. I never even formally announced my retirement. I just never went to spring training in 1980.

That was probably the toughest part, losing that continuity of going to Florida in the spring. Every year when Christmas came I knew that in two months I was going to Florida. I looked forward to the whole routine, packing up, getting ready, and going to St. Petersburg. It was something I had done for nearly twenty years.

And that's one of the greatest pleasures in the game. Spring training is simply the most relaxing, nicest time of the year for a baseball player, especially when you don't have to worry about making the ballclub. You can just enjoy yourself and even spend a lot of time with your family.

Once you're established you can work out in the morning, and by the afternoon you're on the beach with your family. Then you relax at night and start the whole routine over again the next day. It's totally enjoyable, something you love, something you did as a kid for nothing. Now you're getting paid for it to boot. Where else could you have something like that?

So that's a tough thing to lose. Of course, you're also losing whatever share of the limelight you might have had. Fortunately, you maintain a certain amount of it by being in New York. It's the greatest media area in the country, and there are enough things you can do to get some attention. You don't get as much as you did when you played, but there's still a glow there. And because New York is the greatest sports town, I never wanted to go anyplace else. Plus the association I had with the ballclub all those years certainly helped me in business as well.

But there is an emotional letdown. I won't pretend that there isn't. I was out of the game at thirty-five and had been playing baseball for two-thirds of my life. Cut the sport out suddenly and you lose something.

I was lucky because I always went to work. The day after the baseball season ended, I was working. I never knew the difference between the winter of 1979 and the previous winters. Only I never went back to spring training. In the sense of working in the so-called real world, however, I felt I was ready and consider myself fortunate in that sense. A lot of players can't make that adjustment, can't acclimate themselves to working. They've been pampered and catered to, and they're just not ready to go out and do things for themselves.

I think that's one thing baseball people are missing, that the players are missing. It would really help if there was some kind of severance pay for guys who leave the game. Maybe it could be a certain number of dollars for so many years of service. It would help, because it always seems that guys flounder for a year, or a year and a half, often not knowing where to look or what direction to take. So they stay home and don't get a job right away. And before they know it, any little nest egg they built up is gone. A number of players were wiped out financially because of that kind of scenario.

Today, of course, that's much less likely to happen. A guy like Don Mattingly is making two million bucks a year, so if he sits out six months or a year it's really not going to affect him much at all. But back in my time guys didn't make that kind of money.

My top salary was $110,000 my last three years. Not bad for a kid from the Bronx who grew up pretty poor. My father was killed in World War II and my mother raised me by herself. I guess one reason I became so heavily involved with sports was that we didn't have dollars to throw around. When Bubber Jonnard signed me for $85,000, the first thing I did was buy a car and a home for my mom.

I was with the Mets for two weeks in 1962, long enough to make my first West Coast flight and watch Sandy Koufax toss a no-hitter at us. Then I went back to the minors and didn't win a spot with the team until spring training of 1963. I led the club in hitting that spring and opened the season in right field. Even though I got off well I was totally overmatched, and it showed as the year progressed. I was eventually sent out again but came back in September and then stayed for a long time.

Those early Mets teams were loaded with veteran players who had been around for a long time, guys like Roger Craig, Charlie Neal, Richie Ashburn, Gene Woodling, Carlton Willey, Frank Thomas, and Duke Snider. And I've got to say that the vets were all pretty great with me.

Some of them were characters, real flakes. I roomed with Frank Thomas that first year. He was the Mets' first power hitter, but he also had other talents. Whenever he had the chance he would bet that he could catch any ball thrown to him barehanded. A lot of guys would ante up and then fire away. Frank would stand on first, stick out his bare hand, catch the ball, and then collect the money. I can't remember him ever shaking his hand or losing the bet. And he made a lot of extra money with his barehanded challenge.

Duke Snider, of course, was loved in New York because of his years with the Brooklyn Dodgers. There was a story in the papers once that I had a rift with Duke. It was more of a misunderstanding, and all Duke was doing was trying to make me a better player.

We were playing in the old Polo Grounds then and it was a real poke to center field. So one day Casey Stengel, who was still managing then, called me into his office and told me to take some extra batting practice. He said he wanted me to try to hit every ball to the left of second base. "Don't pull the ball," he said. So I'm out there hitting everything to left and Duke is watching me. Suddenly he says, "Why don't you pull the goddam ball!" So I said to him, "Duke, mind your own business, I'm hitting the ball to left field." But he didn't realize that I was following Casey's instructions. And, of course, the press wrote the story and they didn't know, either. And when I told Duke about what Casey had said, he told me if he had known, he would never have said anything. I guess he was embarrassed that I had kind of told him off in front of the press. But we really got along very well.

Casey was a character and you had to get used to his ways. In fact, I really enjoyed playing for him because he was a man's man. One day in St. Louis we were going up against Curt Simmons, a lefty with a herky-jerky motion. I just hadn't been able to touch him. He had struck me out eight straight times and before the game Casey came up to me and said, "You're not feeling good today." I looked at him and thought he was nuts. After all, the guy was seventy-four and I felt great. And when he told me again that I wasn't feeling good I told him he was full of shit. But what he was really trying to do was get me out of the lineup without saying, "Kranepool, you're benched."

But I'll give him credit. He let me play, and in the first inning I got a foul tip off Simmons and that brought a standing ovation from the guys in the dugout. There were two men on then, and wouldn't you know, I blasted a three-run homer. Maybe that was lucky. If I had struck out again I could have been devastated. But I guess I was too stupid to tell Casey, "Yeah, I'm not feeling good."

I played for seven different managers and besides Casey, I guess the two best known ones were Yogi Berra and Gil Hodges. Yogi was the sweetest, nicest guy you'd ever want to meet. But he wasn't rigid enough with his rules and regulations and guys took advantage of him. Still, he was an adequate skipper who knew the game and was great to play for. As long as you played hard he treated you like a man. But he was very simple in his approach to the game and, unfortunately, you can't always be that simple with people.

A manager has to be a leader and there's a difference between being a nice guy and being a leader. Gil Hodges was a leader. He commanded respect. He wanted it and he got it. And his rules and regulations were enforced. So in that sense Gil was the best manager I played for.

My feeling is that a manager shouldn't cost you any ballgames and Gil didn't do that. In fact, a good manager might win five or six games a year, but he won't lose any. I think there are managers today who lose ballgames and just don't make the decisions when they have to. But I always liked a guy who reacted and was consistent with his players. Gil was like that. Once you had a role with Gil he stuck with it. After a while my role was to pinch-hit with men on base late in the ballgame. Because I knew that was my role, I was able to become a very effective pinch-hitter.

So in the second or third inning of a losing ballgame I didn't have to get ready to pinch-hit. But when it came down to the last three innings, I was ready. I mentally prepared myself to think about the pitcher and the situation, and I got my equipment ready. That way, when the manager said pinch-hit, I didn't have to run up to the bat rack and do twenty things in thirty seconds. They were already done, so all I had to do was walk up to the plate and hit.

All of that was mental preparation. In fact, I think the difference between a great major league player and an average player is mental. The great one can handle the crowds, the pressure of the game, and can cope with any situation.

That was one of the things about our 1969 team; we seemed to handle whatever situation arose. Gil, of course, did a great job that year, too. But I think the unsung hero of the team was Rube Walker, our pitching coach. We had a dream staff that year. Seaver, Koosman, Ryan, Tug McGraw. Just look how long all those guys lasted. Rube never forced them when they were young. Instead, I'd say he babied them. They pitched with four days' rest and he counted the pitches. None of those guys hurt their arms and I think Rube deserved credit for that. The team ERA was under three and we led the league with twenty-eight shutouts. Rube made Gary Gentry a winner and knew just how to use the middle guys—Don Cardwell, Jim McAndrew, and Cal Koonce—in just the right spots. And we had Tug and Ron Taylor coming out of the pen. I think that was when we began to get the reputation as an organization that develops pitchers better than most.

In fact, I think that the era during which I played, 1962 to 1979, had more star-caliber players than they have today. Today's athletes may be better conditioned than those of years ago, but I don't think they're better. This is especially true of the pitchers. We had more three hundred-game winners, more Hall of Fame pitchers then, and I don't think you see that in the caliber of pitcher today. When you look at guys like Koufax and Drysdale, Fergie Jenkins and Tom Seaver, Bob Gibson and Juan Marichal, on and on, you just don't have guys like that anymore.

A lot of the pitchers back then used to work the inside of the plate. Gibson always had a thing about pitching inside. So did

Drysdale. The umpires today protect the hitters. And I think the pitchers have a smaller strike zone and are forced to throw the ball right down the middle of the plate. As a consequence, guys are teeing off. They're not getting knocked down. Years ago they did, and they'd have to think about it. And believe me, that works. If a guy who throw ninety-five miles an hour hits you, it hurts.

That's one of the reasons you see more home runs today. Plus I think the players are stronger, the pitching quality is down, and the ball is hopped up. So it's a combination of four or five things.

At the same time, I think the long-term contracts they're giving today take some of the incentive away from the players. Let's face it, the only way a player can really relax is with a guarantee. But certain guys just aren't motivated enough under those circumstances. The numbers show that guys with long-term deals have not done as well after they've signed the long-term deal. So the long-term effect on the game is not healthy. But that's also a reason to admire a guy like Pete Rose. He would play the same way regardless of the salary he received. Dave Winfield is another one. He has been a professional no matter what and has done the job for the Yankees.

Like most players, I saw some crazy things during my career. One of the funniest happened in St. Louis. We were playing the Cards and winning the game 7–0. Suddenly the rains came and they had to stop the game. After we resumed play the Cards rallied and tied the game. During their rally the sun came out and Ron Swoboda missed a goddam fly ball in right. When he came in he was fuming. He threw his sunglasses to the ground, breaking them, and then tried to crush his helmet by stepping on it. Well, he stuck his foot right through the helmet. When it was time to go back on the field his foot was still stuck in the helmet and he was trying to get it out. Casey was managing then, and he kicked Swoboda in the ass and told him never to break the team's equipment. Then he sent him back out on the field with the helmet still on his foot!

Perhaps the strangest thing about being out of baseball is the flashbacks. I'll watch bits and pieces of a game here and there and suddenly really relate to something. It's amazing. At those times I can't really believe I've been out of the game for eight or nine years already. It's almost like you were there last week. And when that happens you suddenly begin thinking you can still play.

Now, if you put me out on the field and gave me a stress test I probably couldn't run a hundred yards. Yet in my mind I think I can still go up there and pinch-hit. You think of it as yesterday when you could do certain things. You loved the game and you miss it. It's something you did almost all of your life. And you still think in your own mind that you can perform.

I don't know if that will ever go away.

BOBBY
THOMSON

♦ **MAJOR LEAGUE EXPERIENCE** ♦

New York Giants, 1946-53
Milwaukee Braves, 1954-1957
New York Giants, 1957
Chicago Cubs, 1958-1959
Boston Red Sox, 1960
Baltimore Orioles, 1960

♦ **CURRENT STATUS** ♦

Sales manager for Stone Container, Inc.,
in Watchung, New Jersey.

Bobby Thomson may have hit the most famous home run in baseball history. It was the dramatic blast that won the 1951 pennant for the New York Giants over the Brooklyn Dodgers. To this day it is aptly labeled, "The Shot Heard Round the World."

Because of the notoriety garnered by that one swing, many fans tend to forget that Bobby Thomson was a fine all-around ballplayer who put up some very good numbers in the late 1940s and early 1950s. A severe ankle injury suffered in 1954 curtailed his effectiveness for several years and more or less relegated him to journeyman status.

Born in Glasgow, Scotland, on October 25, 1923, the man who would someday be known as "The Flying Scot" came to the United States when he was a little over two years old. Like many other youngsters, he took to baseball early and it became his only way of life until retirement forced him to consider other options.

He played alongside and against some of the greatest players the game has known, and for a few years came close to matching some of their feats. But he will always be the man who hit The Shot, and very few players ever have a moment like that.

Leo Durocher likes to tell people that before I came up to face Ralph Branca in the final playoff game in 1951 he called me down to the coaching box at third base and said, "Bobby, remember the pitch he threw you Monday? Well, he's not gonna throw you that one again." Funny, but all I remember him saying is, "Bobby, if you ever hit a home run, hit one now."

Branca had given me a fastball, chest high, in the first playoff game in Brooklyn and I hit it out. It would have been an easy out in the Polo Grounds, but it was what we called an Ebbets Field home run. I would have loved to hit in that ballpark all the time.

Anyway, in the third game, with everything on the line, Ralph threw me a hard strike. And when he threw another one in the same spot I hit it on a line into the lower deck in left. To this day, I can never adequately describe the feeling that went through me as I circled the bases. While I didn't stall during my home run trot, I can remember feeling as if time was just frozen. It was a delirious, delicious moment and when my feet finally touched home plate and I saw my teammates' faces, that's when I realized I had won the pennant with one swing of the bat. And I'd be a liar if I didn't admit that I'll cherish that moment till the day I die.

Yet when I think about it today, I often have the feeling that while the homer put me on a pedestal, a kind of jumping-off place, it was something that I never fully took advantage of. I can even remember feeling self-conscious when I faced Branca for the first time the following season. I didn't want to hit a home run off him.

It's funny, I don't know how many times I've thought about it or people have asked me about it, but I've always wondered why they used Branca in that spot. I always hit Ralph well and had the homer off him in the first playoff game. In most people's eyes, Ralph was the goat. But maybe they should have made [Dodger manager] Charlie Dressen the goat.

In some ways, 1951 was a strange season for me. I started out very slowly that year, even sat on the bench for a short time at the beginning. And when I was in there they had me in center field. That was before Willie [Mays] was brought up. After he came I moved back to my original position, third base, and that's where I played the rest of the year. Yet in my heart I feel I helped that ballclub more than any other club during my career.

We went to the World Series against the Yanks that year and won two of the first three games despite losing Don Mueller, who broke his ankle in the third game of the playoffs. I think that really hurt us. Don was a tough hitter and his swing was tailor-made for Yankee Stadium. Hank Thompson replaced him and didn't have a good Series. But there was also a rainout and that gave Allie Reynolds an extra day of rest.

I remember in one of the games they sent John Mize up to pinch-hit. Dave Koslo was pitching and we all knew that big John couldn't get the bat around anymore. Throw hard and away and he'd probably hit a fly ball to center. But Koslo walked him. He just pitched him too fine. And I started screaming at Dave. I don't know if anyone else thought about it this way, but if we got Mize we'd be out of the inning and we'd have had the ballgame.

That was also the Series where Stanky kicked the ball out of Rizzuto's glove. I could never understand why Phil made such a big deal out of it. Stanky always played that way. He could flat out be a pain in the neck. Sometimes he would jump up and down at second base, trying to distract the hitter. He started a big rhubarb in Philadelphia doing that when Andy Seminick was batting. Eddie got thrown out of the game and when the rhubarb started he was already in the clubhouse. But I guess that's why they called him "The Brat."

The 1951 season was my fifth full year with the Giants. I signed a professional contract out of high school and was sent to Bristol, Virginia, to play in the Class D minors. My memories of those days are of long bus rides, run-down hotels, and greasy food. When I came up with the Giants for good in 1947, I had two nicknames. One was "The Flying Scot," because of my speed and Scottish heritage; and the other was "The Hawk," a name Bill Rigney gave me for the way I chased down fly balls.

Though I was born in Scotland, I came to the United States when I was about two-and-a-half and grew up on Staten Island in New York. So I was practically playing in my back yard. My rookie year of 1947 was a good one. I hit .283 with twenty-nine homers, eighty-five RBIs, and 105 runs scored. And I was part of a team that set a record with 221 home runs. Mize was with us then and had fifty-one, Willard Marshall had thirty-six, and our catcher, Walker Cooper, had thirty-five.

In fact, I'd put my stats up against any other rookie that year. But, if you remember, 1947 was a big year in baseball because that was the year Jackie Robinson joined the Dodgers. Jackie put up some big numbers and the Dodgers won the pennant. Maybe that's why he won the Rookie of the Year Award. But I felt I could have easily won, and so could my teammate, Larry Jansen, who won twenty-one games that season. All three of us had great rookie years.

Leo Durocher became the Giants' manager midway through the 1948 season. I wasn't having a good year, but Leo quickly brought his own aggressive style to the team and I liked that. With Leo, if you had something to say, you said it. Get it out on the table, even if it led to a disagreement. Because with Leo, the next day you started fresh. He didn't hold grudges.

But he liked a certain kind of player. One guy he never liked was Willard Marshall because Willard had a big butt and couldn't run very fast. And he didn't appreciate Walker Cooper, who could really whack the ball. Coop used to give Leo a hard time.

As a manager, though, I always thought Leo was one step ahead of most guys. He knew how to put pressure on the other team, and he knew what it took to win. If you were playing a team with a Jackie Robinson you knew you'd better get that ball back into the infield and not fool around with it. Leo was always reminding us about these things. He played aggressive baseball. By contrast, Charlie Grimm, who managed me at Milwaukee, was just the opposite. He was a great guy who you'd invite home to dinner. But he used to tell us not to make too much of the game. "All it takes is a bat, a ball, and a glove," he would say. Imagine leaving a Durocher and coming to a bat, a ball, and a glove!

In 1949, our entire outfield hit over .300. I batted .309, Marshall hit .307, and Whitey Lockman was at .301. I also hit twenty-seven homers and drove home 109 runs. So it was a really good year for me. And by that time there were people who thought I was the fastest man in the National League. So Durocher always had me running against someone. One time he tried to put together a race between me and Sam Jethroe of the Braves. The winner was supposed to get a grand, and in those days that meant something. But before it came off the commissioner heard about it and stopped it. Gambling wasn't allowed.

Another time we went up to West Point before the season started to play an exhibition game against the Army baseball team. Glenn Davis, the great Army All-American halfback was in the stands and sure enough, Leo tried to arrange a race between us. I was beginning to get nervous about the whole thing when it started raining and we had to cancel it. But the next year we were up there again and Leo asked me to race against their best sprinter. So while I'm out there getting my legs loose, Durocher is smack in the middle of the cadet corps giving everyone the business. Then I run the guy and beat him by ten yards. In fact, I can't ever remember losing a match race like that.

My years with the Giants were filled with a lot of good memories. One guy I won't forget was Davey Williams, the second baseman from Texas who took Stanky's place. When he first joined the team we were in Cincinnati staying at our hotel. Well, I figured I'd take the little guy under my wing, so I said, "Hey, Davey, want to take in a show?" And he shot back, "If there's gonna be any show I'm gonna put it on."

Yet another time in Cincinnati we got into a rhubarb and everyone ran out onto the field. Now if there are two guys on the field who really want to fight, that's a lot. The main thing you watched out for was the spikes. You didn't want to get cut. But anyway, when it finally ended we all walked back to the bench, and who's sitting there but Davey Williams. "Hey, Davey," someone said, "Where the hell were you?" And Davey answered, "They pay me little enough to play baseball. But they don't pay me anything to fight."

Unfortunately, Davey's career was cut short by a back injury that started when Jackie Robinson ran into him. Jackie wrecked the poor guy. Davey had his back turned and there shouldn't have been a play. I remember Al Dark on the bench telling us that the first guy who gets a shot at Robinson better take it. And wouldn't you know, it was Dark. He hit a double the next time we played the Dodgers and never stopped at second. He just kept running and hit Robinson at third. I don't know what kind of a shot he gave him, but Robby never said a word. He knew it was payback for the cheap shot he had given Williams.

I was with the Giants two more years after 1951. They weren't bad years but I think the Giants were a little disappointed in me. Maybe they expected more and maybe I expected more of myself. So even though I hit .288 with twenty-four homers and 106 RBIs in 1953, I could feel a change coming. Willie Mays was coming back from the service for the 1954 season, and in February I was traded to the Braves. Sam Calderone went with me, and the Giants got Johnny Antonelli, Don Liddle, Ebba St. Claire, Billy Klaus, and $50,000.

Even though I suspected I might be traded, I had mixed emotions. But Milwaukee seemed to be an up-and-coming ballclub, so I looked at it as a positive. And I was having a good spring. I had replaced Sid Gordon in left and I was all over the place. The Braves had some real good players then, guys like Joe Adcock, Johnny Logan, Eddie Mathews, Andy Pafko, Bill Bruton, and Del Crandall.

So I really felt I was fitting in well when we played the Yankees in an exhibition game. I remember Mel Allen interviewing me before the game, and I was telling him how I had been lucky to avoid serious injuries and was in great shape. Then during the game I got a hit off Whitey Ford, and when the next guy hit one back to the mound, I took off for second, trying to break up a double play. Well, I stayed up too long and when I tried to get out of the way of Woody Held's throw, I did a kind of half slide and broke my ankle.

The injury really screwed me up. First I had an allergic reaction to the benzoin that held the tape on my leg, and then I tried to come back too soon. So the next year my leg was worse. It really took me a couple of years to get over that. And it was a shame, because we loved living in Milwaukee and the upper management was great to me.

I guess everyone knows the story by now, but a rookie named Hank Aaron took my place and, ironically, broke his ankle later in the season. But I always used to kid with Hank and tell him that no one would ever have heard of him if I hadn't broken my ankle.

The Braves traded me back to the Giants midway through the 1957 season. They desperately needed a second baseman and had the chance to get Red Schoendienst. So they took it. I remember just before being traded having a four-for-five day against a good Phillies team and saying to myself, "Now you're starting to hit." Later in the day I learned I was gone. That was tough, too, because I was just starting to feel like myself.

Back with the Giants I roomed with Johnny Antonelli, the pitcher I had been traded for in the first place. But things were beginning to go downhill. I finished 1957 with the Giants, then three days before breaking camp in the spring of 1958 I was sent to the Cubs, where I was reunited with Al Dark. The Cubs weren't much back then. Ernie Banks was their big star, but I think Al and I helped, because we found ourselves finishing the season in L.A. and playing for fifth place.

That was the first year the Dodgers were in Los Angeles, and they were playing in the Coliseum, which had that crazy left-field wall some 240 or 250 feet away. They had put up a big screen to make it a bit tougher to hit the ball out. Anyway, we were down by one in the last inning and I'm up with Dark on second. The Dodgers bring in Stan Williams to pitch, and Dark is trying to give me signals from second. He signals curveball, and I'm waiting. I remember taking a real good rip and the ball goes straight up in the air. I slam my bat down and start for first. Then I look up and see the ball going over that stupid screen. A home run . . . on a ball the shortstop would normally have backed up and caught. We ended up tied for fifth with St. Louis, but it felt like we won the pennant.

I played one more year for the Cubs, then got traded to the Red Sox prior to the 1960 season. But in late May or early June they released me. Baltimore picked me up, but that didn't last long, either. Paul Richards was running the Orioles then, and he's the only man I met in baseball that I can't say a nice thing about.

One day shortly after I joined the team one of the coaches came up to me and said that Richards wanted me to take some extra batting practice. I thought, gee, he actually knows I'm on the ballclub. But what he really wanted was someone to stand there while Steve Barber, a young lefty, worked on his pitching. The guy got one out of six over the plate and the best I could do was hit a ground ball. What an insult. But I was stupid. I should have gone up to the guy and said, "You SOB. You've got a helluva nerve calling this batting practice." But I didn't. And a short time later they released me, too. And that was it.

I think by then I had lost my confidence. I remember letting a fly ball go over my head in left against the White Sox. Hell, I could play the outfield as well as any of them. And that's bad. It really starts to get into your mind. And I really knew it was over when I didn't even look forward to going to spring training the next year.

What next? Well, this is where I think my Scottish heritage came in. I'm a stubborn guy and I knew what I had to do. I had to go out and make a living. And I wanted to do it my way, get my own job. But I didn't have any real education, so I went to Stevens Institute and took a battery of exams to find out if I should get back on the coaching lines or what. But the results indicated sales capacity. So I used some good common sense, and my wife, Wink, assisted me in my judgment. I took my time interviewing. Every week Wink would ask me if I got a job. But I told her I was going to take my time, and it took a couple of months. We didn't worry about the money running out, but we were concerned. After all, I was starting from scratch at thirty-six or thirty-seven.

And I finally came home with a job and went out into the working world. I got up every morning and realized that a sense of humor is all it takes to hang on to those subway straps with all those other people. My job was as a salesman with the Westvaco Company involved with national accounts. Stone Container eventually took over the company, and I'm still with them as a sales manager. I'm also involved with a "Just Say No to Drugs" program in the schools as part of the Optimist's Club in New Jersey.

In a way, I'd have to say I'm still a little disappointed in my career. I felt I had the ability to do more than I did, maybe hit closer to .300 and drive in a hundred runs on more occasions. Looking back on it and then looking at who I am now, the person I've become and the growth I've made within myself, well, it's something that didn't happen until I left baseball. My wife says I'm a more forceful and aggressive person today, so maybe if I had been that way when I played . . .

But there are certainly memories. How can I forget watching great hitters like Ted Williams and Stan Musial, or a guy like Mays? There were tough pitchers, too, like Ewell Blackwell and Don Drysdale. Blackwell would throw those snakes, and his ball moved so much. He gave you the same motion for the fastball and that slow curve, and he hid the ball better than anyone I've ever seen. Drysdale was always tough. I remember him knocking me on my tail during my last year with Milwaukee. That's how he pitched.

Whenever I talk baseball, though, it usually comes back to the home run. Branca and I weren't really close over the years. If he and I had gotten together and gone out on speaking engagements, we could have made a few bucks. But he always took his side seriously, and I guess I was the fortunate one. Then about a year ago Mike Lupica wrote a pretty nice article about us. It came from a little different direction and made me see Ralph's side of it a little better. Now we're out together more often, going to card shows and things like that.

I guess things are different today. My wife has often said that if it happened today it would really be an incredible thing for us. I guess she's right. Funny, but I can still remember in the spring of '52 Durocher saying to me, "Bobby, I feel you're going to hit one out every time up." Now that's a lot of pressure. But it's in the books and it will stay there, so what the hell.

CHUCK STOBBS

Boston Red Sox, 1947–1951
Chicago White Sox, 1952
Washington Senators, 1953–1958
St. Louis Cardinals, 1958
Washington Senators, 1959–1960
Minnesota Twins, 1961

♦ **CURRENT STATUS** ♦

Retired from baseball as a Cleveland Indians pitching instructor and now has a home on five acres in Sarasota, Florida.

Though he is often remembered for giving up a mammoth home run to Mickey Mantle in 1953, Chuck Stobbs was a fine left-handed pitcher, toiling for the Boston Red Sox and Washington Senators for more than a decade. While he had a number of winning seasons, Stobbs also lost his share of games, especially when working at Washington, where the Senators were perennial cellar-dwellers.

A native of Wheeling, West Virginia, Chuck was born on July 2, 1929, and began his major league career with the Red Sox in 1947. Traded to the Senators in 1953, the six-one, 185-pound Stobbs was then a winning pitcher with a 33–23 career mark. But in his nine years with Washington, the team averaged ninety-two losses a year and he took many of the tough ones.

Yet in 1956, he won 25 percent of his team's victories (15–15) and his sixty-four Senator wins tie him for second among all post-1920 Washington southpaws. Like most pitchers from bygone eras, Chuck Stobbs is acutely aware of the big money being given to today's players, especially lefthanded pitchers. But he feels he played during one of baseball's golden eras and that, he says, is what counts the most.

W hen he hit it, it was just another home run to me. What the heck, I thought, he hit a home run. It wasn't the first one and hopefully I'm gonna be around a few more years so I'll be able to throw some more. Billy Martin hit a home run the same day. Kenny Wood, who was playing left field for us, came in on the ball, but it just went. The wind helped it carry.

So I thought nothing about Mantle's homer until I came to the ballpark the next day. If he hit it 600 feet or 320 feet, it didn't count any more or less. But the papers had a box to show where the ball went and National Bohemian Beer, the sponsor of our games then, put a big baseball up on the old football scoreboard where it hit. Bucky Harris was our manager then, and he got sore and made them take it down.

But then every time a new team came in the players would point and ask, "Is that it, is that where he hit it?" And I'd say, "Yeah, that's it." Whaddaya gonna do? After a while I got over it and didn't really mind answering the questions, depending on how the people asked them.

When I think back about the home run now, I can remember the pitch, a high fastball, high and in, and when Mantle hit it, it just went. I'll tell you what, I'm glad he didn't hit the ball straight back at me. Because if he did it was liable to have been "see ya later."

I guess some people are always gonna remember that homer, but there's so much more. I was barely eighteen when I joined the Red Sox in 1947. They had a bonus rule then that if you got over a certain amount to sign with a big league team they had to keep you with the club for two years. I got thirty-five thousand dollars so they kept me. In two years I got into just ten games. My first game was a relief appearance against the White Sox. Then, late in the season, I got a start against Washington. We took an early 4–0 lead and I even had a base hit my first time up. I'm already thinking that there's nothing to this and then it starts to rain. Wouldn't you know it, the game got rained out and I didn't get my first big league win for more than a year after that. Even my first hit got washed away.

Going to the big leagues wasn't an easy decision for a kid about to turn eighteen years old. I went to high school in Norfolk, Virginia, and graduated in June of 1947. I think if given a choice back then I would have wanted to go to Southern California and play in the Rose Bowl. I had played football, basketball, and baseball in high school and had quite a few scholarship offers. In fact, some of the schools were willing to let me pick the sport.

But the first thing I did was head up to Vermont to play in a summer league with mostly college baseball players. On my way, I stopped in Boston and worked out with the Red Sox for three or four days, a tryout kind of thing. Then I went on to Vermont and pitched in two games before I got a call from my father. The Red Sox wanted to give me money.

My father had always been involved with sports. He played football and baseball at Washington and Jefferson College in Pennsylvania and later coached three sports at Wittenberg College in Ohio. He even coached at the Naval Training Station in Norfolk when I was in high school, so he was the logical one to ask for advice.

No matter what you choose, he said, there will come a time when you'll have a regret. You think about it for a couple of days and let me know your decision. So I thought about it, called him back, and said, "Yeah, I'll sign." Believe it or not, I signed on July 2, my eighteenth birthday.

Funny, but things turned out exactly as my father had predicted. When you're winning and doing well, it's super. But when you're losing—and I certainly lost my share—you begin to wonder why in the heck you got into this in the first place. But the same thing probably would have been true if I had gone to college and done well there. I'd have said this is great. But if it went bad, then I probably would have wished I had done something else. It's really easy to look back and say I shoulda done this and shoulda done that. But I made my decision and forty years later I'm happy I did.

Sitting those first two years was tough. Joe McCarthy was the Red Sox manager then and he liked the old-time veterans. You threw as much as you could, hoping to get into a game, but sometimes it seemed that the game never came around. Plus you're taking up a roster spot and another active player on the roster in '48 might have meant a pennant since the Red Sox lost in a playoff with the Indians.

I finally got a chance to pitch in 1949 and had an 11–6 record. I had heard how tough Fenway Park was for lefthanders with the short left-field wall, but I really didn't find it bad at that time. Maybe that was because we had so many hitters—Williams, Vern Stephens, Bobby Doerr, Birdie Tebbetts, Al Zarilla, Sam Mele, and Dom DiMaggio. We scored a lot of runs, especially at home. So if you held the opposition to four or five runs, you would win most of the time. On the road it was entirely different, but at home you could win like that.

It's funny, but whenever I mention Birdie Tebbetts I remember a piece of advice he gave me back then. Here I was, a twenty-year-old kid coming off a winning season. I was single and had been with the team three years, so I knew already that a baseball player had a lot more opportunities to find women than the average guy. There were always people hanging around the ballplayers.

Well, Birdie told me to be careful. He said never go with a girl that another ballplayer had gone with and if you're gonna go someplace, go by yourself. And if you're gonna be late, you might as well stay out all night. Then go and buy the morning paper, have breakfast, and go back to bed. And that's true. Because if you're late, you're late, doesn't matter if it's ten minutes or all night.

During my early years I threw the ball fairly hard. I had a good change and a good curve. When I got ready to leave Boston, Joe Cronin was the general manager and he thought I ought to come up with a third pitch. So when I went to Chicago I started to develop a slider. But then they tried to change my delivery and I ended up losing my curve. That's when I became more of an off-speed pitcher and it wasn't until the last three or four years of my career that I started throwing a mediocre fastball again. As for the curve, I never really had the same confidence in it after that and it had been one of my best pitches.

Maybe they just should have left me alone, because I had three winning seasons at Boston. Then in 1952 I was traded to the White Sox. The first trade is always the worst. These things happen, of course, but when you're in your early twenties you wonder why they have to happen. I found out when a newspaperman from Chicago called one morning and asked for a statement on the trade. What trade? I had no idea what he was talking about.

The White Sox were starting to come on then. Nellie Fox was there, Chico Carrasquel, Jim Rivera, Sherm Lollar, Jim Busby. I ended up with a 7–12 season, yet one of the best earned run averages of my career. You can't really figure, except that they didn't score runs the way Boston did.

Then after the season was over it happened again. This time I read it in the Sunday paper. I had been traded to Washington for Mike Fornieles, another pitcher. So in 1953 I became a Senator and I guess one of the first things I did that spring was give up the homer to Mantle. But all told, playing in Washington was a good experience. I lived there and worked for the ballclub selling tickets and going to banquets in the winter. My roommate for four or five years was Howard Fox, who was the team's traveling secretary then, and later became president of the club after it moved to Minnesota.

The Senators, of course, never had a great team. I guess everyone knows the old saying about Washington—first in war, first in peace, and last in the American League. The most games I ever won there was fifteen. After that year all they wanted to give me was a five-hundred-dollar raise. Because I had also lost fifteen they said I didn't help the team. And we were in last place. So I held out awhile and got about fifteen hundred dollars more, not a helluva lot.

But I still think that just about everyone who played in Washington liked it. The salaries weren't real good but they weren't the worst, either. They were bad if you were an outstanding player like a Mickey Vernon. Mickey was a great first baseman, great hitter, and great team player. A guy like that could never make what he was really worth in Washington because the club didn't have a lot of money. They only drew four or five hundred thousand a year.

On the other hand, the average type player might make a little bit more in Washington than he would make anyplace else. Even in New York then, the big stars made a lot of money but the average guy didn't make diddly. What they did was pay those guys a small salary, but tell them that they were gonna win the World Series and that would give them five or six thousand more. And in those days five or six thousand was big money.

The Yankees. They were always tough for us. But I'll say this. Back then if you beat New York, everyone in the country knew you won because the Yankees were *the* team. If you beat the Browns or the Phillies, who the hell cared? If you got it in the comic section of the paper you were lucky. So we always tried harder against New York. The year I was 15–15 I started seven times against the Yankees and won three.

Then the next season, 1957, we opened against Baltimore, a team I'd normally have a pretty good chance of beating. But they didn't pitch me. They held me over to pitch against the Yankees in New York. The Yanks beat us by something like 3–2. Then my second start, which again would have been against Baltimore, turned out to be the Yankees again. They beat me once more and I'm 0–2, despite pitching well in both games. Then I pitched well in another couple of games, but still couldn't win. And sooner or later you're gonna be lousy and get creamed. So you begin wondering, am I ever gonna win a game?

So much of pitching is mental. When you're winning and going well, you don't even think about what you're doing. Most of the time you're close to throwing the ball where you want it and you figure if you miss by a little and someone hits it, one of your guys will catch it. Everything will turn out all right.

But if you're going bad, you start saying, I got to get the ball here or there. And if I don't get it there how far is somebody gonna hit it or who's gonna screw up behind me? So you're waiting for something bad to happen and your whole mental outlook changes. And after the bad start that year I ended up 8–20. I'm not saying I never screwed up. I did. But I had some help, too.

I guess the biggest thing in Washington was opening day. You always knew that on no other day would you have the same kind of crowd coming out. The president would throw out the first ball and there would be a big scramble to see who was gonna get it and we'd all be spiking each other. The other celebrities who came out also helped to make it a great day and there was nothing like it in baseball at that time. Then the next day the peanut vendors were out and it was back to normal.

Since there were very few native Washingtonians, there weren't too many dyed-in-the-wool Senator fans. Many of them often rooted for the visiting teams. Sure they'd cheer if [Roy] Sievers hit a homer for us, but they'd cheer a lot louder if someone like [Yogi] Berra hit one for the Yanks. But it was still a super town and most of the fans were great. Maybe they were used to losing, because the loyal ones stayed with us.

My favorite manager in Washington was Bucky Harris. We'd have two meetings a year. On opening day he'd say, boys, you know we're glad you're here and whathaveyou. Then, at the end of the year we'd have another meeting and he'd thank everybody for doing the best they could and say he'd hope to see us all next year. That was it.

By 1958 my years were getting so bad that I think they thought a change of scenery would help. The Senators sent me to the Cards, who had a chance to win the pennant. But they put me in the bullpen in St. Louis and it just didn't work out. At the end of the year I was released. The next year I was back in Washington again and had one more good season in 1960 when I was 12–7. The year after, I went with the team to Minnesota. I hurt my back up there and when you get hurt in Minnesota with the cold weather it never seems to get better.

The team was just starting to jell with Killebrew, Allison, Mincher, Pascual, Kaat, guys like that. But my time was up. I got released after the '61 season.

Being out of baseball wasn't an easy adjustment. I had only been married a couple of years and my oldest daughter was born that year. And I never really worked in the off-season, except for the ballclub. I might have hooked up with an expansion team, but

I always hated to fly and wasn't about to start going to California. It just wasn't worth it.

So I went to work right away as a manufacturer's rep in Virginia, but that lasted for only about six months. Then for a whole year I didn't do anything. I knew I wasn't a salesman, but I tried insurance for a while. You know, you make a living, but you really aren't some super success. I did some broadcasting for a time when the new Senators came into the league in 1961.

Finally, I went back into coaching, first as an assistant at George Washington University, then with the Kansas City Royals baseball academy in Florida. It became full-time and we came to Florida to stay around 1970, 1971. Things got tough in 1975 when my first wife died. We had four children and they were all still young. I spent some time working at a baseball camp in Missouri, about three years. Then I remarried and came back to Bradenton. Around that time I got a tip that the Indians were looking for a minor league pitching coach. I got the job and worked for them for five years.

In 1984 I had major surgery for an aneurysm on the aorta and couldn't work for quite a while. So I decided to take my pension at forty-five. I was out over ten years and the pension would never increase. So I took it.

What did I miss most? Well, I missed the first and fifteenth of the month, paydays. But you miss the rest of it, too. You were brought up in that kind of world and it was the only thing you ever knew. I know I could make a lot of money if I pitched today, no doubt about it. But the game has changed in other ways. I think there was more camaraderie back then. The players spent more time together.

Of course, you always wish you had done a few things differently, but like everything else, it's over and done with. And my dad was right. There are regrets at some time or another. Yet I think I'm one of the few people who went through my whole career and put food on the table and enjoyed what I was doing.

Then there are all the memories. They never leave you. I remember one opening day against the Yanks when I went about eight and two-thirds innings and pitched real well. Vernon hit a homer in the tenth to win it and we ended up getting letters from senators and others telling us how well we played. That kind of thing always felt good.

Plus there were the different guys I met. I roomed with Walt Dropo in Boston. He had a super rookie year, tied for the league lead in RBIs. If I remember, the next year in spring training he got hit on the arm or the hand by a pitch and he came back a little too soon, changed his stroke a bit and was never the same.

Then there was Rocky Bridges with the Senators. He lived with Vern Stephens and Bob Lemon in San Diego. They all had a few drinks now and then and would tell great stories. Wonderful guys. They used to drive from Washington to San Diego after the season. Bridges could never tell you how many miles it was, just how many beers and how many cigars it took. That, he always knew.

And Ted Williams. It was during one of those first years in Boston when I was hardly pitching. Ted was hitting over .300 as usual, but he didn't feel right at the plate. So he asked me to throw a little batting practice to him. Well, he hit for about an hour, the first half hour telling me what to throw, and the second telling me to throw anything. And in that hour he didn't hit one home run. He said, "Chuck, there was something about you today. I just couldn't hit you." Whenever I pitched against him I remembered that, and it helped.

Then there was 1949. We [Boston] had a one-game lead over the Yanks with two games left against them. I pitched the day before in Washington and I'm leading 1–0—knocked in the only run myself—going into the ninth inning. We had two twenty-game winners that year, Mel Parnell and Ellis Kinder, and both of them came in to relieve. What happens? They get base hits off Kinder and Parnell comes in and throws a wild pitch and we end up losing, 2–1.

Then the Yanks beat us twice and we lost the pennant by one game. Heck, if we hadn't blown the game against Washington I coulda been a hero.

J. W.
PORTER

♦ **MAJOR LEAGUE EXPERIENCE** ♦

St. Louis Browns, 1952
Detroit Tigers, 1955–1957
Cleveland Indians, 1958
Washington Senators, 1959
St. Louis Cardinals, 1959

♦ **CURRENT STATUS** ♦

Works for J. & K. Appliances in Jupiter, Florida. Lives in West Palm Beach Gardens with his wife and three children and participates in an innovative Baseball Chapel program throughout the state.

J. W. Porter was one of the highest-paid "bonus babies" of the 1950s, signing with the Chicago White Sox for $67,500 in 1951. Born in Shawnee, Oklahoma, on January 17, 1933, Porter grew *up in California where he became a catcher with a rifle for an arm, a legitimate "can't miss" prospect who had just led his American Legion team to the only back-to-back junior Legion titles in history.*

But baseball can sometimes alter even the best-laid plans. Traded to the St. Louis Browns in 1952, Porter spent the next seven years trying to find his place in the game and dispel the "utility" label that had been placed upon him.

During his quest, Porter had to deal with the painful reality that he wasn't going to be a Hall of Fame player, the superstar that everyone expected. Oddly enough, his greatest success came in the minors and that's where his fondest memories remain.

Still, he was part of a great era in baseball, playing with and against many of the top performers of his time. Having to over-come personal tragedy and other adversity during his career, J. W. Porter is a happy man today, having found peace and tran-quility through Christ.

If I had signed with the Yankees a lot of things might have been different. Look at it this way. Had I become [Yogi] Berra's backup, I'd have been in ten World Series, which would have meant a lot of money. But even if I never caught an inning with the Yankees, just signing with them could have changed things for me.

Looking around the American League in 1956, I think every team but the Red Sox had a former Yankee as a catcher. There were guys like [Jim] Hegan, [Sherm] Lollar, Hal Smith, [Lou] Berberet, [Clint] Courtney, [Gus] Triandos in Baltimore, and I had started my career with two of the greatest years you could ever have in the minor leagues. If I had that background in a pin-striped uniform and had been traded, another team would have given me two or three years to play my way into or out of the lineup.

But you have those same statistics with a White Sox farm team and . . . well, who ever heard of the White Sox? The funny thing was the White Sox were very, very happy with me the first two years. Then they traded me before I ever put on the uniform, despite the fact that they had so much money invested in me.

It was one of those deals that clubs make every year. The White Sox thought they could win the pennant in 1952, but they had to catch the Yankees. When the trade was made in late July they were just five games back, and they didn't have a center fielder. The guy they wanted was Jim Rivera, who was with the Browns. They thought he was the difference between winning and losing. I was dealt to St. Louis, Rivera came to the White Sox, and they finished fourteen games behind the Yankees. So much for pennant-winning trades.

Of course, St. Louis didn't make the deal out of the blue, either. Bill Veeck, who owned the Browns, saw me in spring training that year and I guess he really liked what he saw. He was trying very hard to build a team in St. Louis and he wanted to trade for youth. I started the year at Memphis mostly as a catcher. But because Clint Courtney was having a good year behind the plate in St. Louis, Veeck was interested in me as an outfielder. So they dropped me down a notch to A ball at Colorado Springs and put me in the outfield.

I was having a helluva year there, hitting around .340. Everything was beautiful in Colorado Springs. I had been married for eight months and my wife was five months pregnant. I was getting three hits every day and making love all night. We were on the road in Lincoln when Bill [Veeck] called to say the trade had been made and asked if I could get to St. Louis right away by plane.

When I told him I had a new wife and we had just bought a car that she couldn't drive, he told me not to worry. He had called her first to discuss the trade and said she was happy I was going to St. Louis. She had called her father, who was flying to Colorado Springs to drive her in our car to meet me. So I flew there thinking that things couldn't be better. But on the way to St. Louis from Colorado Springs, both my wife and my father-in-law were killed instantly in an automobile accident!

I was born in Oklahoma and raised in California. Like a lot of laborers and farmers, my father had to go west to make a living. He worked in shipyards and factories, and I played baseball. My first real notoriety came in American Legion ball. I was lucky enough to play on two consecutive Legion junior championship teams in 1949 and '50. No Legion team has ever repeated before or since, and I won the batting title of the World Legion ball both those years, hitting .551 in 1949 and .488 the next year.

Once you became state champs, those averages begin counting, because next you play in the regionals, then the sectionals, and then the Legion Series. And once we got out of the city, we never played a game where there weren't about fifteen or twenty scouts. We had an outstanding coach by the name of George Powles. I was his first top player, but coming right behind me were Frank Robinson, Vada Pinson, Curt Flood, Jesse Gonder, Charlie Beamon, and Tommy Harper. We all came from the same high school and during a five-year period George just spit us out like watermelon seeds. It was really fabulous.

I remember Frank Robinson when he was only a ninth-grader. He was already showing signs of greatness. He never did pull the ball much as a kid and he had the smallest legs you ever saw, little skinny ankles. But he was big from the waist up and the first ball I ever saw him hit went about five hundred feet to right center.

So the scouts came. I remember a Cincinnati scout who actually took an apartment in Oakland just to watch us. I guess the Reds wanted me, but he told me they couldn't afford me because I was gonna get a bunch of money. There was also a story that the Yanks and Red Sox both wanted to make me the highest-paid bonus baby to that time. But, to be honest, both those teams were kind of snobbish. They sent a whole planeload of superscouts and the hierarchy to see me play my senior year. And they'd take you out to wine and dine you, with your folks and your girlfriend and all that. But then they would just assume because they were the Yankees or Red Sox and were offering more money than anyone else, that you were gonna put your name on their contract.

I had a chance to sign in September of 1950, but the story was that the bonus rule that kept young players in the majors for two years was about to be kicked out, so I waited. Sure enough, it was voted out that winter, and by that time I was leaning toward the White Sox. Their scouting had been the nicest. An old major league pitcher by the name of Hollis "Sloppy" Thurston was their Southern California scout and had seen me many times. So I finally signed for $67,500. I think the only player who got more to that time was Paul Pettit, a lefthanded pitcher out of North Hollywood who signed with the Pirates, though unknown to them he already had a bad arm.

But I signed and went to Waterloo in 1951, and after a terrible start came on with a rush and hit around .308 or .310, with fifteen homers and ninety-five RBIs. And it was fun. To an eighteen-year-old kid even a bus trip is fun. You hope the bus breaks down in the middle of a cornfield so you can have a war with the corncobs and just scream at the pigs out the window and watch them scatter.

They were good times. I stayed with a suburban family who took in a couple of young ballplayers every year. And I'll tell you, having been, as it turned out, an average major league player and a star minor league player, when I lie awake at night and my mind goes back to those days, it is more apt to go back to the minor leagues, because that's where the fun was.

The majors didn't start well because of the car accident. But I had to go on and I went to St. Louis where I got into around thirty games. Then in December, I was traded to Detroit. The Tigers had just finished last for the one and only time in the history of the franchise. They had brought in Fred Hutchinson to manage and he had decided to clean house. So I figured I really had a shot to compete for the catching job. Then on the Friday before I was due to report to Lakeland for spring training I got a "Greetings" letter from Uncle Sam!

It was during the Korean War and apparently there were a lot of mothers around the country who felt that ballplayers were not being drafted just because they were ballplayers. So they bombarded Washington with letters and Uncle Sam picked up a few of us to make examples and quiet the whole thing down. I was actually taken a year and a half before my high school classmates were.

But I didn't go to Korea. I spent the whole time in California and played one hundred games both years. In fact, I managed the Fort Ord team and we won the all-Army championship and all-Service championship. So it wasn't bad. Only being in the army for two years didn't help my career. By the time I returned to the Tigers things were pretty much set and they had given the catching job to Frank House. I was just twenty-two years old when I came back in 1955. Yet if I hadn't gone I might have been part of Hutchinson's youth movement and earned a spot. Now they said they just hadn't seen enough of me.

And to make matters worse, Hutchinson demanded more than a one-year contract and was replaced by Bucky Harris. I must have played for thirty managers in my life and I've got to say the worst was Bucky Harris. We all heard about this young giant, this guy who literally in 1925 or '26, when an umpire turned to brush off home plate, had kicked him right in the ass.

But on opening day of spring training in 1955 he got everyone around him at the mound. There must have been sixty-five guys there and here's exactly what he said. He said, "Guys, you're major leaguers. If you don't know how to play this fucking game now, you never will." And he dropped the bag of balls on the mound, went and sat in the dugout and stayed there for two years until they ran him off.

Because of that, we were losing on fundamentals. We had twenty-game winners, the league's leading hitter in Al Kaline, and a strong team. But we blew it on missing cutoff men and things like that. The situation got so bad that Joe Gordon quit as one of his coaches. And he had other great people around him—Billy

Hitchcock, Schoolboy Rowe, Whitlow Wyatt—but he didn't use them.

It was a strange spring training in '55. I thought I had a good chance to be the team's right fielder. I had a great spring, a fantastic spring. Played every inning, hit more home runs than anyone else. So I opened the season in right and was given a four-game trial. We played two in Kansas City and then went home. It was cold as a welder's ass back there. And I had to hit against Mike Garcia and Bob Lemon of the Indians. Then it was all over. It wasn't that Harris took me out against righthanders or anything like that. He just took me out, period. And I had had a good opening series in Kansas City. Doubled the first day and was given a big transoceanic radio for hitting the first major league double in Kansas City. Hit it off Alex Kellner. I might have been overmatched against Garcia, because I remember him tearing the bat out of my hands. And that was the game when Kaline seemed to become a man. I had twice the spring he had and I think it came as a total surprise when he went on to lead the league in hitting. But he had two triples against Garcia that night and then really went on a tear. From the third game of the season he was the league's leading hitter and, of course, he became the right fielder.

I was so disappointed that I wasn't playing in any form or fashion that I told Harris to send me to the minors. I'm going nuts, I said, and sending me out was fine with him. So I went to Little Rock for a few weeks, then to Buffalo. I was back the next year and still didn't play much. But I'll say this. I warmed up some of the finest pitchers this game has ever known.

Then in '57 I was traded again, this time to Cleveland. It was tough, but I don't believe I ever totally lost confidence in myself or my ability to hit. Because every time I was given the opportunity to play and put games back to back, I hit, at any level. There was one two-week period in Detroit where [Bill] Tuttle had something wrong with him and they moved Kaline to center and put me in right. We won about ten games and lost four, and I hit.

I hit about .400 for a couple of solid weeks. Yet the minute Tuttle improved I went back to the bullpen, back to the dugout, and it was just like I wasn't there.

When I went to Cleveland in the winter of 1957 I was traded for the most popular player in the history of Indians baseball, Jim Hegan. A newspaper poll said that. I think it was somewhere at this point that I got my head screwed on straight to the fact that Jay, you're not gonna be this Hall of Famer, so just be the best ballplayer you can.

Naturally, Cleveland already had two young catchers they were breaking in, Russ Nixon and Dick Brown. So I just relaxed and tried to become a better pinch-hitter. I remember hitting a pinch homer in the bottom of the ninth and another in an extra-inning game. If I don't die before I touch home plate the game's over. Yet the fans, en masse, what few there were, were booing me all the way around the bases. That's how much they loved Hegan.

Finally, Frank Lane, Trader Lane, the general manager, said, "Jay, you've done everything we've expected, played some, filled in, and hit well. But I've got to trade you for your own benefit. You must be miserable here." And I said, "Frank, I sneak in and out of this place every day." So it was on to the Senators in '59, and they had the makings of a great team with Killebrew, Allison, and that group.

I didn't finish the season with the Senators. Toward the end of July I was shipped to the Cards for the waiver price. They already had a good catcher in Hal Smith and were about to bring up Tim McCarver. So I hardly played at all. But one thing I'll always remember in St. Louis was catching Bob Gibson's first big league victory and hitting a three-run homer off Taylor Phillips. That was the highlight. After '59 I was finished in the majors at the age of twenty-six.

So I went back to the minors. I played in Sacramento, Denver, and Toronto, still hitting and still making the all-star teams. I was playing first, catching, and also playing the outfield. And I still had some good defensive years. I could always throw. In fact, I once cut down Luis Aparicio three times in a game when I was with Washington. I think if I had been left alone as a catcher I would have improved even more defensively. But you'll never be the best defensive catcher who came down the pike when you wear a catcher's glove one day, a first baseman's the next, and a fielder's the day after.

I was in the Braves organization for a while, playing and coaching in the minors, and finished my career with the Atlanta Crackers in 1967 and '68. By then the feet were starting to hurt, the arm was starting to go, and the eyes a little bit as well. Playing in the Texas League didn't help. In West Texas you get those dust storms. I once had to leave a game in Amarillo because I just couldn't see.

There were two reasons why I don't think I was ever recalled after that. One was my reputation as a utility player. It might have kept me in the majors early, but it hurt me in the latter stages of my career. People looked at me as a guy who could fill in, rather than a guy who could play.

And the other reason was, frankly, that my reputation then was no good. Because of not playing I always had a lot of excess energy, a lot of frustration that had to be released. I couldn't release it on the field, so I released it at night. I never drank much, but I womanized and there was a paternity suit thrown in that made headlines in those days. It seems that everyone who signed for money had one, whether he was guilty or not. There was even a lady in Boston who had a teenage group of young ladies trying to get pregnant by major league bonus babies. I know that she thought you could come out with a grand or two or five to keep it out of the newspapers. In fact, ballclubs bought her off many, many times to save the reputations of their players. We went as far as blood tests and everything else to try to prove our innocence.

Now that it's over, though, I look back and I don't think anyone would argue that the best decade in baseball was the fifties. It opened with DiMaggio and ended with Mays and Mantle. Tough to beat.

I started working at Sears toward the end of my baseball career on an interim basis. And even though I went back to baseball briefly to manage in the minors for the Expos in '69 and '70, I stayed at Sears for ten or eleven years and learned the appliance business. I also met my present wife and the joy of my life at a Sears store in Atlanta.

Even though the teams I managed did well and for a while it flipflopped in my mind that I was going to become Casey Stengel and John McGraw rolled into one, sadly it didn't happen. It seems to be the guys who get the reputations, like Roger Craig as a pitching coach or Charley Lau as a batting coach, who get the jobs. Also guys who are sort of rebels, or maybe free thinkers is a better word. But I'm thinking of the Billy Martins, the Tom Larsordas, the Whitey Herzogs.

I did have one more offer to manage for the Expos in Yakima, Washington, but by then we were too deeply committed down here. My wife gave me a couple of daughters and a son, and that's been beautiful. From my wife, I also became part of the church. I went to a retreat weekend with her and since then my whole life has been different. The organization is called Cursillo, a Spanish word meaning a short lesson in Christ. I have also become involved in bringing this message into one of the prisons down here, the Glades Correctional Institute. That has also become a big part of my life. And I'm also associated with a program called Baseball Chapel, which has spread all through Florida and makes us available at ballparks for any players who might want to talk.

GARY
PETERS

◆ **MAJOR LEAGUE EXPERIENCE** ◆

Chicago White Sox, 1959–1969
Boston Red Sox, 1970–1972

◆ **CURRENT STATUS** ◆

General superintendent of E. E. "Gene"
Simmons Construction Company in Sarasota, Florida, where he lives with his wife
and enjoys hunting, fishing, and golf.

Gary Peters made a perfect addition to the "Go-Go" Chicago White Sox team in 1963. A good-pitch, no-hit team for several years before that, the Sox nevertheless always stayed close to the top. A stylish southpaw with a good sinker and slider, Peters won nineteen games that year and was named American League Rookie of the Year.

The next season, Gary became a twenty-game winner as his Sox finished just a game behind the pennant-winning New York

Yankees. *Though he never won that many again, Peters remained*
one of the American League's top lefthanders through 1971, a
pitcher especially tough on lefthanded batters.

Born in Grove City, Pennsylvania, on April 21, 1937, Gary
didn't play high school baseball. But he played alongside his father
in semipro leagues from the time he was fourteen years old. And
after signing with the White Sox, he still found time to play three
years of college basketball.

A solid stickman, Gary was often called upon to pinch-hit during
his career, a practice that could be dangerous in an age when
pitchers often worked the inside part of the plate. To Gary Peters,
it was a better game then, and he finds that today clubhouses are
too often devoid of fun and laughter, with players all tending to
business.

I never wanted to play too long. From time to time I had seen
some guys on television who were just playing a few years after
they should have quit. There were pitchers who were still pitching because they had had good years, not because they were
pitching well. Willie Mays was another big example. That really
bothered me and I didn't want to do that.

My last year was 1972 when I went 3–3 with the Red Sox.
After they released me I went to spring training the next year
with the Royals. But I could see a big difference in myself from
the last good year I had in 1971. My slider just didn't have the
sharp break it once did, and while things were still going in the
right direction, the pitches didn't have the same stuff. I could throw
to the right place, but the ball didn't move the way it once had.

It always hurts a little bit to pitch, but I noticed in '72 that it
hurt a little more. Plus the Royals wanted me to be a relief

pitcher, something I had never done before. I just didn't think I could do a good job, so I called it quits.

I was primarily a sinker-slider pitcher, although I threw a curveball to certain hitters. I also threw a straight change and I had to get two of them over. The change I could get over any time, and usually the sinker and slider. Those were the three pitches I felt I could throw three and oh if I had to. But I only threw the curve when I was ahead. Of course, I could throw the fastball any time, as well. Most of the guys on the White Sox, especially Joe Horlen and myself, as well as Tommy John a little later, threw two kinds of fastballs. We threw a sinking fastball, and also what I called a runner, a ball that would run inside to righthanders. I used that quite often after the first few years and jammed a lot of hitters.

Everyone worked inside back then. The hitters expected it and the pitchers didn't disappoint them. If a guy crowded the plate, you moved him back. It was as simple as that. I'll never forget the best knockdown pitch I ever threw. Al Kaline was hitting and after throwing a few outside sinkers, I tried to throw one up and in, and it sailed. It sailed about a foot and got him in the neck. He told me years later that he tried not to let the pitch bother him, but it made me a little tougher to hit after it happened.

I got hit a few times in retaliation, but that element is gone from the game today. Still, I was enough of a hitter to know that if I had even a little doubt in my mind it would take something away when I was at the plate, because I'd be standing a little lighter in there. Kaline said the same thing. Of course, he was a great hitter and he still did pretty good against me. But he always said that was one of the best knockdown pitches he ever saw.

The knockdown, or purpose pitch, was also the biggest cause of fights when I pitched. You know, guys come out to the mound, just like they do today. I hit Yaz one year in Boston and they were all going to come out. But I got the ball back quickly and it quieted down. We also used to have some pretty regular fights with Kansas City. I remember one game where we were ahead by a few runs when Jack Aker came in and hit Pete Ward. Pete had already driven in a couple, so we all knew what was happening.

When I went back to the mound Rick Monday was the first guy up. I was just gonna knock him down to let them know we didn't appreciate Aker hitting Pete. But the ball tailed and hit him in the face, breaking his jaw. After that we had several more altercations with the Royals. In fact, Monday was out for quite some time and the next time I found myself facing him, the exact same situation existed.

They had a tall righthander who hit Pete Ward. Eddie Stanky was our manager then, and while he would never tell us to throw at somebody, he would come over and say something like, "You know what you need to do." So when they hit Pete he came halfway down the bench and I said, "I know, I know." Then I went out to the mound and there was Monday. I threw the first ball behind him and it actually broke his bat. The next one was in close and it hit his bat for a second time . . . and broke it again. I knew he was leery of me anyway, so I threw him a slider and struck him out.

I can't really say I felt terrible when I broke his jaw. If I had been intentionally throwing at his head I would have, but he was looking for a breaking ball, guessing slider, and he stepped right into it. When the ball jumped up, it hit him.

A lot of people always had problems with Eddie Stanky as a manager, but I always thought he was pretty good. Unfortunately for Eddie, the White Sox had had a lot of success under Al Lopez and when Stanky took over the team was going downhill. Lopez was also a good baseball man and probably a better psychologist. Eddie had a bad temper and was especially hard on the young guys. He terrorized them a little bit. But I was more of an established player by the time he came over.

He would scream a lot when he lost his temper and really work the young guys over. I think they were a little scared, and you can't play well when you're scared. He'd scream at us sometimes after a tough loss, but we'd just tell him we'd get 'em next time.

But as far as thinking ahead and managing, and the strategy of the game itself, Eddie was great. Just as good as Lopez, only Al got more out of everybody because he was such a good psychologist.

I may sound like a seasoned veteran, but I was by no means an overnight sensation. Maybe I got something of a late start because my high school in Mercer, Pennsylvania, didn't have a baseball team. But my father was a fine semipro player who kept playing until he was about fifty. I started going with him to the games when I was about thirteen and began playing alongside him a year later. We played semipro ball together for four years and I also played a year of Legion. My father was an influence, obviously, but he never forced me to play, only exposed me to the game every chance he had.

I signed with the White Sox right out of high school, but only with the agreement that I could go to college full-time and play baseball as a summer job. In fact, I played a year in D ball, a year in B ball, and one year in Triple A ball, and at the same time played college basketball for all three years. In fact, I probably played more organized basketball than baseball then, but the Sox still signed me. My first tryout was as a first baseman. I had pitched a little in the semipro league then, threw pretty hard, but nothing else. In fact, my father wasn't too keen on me being a pitcher, and he always told me if I threw curveballs I'd hurt my arm.

A White Sox scout named Freddie Schaeffer was the guy who signed me. He covered mostly the high schools and colleges, but he made it to a couple of our games and was really the only scout who saw me. In fact, he was at one of the games I pitched and I happened to throw a seven-inning no-hitter. I guess that's one reason he took me to Chicago.

I worked out as a first baseman when I first got there and even hit a couple out. But gradually they decided that if I had a future it would be as a pitcher. Then I was in the minors for the better part of four seasons, so it really took me a long time to get to the big leagues. The White Sox had a very good pitching staff when I signed. They had [Early] Wynn and [Bob] Shaw, the core of the staff that won the pennant in 1959. That was my first year in Triple A ball. I came up at the end of the year, threw one inning, and got to go to the World Series as a batting practice pitcher.

But knowing the kind of pitchers the Sox had only made me work harder. Ray Berres, a former big league catcher, was the man who really taught me how to pitch. I was at Indianapolis in '59, two years in San Diego, then back to Indianapolis. Then after the 1962 season I went to Puerto Rico to play winter ball and that's where things finally began coming together. My ball was moving better, going where I wanted it to, and my breaking ball was also much better. It took awhile, but the things Ray Berres had taught me about pitching were finally sinking in.

I stuck with the club through spring training in 1963. For a while, I thought I might even be traded. But I remember that Juan Pizarro was supposed to start the opening game in Kansas City and he got the flu. So I got the start, beat them, and hit a home run. Jim Brosnan saved it for me, and I was in the rotation from that point on.

It's not easy coming to the big leagues, no matter how old you are. I was twenty-six in 1963 and the guy who really helped me was Nellie Fox, who was a star second baseman at that time. Nellie was from Pennsylvania, too, the other side of the state. But he grew up in a little town, was a deer hunter, and we had a lot in common. So he kind of took me under his wing and was very nice to me. He showed me around, told me about salary negotiations, suggested a neighborhood to live in, and even helped me to get a place.

He was also an amazing ballplayer. He probably did more with less talent than almost anybody. Physically, he didn't have much. He was small, but he was a hard worker, a guy who always led by example. One year he struck out only eleven times all year, and that's almost inconceivable. So I was really glad to have him as a friend.

In a way, though, Nellie typified the White Sox back then. We had good pitching and a good defensive club. We also had great speed, but we weren't a good-hitting team. What we needed was a couple of RBI men. I think one year Pete Ward led the club with fifty-some RBIs, and Juan Pizarro and myself combined for only about five less.

Pizarro had a couple of real fine years for us and I thought he was a good guy to get along with and a good team man. And could he throw. He had a great fastball. I remember him telling me at the end of one season that he planned to lift weights during the winter. That was before people thought much about weights. He said he was going on weights and would throw faster. I said, "Gosh, Juan, you can't be any faster." But he lifted the weights, and when he came to spring training the next year he was musclebound, and it was like night and day. From one fall to the next spring, and he was never the same pitcher again.

But anyway, my rookie year turned out to be a good one. I won nineteen games and was named Rookie of the Year. Pete Rose won it in the National League that year and in spring training before the following season they gave each of us a big ol' trophy. I think I've got it up in the attic somewhere. My family room has ducks and hunting trophies, and a few golf trophies.

In '64 I had another good year, winning twenty games and making the All-Star team for one of the two times in my career. I also pitched a game against Baltimore that year in which I had the best stuff I ever had in my entire career. It was so good that I was pitching a perfect game and the guy who broke it up was Robin Roberts, the Orioles' pitcher that day. He came up in the sixth inning and I threw him a fastball inside. He took a little swing and the ball just went over the second baseman's head. He was the only guy to get on base. In fact, he lives nearby and whenever I see him he reminds me of that hit.

But I really had it that day. All I had to do was throw my slider over. It was breaking so hard that the righthanders couldn't touch it. I'll admit it wasn't like that too many times. Usually I had to be

careful and really locate my ball. Control was my forte. I threw
fairly hard and my ball moved and sank well. But I wasn't the kind
of pitcher who could throw the ball in the middle of the strike
zone. There aren't many like that now. Back in those days
[Denny] McLain could do it, [Jim] Palmer could do it, [Sandy]
Koufax could do it. [Nolan] Ryan still does it.

Things continued to go fairly well until 1968. Then I had some
physical problems. I pitched the first game of a doubleheader
early in the year in Chicago, and it was cold. When the second
game started, I stayed in the clubhouse. I guess our starter gave
up a lot of runs early, because in the fourth or fifth inning,
somebody came in and told me to hurry up to the dugout because
Stanky wanted me to pinch-hit. I remember going out and still
feeling kind of stiff from the first game.

There was a guy on first base and I knew he wanted me to pull
the ball and try to get the runner around. So I tried to pull an
outside pitch and got a spasm in my back. I never even got to
first base, even though I hit the ball. I fought the thing all year
and in the fall was still limping around with it.

It turned into a bad year, the worst, and while the next year
was a bit better, I was still below .500. And that's when I was
traded to the Red Sox. A lot of people thought lefties couldn't
pitch in Fenway Park, but I had pitched there a number of times
with the White Sox, so it didn't bother me. In fact, I remember
going in there my rookie year for a doubleheader, and the way
the rotation was set up, Pizarro and I were scheduled to go. All
the Boston writers said Lopez was crazy for starting two lefthanders. But we both shut them out. That's when they had Dick
Stuart playing first base and I think the two of us struck him out
eight times that day.

The second year I was in Boston the White Sox sent Luis
Aparicio over. It was always good to have Luis playing behind
you. He was great. There are a lot of good shortstops, but it
would be hard for me to say anybody was better than he was
because I saw him do so many things. In fact, I saw him do the

things Ozzie [Smith] is doing now, only he wasn't as acrobatic. But I think he was just as quick and had just as much range.

I had two good years in Boston and enjoyed playing there. I guess my only regret is that I never got to pitch in the World Series. I got a taste of it when I pitched batting practice at the Series in '59, and we were close several other times. In '64 we had about ten or eleven games left and were just two games behind the Yanks. I think we got hot and won them all, but the Yanks only lost once and beat us by one game. Then with Boston we barely missed in '72.

Looking back, I think the most money I made in a season was somewhere in the fifties. The White Sox weren't big payers. They cut corners. Ed Short was the general manager and he had just so much for salary. If I hadn't been tough, I probably would have been playing for less. I held out a little every year until I went to Boston. That was a whole different story. They'd ask you what you wanted and they'd pay you. Their pay scale was considerably higher than the White Sox and if I had had those good years in Boston I'd have probably made twenty or thirty thousand more a year.

As I said, the White Sox were very businesslike and watched the bucks. I remember one night when it was raining at Comiskey Park and they had a big presale. The White Sox would always wait forever to call off a ballgame. So we waited and waited, and it kept pouring down rain. One of my hobbies is scuba diving and I happened to have some of my equipment in the clubhouse that night. So I put a tank on, got my flippers and mask, and walked up to home plate and took a few practice swings in the rain. There were about thirty thousand fans there and they thought it was great. Didn't even know who I was. But Ed Short said it was gonna cost me one thousand dollars because I was showing him up. They never did officially fine me, though, because the Players' Association kept on top of it.

I wasn't really worried when my career was ending. I had studied engineering in college and had always read and stayed interested. Plus I always liked the building business and kind of knew that's what I was going to do when I got out. So now I work for a construction company, called E. E. "Gene" Simmons, as a general superintendent. I control the field work and quality control. I've lived in Florida since 1959 and began working with them as soon as I retired from baseball.

My wife and I have been married for thirty years and we've got two daughters. One's an attorney in Chattanooga and the other is director of Retirement Systems in Atlanta.

I had a few opportunities to stay in baseball with a couple of clubs, especially when I first got out. And even now, someone occasionally calls about it. Who knows, now that the kids are grown and my wife could go with me, we might think about it. I also do a couple of Equitable [old-timers'] games every year. But once you start going to card shows they want you to go all the time, and I don't want to do that, even though the money is pretty good.

All in all, I think I preferred the game when I played. Not only did we have more fun, but I think it was a better game then. I certainly don't have anything against money, but it has affected the game a lot. Whenever I go into a clubhouse now for an old-timers' game or something, there never seems to be anyone laughing. All the players are busy talking to an agent or another kind of representative. It seems to be all business.

It's just not like it used to be.

◆ APPENDIX ◆
CAREER STATISTICS

Tom Tresh

TRESH, THOMAS MICHAEL
Son of Mike Tresh.
B. Sept. 20, 1937, Detroit, Mich.

BB TR 6'1" 180 lbs.

	G	AB	H	2B	3B	HR	HR%	R	RBI	BB	SO	SB	BA	SA	Pinch Hit AB	Pinch Hit H	G by POS
1961 NY A	9	8	2	0	0	0	0.0	1	0	0	1	0	.250	.250	3	1	SS-3
1962	157	622	178	26	5	20	3.2	94	93	67	74	4	.286	.441	2	0	SS-111, OF-43
1963	145	520	140	28	5	25	4.8	91	71	83	79	3	.269	.487	1	0	OF-144
1964	153	533	131	25	5	16	3.0	75	73	73	110	13	.246	.402	7	1	OF-146
1965	156	602	168	29	6	26	4.3	94	74	59	92	5	.279	.477	2	0	OF-154
1966	151	537	125	12	4	27	5.0	76	68	86	89	5	.233	.421	3	1	OF-84, 3B-64
1967	130	448	98	23	3	14	3.1	45	53	50	86	1	.219	.377	10	1	OF-118
1968	152	507	99	18	3	11	2.2	60	52	76	97	10	.195	.308	6	1	SS-119, OF-27
1969 2 teams	NY A (45G – .182)			DET A (94G – .224)													
" total	139	474	100	18	3	14	3.0	59	46	56	70	4	.211	.350	10	1	SS-118, OF-11, 3B-1
9 yrs.	1192	4251	1041	179	34	153	3.6	595	530	550	698	45	.245	.411	44	6	OF-727, SS-351, 3B-65
WORLD SERIES																	
1962 NY A	7	28	9	1	0	1	3.6	5	4	1	4	2	.321	.464	0	0	OF-7
1963	4	15	3	0	0	1	6.7	1	2	1	6	0	.200	.400	0	0	OF-4
1964	7	22	6	2	0	2	9.1	4	7	6	7	0	.273	.636	0	0	OF-7
3 yrs.	18	65	18	3	0	4	6.2	10	13	8	17	2	.277	.508	0	0	OF-18

Dale Long

LONG, RICHARD DALE
B. Feb. 6, 1926, Springfield, Mo.

BL TL 6'4" 205 lbs.

	G	AB	H	2B	3B	HR	HR%	R	RBI	BB	SO	SB	BA	SA	Pinch Hit AB	Pinch Hit H	G by POS
1951 2 teams	PIT N (10G – .167)			STL A (34G – .238)													
" total	44	117	27	5	1	3	2.6	12	12	10	25	0	.231	.368	13	1	1B-29, OF-1
1955 PIT N	131	419	122	19	13	16	3.8	59	79	48	72	0	.291	.513	13	4	1B-119
1956	148	517	136	20	7	27	5.2	64	91	54	85	1	.263	.485	12	2	1B-138
1957 2 teams	PIT N (7G – .182)			CHI N (123G – .305)													
" total	130	419	125	20	0	21	5.0	55	67	56	73	1	.298	.496	18	6	1B-111
1958 CHI N	142	480	130	26	4	20	4.2	68	75	66	64	2	.271	.467	5	2	1B-137, C-2
1959	110	296	70	10	3	14	4.7	34	37	31	53	0	.236	.432	27	6	1B-85
1960 2 teams	SF N (37G – .167)			NY A (26G – .366)													
" total	63	95	24	3	1	6	6.3	10	16	12	13	0	.253	.495	39	11	1B-21
1961 WAS A	123	377	94	20	4	17	4.5	52	49	39	41	0	.249	.459	24	3	1B-95
1962 2 teams	WAS A (67G – .241)			NY A (41G – .298)													
" total	108	285	74	12	0	8	2.8	29	41	36	31	6	.260	.386	28	3	1B-82
1963 NY A	14	15	3	0	0	0	0.0	1	0	1	3	0	.200	.200	11	2	1B-2
10 yrs.	1013	3020	805	135	33	132	4.4	384	467	353	460	10	.267	.464	190	40	1B-819, C-2, OF-1
WORLD SERIES																	
1960 NY A	3	3	1	0	0	0	0.0	0	0	0	0	0	.333	.333	3	1	
1962	2	5	1	0	0	0	0.0	0	1	0	1	0	.200	.200	0	0	1B-2
2 yrs.	5	8	2	0	0	0	0.0	0	1	0	1	0	.250	.250	3	1	1B-2

Note: tables reprinted from *The Baseball Encyclopedia*, seventh edition (Macmillan, 1988).

Mel Parnell

	W	L	PCT	ERA	G	GS	CG	IP	H	BB	SO	ShO	Relief Pitching W	L	SV	BATTING AB	H	HR	BA

PARNELL, MELVIN LLOYD (Dusty)
B. June 13, 1922, New Orleans, La.
BL TL 6' 180 lbs.

	W	L	PCT	ERA	G	GS	CG	IP	H	BB	SO	ShO	W	L	SV	AB	H	HR	BA
1947 BOS A	2	3	.400	6.39	15	5	1	50.2	60	27	23	0	1	1	0	18	1	0	.056
1948	15	8	.652	3.14	35	27	16	212	205	90	77	1	0	2	0	80	13	0	.163
1949	25	7	.781	2.77	39	33	27	295.1	258	134	122	4	1	1	2	114	29	0	.254
1950	18	10	.643	3.61	40	31	21	249	244	106	93	2	0	1	3	98	19	0	.194
1951	18	11	.621	3.26	36	29	11	221	229	77	77	3	2	0	2	81	25	0	.309
1952	12	12	.500	3.62	33	29	15	214	207	89	107	3	0	0	2	84	8	1	.095
1953	21	8	.724	3.06	38	34	12	241	217	116	136	5	1	0	0	94	21	0	.223
1954	3	7	.300	3.70	19	15	4	92.1	104	35	38	1	0	0	0	34	3	0	.088
1955	2	3	.400	7.83	13	9	0	46	62	25	18	0	0	0	1	19	6	0	.316
1956	7	6	.538	3.77	21	20	6	131.1	129	59	41	1	0	1	0	46	7	0	.152
10 yrs.	123	75	.621	3.50	289	232	113	1752.2	1715	758	732	20	5	6	10	668	132	1	.198

Jake Gibbs

	G	AB	H	2B	3B	HR	HR%	R	RBI	BB	SO	SB	BA	SA	Pinch Hit AB	H	G by POS

GIBBS, JERRY DEAN
B. Nov. 7, 1938, Grenada, Miss.
BL TR 6' 180 lbs.

	G	AB	H	2B	3B	HR	HR%	R	RBI	BB	SO	SB	BA	SA	AB	H	G by POS
1962 NY A	2	0	0	0	0	0	–	0	0	0	0	0	–	–	0	0	3B-1
1963	4	8	2	0	0	0	0.0	1	0	0	1	0	.250	.250	3	2	C-1
1964	3	6	1	0	0	0	0.0	1	0	0	2	0	.167	.167	1	1	C-2
1965	37	68	15	1	0	2	2.9	6	7	4	20	0	.221	.324	16	3	C-21
1966	62	182	47	6	0	3	1.6	19	20	19	16	5	.258	.341	5	1	C-54
1967	116	374	87	7	1	4	1.1	33	25	28	57	7	.233	.289	17	3	C-99
1968	124	423	90	12	3	3	0.7	31	29	27	68	9	.213	.277	4	1	C-121
1969	71	219	49	9	2	0	0.0	18	18	23	30	3	.224	.283	2	0	C-66
1970	49	153	46	9	2	8	5.2	23	26	7	14	2	.301	.542	5	1	C-44
1971	70	206	45	9	0	5	2.4	23	21	12	23	2	.218	.335	16	1	C-51
10 yrs.	538	1639	382	53	8	25	1.5	157	146	120	231	28	.233	.321	69	13	C-459, 3B-1

Al Smith

	G	AB	H	2B	3B	HR	HR%	R	RBI	BB	SO	SB	BA	SA	Pinch Hit AB	H	G by POS

SMITH, ALPHONSE EUGENE (Fuzzy)
B. Feb. 7, 1928, Kirkwood, Mo.
BR TR 6'½" 189 lbs.

	G	AB	H	2B	3B	HR	HR%	R	RBI	BB	SO	SB	BA	SA	AB	H	G by POS
1953 CLE A	47	150	36	9	0	3	2.0	28	14	20	25	2	.240	.360	2	1	OF-39, 3B-2
1954	131	481	135	29	6	11	2.3	101	50	88	65	2	.281	.435	2	0	OF-109, 3B-21, SS-4
1955	154	607	186	27	4	22	3.6	123	77	93	77	11	.306	.473	0	0	OF-120, 3B-45, SS-5, 2B-1
1956	141	526	144	26	5	16	3.0	87	71	84	72	6	.274	.433	1	0	OF-122, 3B-28, 2B-1
1957	135	507	125	23	5	11	2.2	78	49	79	70	12	.247	.377	1	0	3B-84, OF-50
1958 CHI A	139	480	121	23	5	12	2.5	61	58	48	77	3	.252	.396	3	1	OF-138, 3B-1
1959	129	472	112	16	4	17	3.6	65	55	46	74	7	.237	.396	1	0	OF-128, 3B-1
1960	142	536	169	31	3	12	2.2	80	72	50	65	8	.315	.451	1	0	OF-141
1961	147	532	148	29	4	28	5.3	88	93	56	67	4	.278	.506	5	2	3B-80, OF-71
1962	142	511	149	23	8	16	3.1	62	82	57	60	3	.292	.462	4	2	3B-105, OF-39
1963 BAL A	120	368	100	17	1	10	2.7	45	39	32	74	9	.272	.405	21	5	OF-97
1964 2 teams			CLE A (61G – .162)					BOS A (29G – .216)									
" total	90	187	33	5	1	6	3.2	25	16	21	42	0	.176	.310	30	4	OF-56, 3B-12
12 yrs.	1517	5357	1458	258	46	164	3.1	843	676	674	768	67	.272	.429	71	15	OF-1110, 3B-379, SS-9, 2B-2
WORLD SERIES																	
1954 CLE A	4	14	3	0	0	1	7.1	2	2	2	2	0	.214	.429	0	0	OF-4
1959 CHI A	6	20	5	3	0	0	0.0	1	1	4	4	0	.250	.400	0	0	OF-6
2 yrs.	10	34	8	3	0	1	2.9	3	3	6	6	0	.235	.412	0	0	OF-10

Al Weis

	G	AB	H	2B	3B	HR	HR%	R	RBI	BB	SO	SB	BA	SA	Pinch Hit AB	H	G by POS

WEIS, ALBERT JOHN
B. Apr. 2, 1938, Franklin Square, N. Y.
BB TR 6' 160 lbs.
BR 1969

	G	AB	H	2B	3B	HR	HR%	R	RBI	BB	SO	SB	BA	SA	AB	H	G by POS
1962 CHI A	7	12	1	0	0	0	0.0	2	0	2	3	1	.083	.083	0	0	SS-4, 3B-1, 2B-1
1963	99	210	57	9	0	0	0.0	41	18	18	37	15	.271	.314	9	2	2B-48, SS-27, 3B-1
1964	133	328	81	4	4	2	0.6	36	23	22	41	22	.247	.302	6	1	2B-116, SS-9, OF-2
1965	103	135	40	4	3	1	0.7	29	12	12	22	4	.296	.393	6	2	2B-74, SS-7, OF-2, 3B-2
1966	129	187	29	4	1	0	0.0	20	9	17	50	3	.155	.187	0	0	2B-96, SS-18
1967	50	53	13	2	0	0	0.0	9	4	1	7	3	.245	.283	0	0	2B-32, SS-13
1968 NY N	90	274	47	6	0	1	0.4	15	14	21	63	3	.172	.204	3	0	SS-59, 2B-29, 3B-2
1969	103	247	53	9	2	2	0.8	20	23	15	51	3	.215	.291	3	0	SS-52, 2B-43, 3B-1
1970	75	121	25	7	1	1	0.8	20	11	7	21	1	.207	.306	2	0	2B-44, SS-15
1971	11	11	0	0	0	0	0.0	3	3	2	4	0	.000	.000	4	0	2B-5, 3B-1
10 yrs.	800	1578	346	45	11	7	0.4	195	115	117	299	55	.219	.275	33	5	2B-488, SS-204, 3B-9, OF-4
LEAGUE CHAMPIONSHIP SERIES																	
1969 NY N	3	1	0	0	0	0	0.0	0	0	0	0	0	.000	.000	0	0	2B-3
WORLD SERIES																	
1969 NY N	5	11	5	0	0	1	9.1	1	3	4	2	0	.455	.727	0	0	2B-5

Clem Labine

	W	L	PCT	ERA	G	GS	CG	IP	H	BB	SO	ShO	Relief Pitching W	L	SV	BATTING AB	H	HR	BA
								LABINE, CLEMENT WALTER B. Aug. 6, 1926, Lincoln, R. I.								BR TR 6'		180 lbs.	
1950 BKN N	0	0	–	4.50	1	0	0	2	2	1	0	0	0	0	0	0	0	0	–
1951	5	1	.833	2.20	14	6	5	65.1	52	20	39	2	0	0	0	21	3	0	.143
1952	8	4	.667	5.14	25	9	0	77	76	47	43	0	6	1	0	22	1	0	.045
1953	11	6	.647	2.77	37	7	0	110.1	92	30	44	0	10	4	7	28	2	0	.071
1954	7	6	.538	4.15	47	2	0	108.1	101	56	43	0	6	5	5	30	1	0	.033
1955	13	5	.722	3.24	60	8	1	144.1	121	55	67	0	10	2	11	31	3	3	.097
1956	10	6	.625	3.35	62	3	1	115.2	111	39	75	0	9	6	19	23	2	0	.087
1957	5	7	.417	3.44	58	0	0	104.2	104	27	67	0	5	7	17	20	2	0	.100
1958 LA N	6	6	.500	4.15	52	2	0	104	112	33	43	0	5	5	14	18	1	0	.056
1959	5	10	.333	3.93	56	0	0	84.2	91	25	37	0	5	10	9	16	0	0	.000
1960 3 teams	LA	N	(13G 0–1)		DET	A	(14G 0–3)	PIT	N	(15G 3–0)									
" total	3	4	.429	3.65	42	0	0	66.2	74	31	42	0	3	4	6	8	1	0	.125
1961 PIT N	4	1	.800	3.69	56	1	0	92.2	102	31	49	0	4	1	8	10	1	0	.100
1962 NY N	0	0	–	11.25	7	0	0	4	5	1	2	0	0	0	0	0	0	0	–
13 yrs.	77	56	.579	3.63	513	38	7	1079.2	1043	396	551	2	63	45	96	227	17	3	.075
WORLD SERIES																			
1953 BKN N	0	2	.000	3.60	3	0	0	5	10	1	3	0	0	2	1	2	0	0	.000
1955	1	0	1.000	2.89	4	0	0	9.1	6	2	2	0	1	0	1	4	0	0	.000
1956	1	0	1.000	0.00	2	1	1	12	8	3	7	1	0	0	0	4	1	0	.250
1959 LA N	0	0	–	0.00	1	0	0	1	0	1	0	0	0	0	0	0	0	0	–
1960 PIT N	0	0	–	13.50	3	0	0	4	13	1	2	0	0	0	0	0	0	0	–
5 yrs.	2	2	.500	3.16	13 6th	1	1	31.1	37	7	15	1	1	2 2nd	2	10	1	0	.100

Bob Veale

	W	L	PCT	ERA	G	GS	CG	IP	H	BB	SO	ShO	Relief Pitching W	L	SV	BATTING AB	H	HR	BA
								VEALE, ROBERT ANDREW B. Oct. 28, 1935, Birmingham, Ala.								BB TL 6'6"		212 lbs.	
1962 PIT N	2	2	.500	3.74	11	6	2	45.2	39	25	42	0	0	0	1	16	4	0	.250
1963	5	2	.714	1.04	34	7	3	77.2	59	40	68	2	1	0	3	23	2	0	.087
1964	18	12	.600	2.74	40	38	14	279.2	222	124	250	1	0	0	0	96	15	0	.156
1965	17	12	.586	2.84	39	37	14	266	221	119	276	7	0	0	0	93	8	0	.086
1966	16	12	.571	3.02	38	37	12	268.1	228	102	229	3	0	0	0	94	13	0	.138
1967	16	8	.667	3.64	33	31	6	203	184	119	179	1	0	0	0	69	3	0	.043
1968	13	14	.481	2.05	36	33	13	245.1	187	94	171	4	0	1	0	82	9	0	.110
1969	13	14	.481	3.23	34	34	9	226	232	91	213	1	0	0	0	79	4	0	.051
1970	10	15	.400	3.92	34	32	5	202	189	94	178	1	0	0	0	67	11	0	.164
1971	6	0	1.000	7.04	37	0	0	46	59	24	40	0	6	0	2	9	3	0	.333
1972 2 teams	PIT	N	(5G 0–0)		BOS	A	(6G 2–0)												
" total	2	0	1.000	3.18	11	0	0	17	12	10	16	0	2	0	2	2	0	0	.000
1973 BOS A	2	3	.400	3.50	32	0	0	36	37	12	25	0	2	3	11	0	0	0	–
1974	0	1	.000	5.54	18	0	0	13	15	4	16	0	0	1	2	0	0	0	–
13 yrs.	120	95	.558	3.08	397	255	78	1925.2	1684	858	1703	20	11	5	21	630	72	0	.114
WORLD SERIES																			
1971 PIT N	0	0	–	13.50	1	0	0	.2	1	2	0	0	0	0	0	0	0	0	–

Ray Boone

	G	AB	H	2B	3B	HR	HR %	R	RBI	BB	SO	SB	BA	SA	Pinch Hit AB	H	G by POS
							BOONE, RAYMOND OTIS (Ike) Father of Bob Boone. B. July 27, 1923, San Diego, Calif.								BR TR 6'		172 lbs.
1948 CLE A	6	5	2	1	0	0	0.0	0	1	0	1	0	.400	.600	1	0	SS-4
1949	86	258	65	4	4	4	1.6	39	26	38	17	0	.252	.345	7	1	SS-76
1950	109	365	110	14	6	7	1.9	53	58	56	27	4	.301	.430	6	0	SS-102
1951	151	544	127	14	1	12	2.2	65	51	48	36	5	.233	.329	0	0	SS-151
1952	103	316	83	8	2	7	2.2	57	45	53	33	0	.263	.367	4	0	SS-96, 3B-2, 2B-1
1953 2 teams	CLE	A	(34G	–	.241)		DET	A	(101G	–	.312)						
" total	135	497	147	17	8	26	5.2	94	114	72	68	3	.296	.519	4	1	3B-97, SS-34
1954 DET A	148	543	160	19	7	20	3.7	76	85	71	53	4	.295	.466	0	0	3B-148, SS-1
1955	135	500	142	22	7	20	4.0	61	116	50	49	1	.284	.476	8	2	3B-126
1956	131	481	148	14	6	25	5.2	77	81	77	46	0	.308	.518	0	0	3B-130
1957	129	462	126	25	3	12	2.6	48	65	57	47	1	.273	.418	5	1	1B-117, 3B-4
1958 2 teams	DET	A	(39G	–	.237)		CHI	A	(77G	–	.244)						
" total	116	360	87	16	2	13	3.6	41	61	32	46	1	.242	.406	21	2	1B-95
1959 3 teams	CHI	A	(9G	–	.238)		KC	A	(61G	–	.273)		MIL	N	(13G	–	.200)
" total	83	168	44	6	0	4	2.4	25	19	38	24	2	.262	.369	37	11	1B-47, 3B-3
1960 2 teams	MIL	N	(7G	–	.250)		BOS	A	(34G	–	.205)							
" total	41	90	19	2	0	1	1.1	9	16	16	0	0	.211	.267	15	3	1B-26
13 yrs.	1373	4589	1260	162	46	151	3.3	645	737	608	463	21	.275	.429	108	21	3B-510, SS-464, 1B-285, 2B-1
WORLD SERIES																	
1948 CLE A	1	1	0	0	0	0	0.0	0	0	0	1	0	.000	.000	1	0	

Bob Boyd

BOYD, ROBERT RICHARD (The Rope)
B. Oct. 1, 1926, Potts Camp, Miss.

BL TL 5'10" 170 lbs.

	G	AB	H	2B	3B	HR	HR%	R	RBI	BB	SO	SB	BA	SA	Pinch Hit AB	Pinch Hit H	G by POS
1951 CHI A	12	18	3	0	1	0	0.0	3	4	3	3	0	.167	.278	5	1	1B-6
1953	55	165	49	6	2	3	1.8	20	23	13	11	1	.297	.412	8	4	1B-29, OF-16
1954	29	56	10	3	0	0	0.0	10	5	4	3	2	.179	.232	2	0	OF-13, 1B-12
1956 BAL A	70	225	70	8	3	2	0.9	28	11	30	14	0	.311	.400	10	3	1B-60, OF-8
1957	141	485	154	16	8	4	0.8	73	34	55	31	2	.318	.408	15	6	1B-132, OF-1
1958	125	401	124	21	5	7	1.7	58	36	25	24	1	.309	.439	32	4	1B-99
1959	128	415	110	20	2	3	0.7	42	41	29	14	3	.265	.345	20	4	1B-109
1960	71	82	26	5	2	0	0.0	9	9	6	5	0	.317	.427	56	17	1B-17
1961 2 teams	KC	A (26G –		.229)		MIL	N (36G –	.244)									
" total	62	89	21	2	0	0	0.0	10	12	2	9	0	.236	.258	49	9	1B-11
9 yrs.	693	1936	567	81	23	19	1.0	253	175	167	114	9	.293	.388	197	48	1B-475, OF-38

Bob Hazle

HAZLE, ROBERT SIDNEY (Hurricane)
B. Dec. 9, 1930, Laurens, S. C.

BL TR 6' 190 lbs.

	G	AB	H	2B	3B	HR	HR%	R	RBI	BB	SO	SB	BA	SA	Pinch Hit AB	Pinch Hit H	G by POS
1955 CIN N	6	13	3	0	0	0	0.0	0	0	0	3	0	.231	.231	3	1	OF-4
1957 MIL N	41	134	54	12	0	7	5.2	26	27	18	15	1	.403	.649	1	1	OF-40
1958 2 teams	MIL	N (20G –	.179)		DET	A (43G –	.241)										
" total	63	114	24	2	0	2	1.8	11	10	14	17	0	.211	.281	29	6	OF-32
3 yrs.	110	261	81	14	0	9	3.4	37	37	32	35	1	.310	.467	33	8	OF-76
WORLD SERIES																	
1957 MIL N	4	13	2	0	0	0	0.0	2	0	1	2	0	.154	.154	0	0	OF-4

Roy Face

FACE, ELROY LEON
B. Feb. 20, 1928, Stephentown, N. Y.

BB TR 5'8" 155 lbs.
BR 1953-59

	W	L	PCT	ERA	G	GS	CG	IP	H	BB	SO	ShO	Relief Pitching W	Relief Pitching L	Relief Pitching SV	BATTING AB	BATTING H	BATTING HR	BA
1953 PIT N	6	8	.429	6.58	41	13	2	119	145	30	56	0	3	2	0	30	4	0	.133
1955	5	7	.417	3.58	42	10	4	125.2	128	40	84	0	1	1	5	26	3	0	.115
1956	12	13	.480	3.52	68	3	0	135.1	131	42	96	0	11	12	6	26	5	0	.192
1957	4	6	.400	3.07	59	1	0	93.2	97	24	53	0	4	6	10	16	2	0	.125
1958	5	2	.714	2.89	57	0	0	84	77	22	47	0	5	2	20	7	0	0	.000
1959	18	1	.947	2.70	57	0	0	93.1	91	25	69	0	18	1	10	13	3	0	.231
1960	10	8	.556	2.90	68	0	0	114.2	93	29	72	0	10	8	24	17	7	0	.412
1961	6	12	.333	3.82	62	0	0	92	94	10	55	0	6	12	17	11	3	0	.273
1962	8	7	.533	1.88	63	0	0	91	74	18	45	0	8	7	28	12	1	0	.083
1963	3	9	.250	3.23	56	0	0	69.2	75	19	41	0	3	9	16	8	2	0	.250
1964	3	3	.500	5.20	55	0	0	79.2	82	27	63	0	3	3	4	4	0	0	.000
1965	5	2	.714	2.66	16	0	0	20	7	19	0	5	2	0	1	0	0	.000	
1966	6	6	.500	2.70	54	0	0	70	68	24	67	0	6	6	18	11	0	0	.000
1967	7	5	.583	2.42	61	0	0	74.1	62	22	41	0	7	5	17	6	0	0	.000
1968 2 teams	PIT	N (43G 2-4)		DET	A (2G 0-0)														
" total	2	4	.333	2.55	45	0	0	53	48	8	35	0	2	4	13	4	0	0	.000
1969 MON N	4	2	.667	3.94	44	0	0	59.1	62	15	34	0	4	2	5	2	1	0	.500
16 yrs.	104	95	.523	3.48	848	27	6	1375	1347	362	877	0	96 6th	82 8th	193	194	31	0	.160
WORLD SERIES																			
1960 PIT N	0	0	–	5.23	4	0	0	10.1	9	2	4	0	0	0	3 4th	3	0	0	.000

Roy Sievers

SIEVERS, ROY EDWARD (Squirrel)
B. Nov. 18, 1926, St. Louis, Mo.

BR TR 6'1" 195 lbs.

	G	AB	H	2B	3B	HR	HR%	R	RBI	BB	SO	SB	BA	SA	Pinch Hit AB	Pinch Hit H	G by POS
1949 STL A	140	471	144	28	1	16	3.4	84	91	70	75	1	.306	.471	7	2	OF-125, 38-7
1950	113	370	88	20	4	10	2.7	46	57	34	42	1	.238	.395	15	2	OF-78, 38-21
1951	31	89	20	2	1	1	1.1	10	11	9	21	0	.225	.303	8	1	OF-25
1952	11	30	6	3	0	0	0.0	3	5	1	4	0	.200	.300	5	0	1B-7
1953	92	285	77	15	0	8	2.8	37	35	32	47	0	.270	.407	17	3	1B-76
1954 WAS A	145	514	119	26	6	24	4.7	75	102	80	77	2	.232	.446	5	0	OF-133, 1B-8
1955	144	509	138	20	8	25	4.9	74	106	73	66	1	.271	.489	2	0	OF-129, 1B-17, 3B-2
1956	152	550	139	27	2	29	5.3	92	95	100	88	0	.253	.467	0	0	OF-78, 1B-76
1957	152	572	172	23	5	42	7.3	99	114	76	55	1	.301	.579	2	2	OF-130, 1B-21
1958	148	550	162	18	1	39	7.1	85	108	53	63	3	.295	.544	4	1	OF-114, 1B-33
1959	115	385	93	19	0	21	5.5	55	49	53	62	1	.242	.455	7	1	1B-93, OF-13
1960 CHI A	127	444	131	22	0	28	6.3	87	93	74	69	1	.295	.534	9	1	1B-114, OF-6
1961	141	492	145	26	6	27	5.5	76	92	61	62	1	.295	.537	10	4	1B-132
1962 PHI N	144	477	125	19	5	21	4.4	61	80	56	80	2	.262	.455	12	1	1B-130, OF-7
1963	138	450	108	19	2	19	4.2	46	82	43	72	0	.240	.418	18	6	1B-126
1964 2 teams	PHI	N (49G –	.183)		WAS	A (33G –	.172)										
" total	82	178	32	4	1	8	4.5	12	27	22	34	0	.180	.348	29	6	1B-48
1965 WAS A	12	21	4	1	0	0	0.0	3	0	4	3	0	.190	.238	4	1	1B-7
17 yrs.	1887	6387	1703	292	42	318	5.0	945	1147	841	920	14	.267	.475	154	31	1B-888, OF-838, 3B-30

Bill Bruton

BRUTON, WILLIAM HARON
B. Dec. 22, 1929, Panola, Ala.
BL TR 6'½" 169 lbs.

	G	AB	H	2B	3B	HR	HR %	R	RBI	BB	SO	SB	BA	SA	Pinch Hit AB	Pinch Hit H	G by POS
1953 MIL N	151	613	153	18	14	1	0.2	82	41	44	100	26	.250	.330	1	0	OF-150
1954	142	567	161	20	7	4	0.7	89	30	40	78	34	.284	.365	3	2	OF-141
1955	149	636	175	30	12	9	1.4	106	47	43	72	25	.275	.403	2	0	OF-149
1956	147	525	143	23	15	8	1.5	73	56	26	63	8	.272	.419	4	0	OF-145
1957	79	306	85	16	9	5	1.6	41	30	19	35	11	.278	.438	1	0	OF-79
1958	100	325	91	11	3	3	0.9	47	28	27	37	4	.280	.360	5	0	OF-96
1959	133	478	138	22	6	6	1.3	72	41	35	54	13	.289	.397	6	2	OF-133
1960	151	629	180	27	13	12	1.9	112	54	41	97	22	.286	.428	3	0	OF-149
1961 DET A	160	596	153	15	5	17	2.9	99	63	61	66	22	.257	.384	6	1	OF-155
1962	147	561	156	27	5	16	2.9	90	74	55	67	14	.278	.430	5	1	OF-145
1963	145	524	134	21	8	8	1.5	84	48	59	70	14	.256	.372	11	6	OF-138
1964	106	296	82	11	5	5	1.7	42	33	32	54	14	.277	.399	26	6	OF-81
12 yrs.	1610	6056	1651	241	102	94	1.6	937	545	482	793	207	.273	.393	73	18	OF-1561

WORLD SERIES

	G	AB	H	2B	3B	HR	HR %	R	RBI	BB	SO	SB	BA	SA	Pinch Hit AB	Pinch Hit H	G by POS
1958 MIL N	7	17	7	0	0	1	5.9	2	2	5	5	0	.412	.588	1	0	OF-7

Davey Williams

WILLIAMS, DAVID CARLOUS
B. Nov. 2, 1927, Dallas, Tex.
BR TR 5'10" 160 lbs.

	G	AB	H	2B	3B	HR	HR %	R	RBI	BB	SO	SB	BA	SA	Pinch Hit AB	Pinch Hit H	G by POS
1949 NY N	13	50	12	1	1	1	2.0	7	5	7	4	0	.240	.360	0	0	2B-13
1951	30	64	17	1	0	2	3.1	17	8	5	8	1	.266	.375	2	0	2B-22
1952	138	540	137	26	3	13	2.4	70	55	48	63	2	.254	.385	0	0	2B-138
1953	112	340	101	11	2	3	0.9	51	34	44	19	2	.297	.368	10	3	2B-95
1954	142	544	121	18	3	9	1.7	65	46	43	33	1	.222	.316	1	0	2B-142
1955	82	247	62	4	1	4	1.6	25	15	17	17	0	.251	.324	12	4	2B-71
6 yrs.	517	1785	450	61	10	32	1.8	235	163	164	144	6	.252	.351	25	7	2B-481

WORLD SERIES

	G	AB	H	2B	3B	HR	HR %	R	RBI	BB	SO	SB	BA	SA	Pinch Hit AB	Pinch Hit H	G by POS
1951 NY N	2	1	0	0	0	0	0.0	0	0	0	0	0	.000	.000	1	0	
1954	4	11	0	0	0	0	0.0	0	1	2	2	0	.000	.000	0	0	2B-4
2 yrs.	6	12	0	0	0	0	0.0	0	1	2	2	0	.000	.000	1	0	2B-4

Dick Ellsworth

ELLSWORTH, RICHARD CLARK
B Mar. 22, 1940, Lusk, Wyo.
BL TL 6'3½" 180 lbs.

	W	L	PCT	ERA	G	GS	CG	IP	H	BB	SO	ShO	Relief Pitching W	Relief Pitching L	Relief Pitching SV	BATTING AB	BATTING H	BATTING HR	BATTING BA
1958 CHI N	0	1	.000	15.43	1	1	0	2.1	4	3	0	0	0	0	0	1	0	0	.000
1960	7	13	.350	3.72	31	27	6	176.2	170	72	94	0	0	0	0	48	2	0	.042
1961	10	11	.476	3.86	37	31	7	186.2	213	48	91	1	1	0	0	56	2	0	.036
1962	9	20	.310	5.09	37	33	6	208.2	241	77	113	0	1	1	1	62	7	0	.113
1963	22	10	.688	2.11	37	37	19	290.2	223	75	185	4	0	0	0	94	9	0	.096
1964	14	18	.438	3.75	37	36	16	256.2	267	71	148	1	0	1	0	87	4	0	.046
1965	14	15	.483	3.81	36	34	8	222.1	227	57	130	0	1	0	1	73	7	0	.096
1966	8	22	.107	8.98	00	34	8	2W1	341	3	144	0	0	0	0	90	14	0	.156
1967 PHI N	6	7	.462	4.00	32	21	3	125.1	152	36	45	1	0	0	0	8F	1	0	.178
1968 BOS A	16	7	.696	3.03	31	28	10	196	196	37	106	1	1	0	1	72	4	0	.056
1969 2 teams			BOS A (2G 0-0)				CLE A (34G 6-9)												
" total	6	9	.400	4.10	36	24	3	147	178	44	52	1	1	0	0	48	6	0	.125
1970 2 teams			CLE A (29G 3-3)				MIL A (14G 0-0)												
" total	3	3	.500	3.79	43	1	0	59.1	60	17	22	0	3	2	3	4	0	0	.000
1971 MIL A	0	1	.000	4.80	11	0	0	15	22	7	10	0	0	1	0	1	0	0	.000
13 yrs.	115	137	.456	3.72	407	310	87	2156	2274	595	1140	9	7	5	5	673	59	0	.088

Ed Kranepool

KRANEPOOL, EDWARD EMIL
B. Nov. 8, 1944, New York, N. Y.

BL TL 6'3" 205 lbs.

	G	AB	H	2B	3B	HR	HR %	R	RBI	BB	SO	SB	BA	SA	Pinch Hit AB	Pinch Hit H	G by POS
1962 NY N	3	6	1	1	0	0	0.0	0	0	0	1	0	.167	.333	0	0	1B-3
1963	86	273	57	12	2	2	0.7	22	14	18	50	4	.209	.289	13	3	OF-55, 1B-20
1964	119	420	108	19	4	10	2.4	47	45	32	50	0	.257	.393	10	2	1B-104, OF-6
1965	153	525	133	24	4	10	1.9	44	53	39	71	1	.253	.371	11	4	1B-147
1966	146	464	118	15	2	16	3.4	51	57	41	66	1	.254	.399	7	1	1B-132, OF-11
1967	141	469	126	17	1	10	2.1	37	54	37	51	0	.269	.373	9	1	1B-139
1968	127	373	86	13	1	3	0.8	29	20	19	39	0	.231	.295	16	3	1B-113, OF-2
1969	112	353	84	9	2	11	3.1	36	49	37	32	3	.238	.368	7	1	1B-106, OF-2
1970	43	47	8	0	0	0	0.0	2	3	5	2	0	.170	.170	31	4	1B-8
1971	122	421	118	20	4	14	3.3	61	58	38	33	0	.280	.447	8	2	1B-108, OF-11
1972	122	327	88	15	1	8	2.4	28	34	34	35	1	.269	.394	16	4	1B-108, OF-1
1973	100	284	68	12	2	1	0.4	28	35	30	28	1	.239	.306	16	2	1B-51, OF-32
1974	94	217	65	11	1	4	1.8	20	24	18	14	1	.300	.415	35	17	OF-33, 1B-24
1975	106	325	105	16	0	4	1.2	42	43	27	21	1	.323	.409	20	8	1B-82, OF-4
1976	123	415	121	17	1	10	2.4	47	49	35	38	1	.292	.410	10	4	1B-86, OF-31
1977	108	281	79	17	0	10	3.6	28	40	23	20	1	.281	.448	29	13	OF-42, 1B-41
1978	66	81	17	2	0	3	3.7	7	19	8	12	0	.210	.346	50	15	OF-12, 1B-3
1979	82	155	36	5	0	2	1.3	7	17	13	18	0	.232	.303	37	6	1B-29, OF-8
18 yrs.	1853	5436	1418	225	25	118	2.2	536	614	454	581	15	.261	.377	325	90	1B-1304, OF-250
LEAGUE CHAMPIONSHIP SERIES																	
1969 NY N	3	12	3	1	0	0	0.0	2	1	1	2	0	.250	.333	0	0	1B-3
1973	1	2	1	0	0	0	0.0	0	2	0	0	0	.500	.500	0	0	OF-1
2 yrs.	4	14	4	1	0	0	0.0	2	3	1	2	0	.286	.357	0	0	1B-3, OF-1
WORLD SERIES																	
1969 NY N	1	4	1	0	0	1	25.0	1	1	0	0	0	.250	1.000	0	0	1B-1
1973	4	3	0	0	0	0	0.0	0	0	0	0	0	.000	.000	3	0	
2 yrs.	5	7	1	0	0	1	14.3	1	1	0	0	0	.143	.571	3	0	1B-1

Bobby Thomson

THOMSON, ROBERT BROWN (The Staten Island Scot)
B. Oct. 25, 1923, Glasgow, Scotland

BR TR 6'2" 180 lbs.

	G	AB	H	2B	3B	HR	HR %	R	RBI	BB	SO	SB	BA	SA	Pinch Hit AB	Pinch Hit H	G by POS
1946 NY N	18	54	17	4	1	2	3.7	8	9	4	5	0	.315	.537	2	0	3B-16
1947	138	545	154	26	5	29	5.3	105	85	40	78	1	.283	.508	3	0	OF-127, 2B-9
1948	138	471	117	20	2	16	3.4	75	63	30	77	2	.248	.401	9	3	OF-125
1949	156	641	198	35	9	27	4.2	99	109	44	45	10	.309	.518	0	0	OF-156
1950	149	563	142	22	7	25	4.4	79	85	55	45	3	.252	.449	0	0	OF-149
1951	148	518	152	27	8	32	6.2	89	101	73	57	5	.293	.562	2	0	OF-77, 3B-69
1952	153	608	164	29	14	24	3.9	89	108	52	74	5	.270	.482	0	0	3B-91, OF-63
1953	154	608	175	22	6	26	4.3	80	106	43	57	4	.288	.472	0	0	OF-154
1954 MIL N	43	99	23	3	0	2	2.0	7	15	12	29	0	.232	.323	14	5	OF-26
1955	101	343	88	12	3	12	3.5	40	56	34	52	2	.257	.414	13	2	OF-91
1956	142	451	106	10	4	20	4.4	59	74	43	75	2	.235	.408	5	0	OF-136, 3B-3
1957 2 teams	MIL N (41G – .236)							NY N (81G – .242)									
" total	122	363	87	12	7	12	3.3	39	61	27	66	3	.240	.410	13	2	OF-109, 3B-1
1958 CHI N	152	547	155	27	5	21	3.8	67	82	56	76	0	.283	.466	1	1	OF-148, 3B-4
1959	122	374	97	15	2	11	2.9	55	52	35	50	1	.259	.398	9	4	OF-116
1960 2 teams	BOS A (40G – .263)							BAL A (3G – .000)									
" total	43	120	30	3	1	5	4.2	12	20	11	18	0	.250	.417	13	3	OF-29, 1B-1
15 yrs.	1779	6305	1705	267	74	264	4.2	903	1026	559	804	38	.270	.462	84	20	OF-1506, 3B-184, 2B-9, 1B-1
WORLD SERIES																	
1951 NY N	6	21	5	1	0	0	0.0	1	2	5	0	0	.238	.286	0	0	3B-6

Chuck Stobbs

STOBBS, CHARLES KLEIN
B. July 2, 1929, Wheeling, W. Va.

BL TL 6'1" 185 lbs.

	W	L	PCT	ERA	G	GS	CG	IP	H	BB	SO	ShO	Relief Pitching W	Relief Pitching L	Relief Pitching SV	BATTING AB	BATTING H	BATTING HR	BA
1947 BOS A	0	1	.000	6.00	4	1	0	9	10	5	5	0	0	0	0	1	0	0	.000
1948	0	0	–	6.43	6	0	0	7	9	7	4	0	0	0	0	1	0	0	.000
1949	11	6	.647	4.03	26	19	10	152	145	75	70	0	0	2	0	53	11	0	.208
1950	12	7	.632	5.10	32	21	6	169.1	158	88	78	0	1	1	1	57	14	0	.246
1951	10	9	.526	4.76	34	25	6	170	180	74	75	0	0	0	0	61	11	0	.180
1952 CHI A	7	12	.368	3.13	38	17	2	135	118	72	73	0	3	1	1	38	3	0	.079
1953 WAS A	11	8	.579	3.29	27	20	8	153	146	44	67	0	0	0	0	44	10	0	.227
1954	11	11	.500	4.10	31	24	10	182	189	67	67	3	1	0	0	51	7	0	.137
1955	4	14	.222	5.00	41	16	2	140.1	169	57	60	0	3	3	3	35	6	0	.171
1956	15	15	.500	3.60	37	33	15	240	264	54	97	1	1	0	1	84	15	0	.179
1957	8	20	.286	5.36	42	31	5	211.2	235	80	114	2	1	2	1	76	16	0	.211
1958 2 teams	WAS A (19G 2–6)							STL N (17G 1–3)											
" total	3	9	.250	5.04	36	8	0	96.1	127	30	48	0	2	3	1	16	1	0	.063
1959 WAS A	1	8	.111	2.98	41	7	0	90.2	82	24	50	0	0	3	7	19	2	0	.105
1960	12	7	.632	3.32	40	13	1	119.1	115	38	72	1	6	2	2	34	3	0	.088
1961 MIN A	2	3	.400	7.46	24	3	0	44.2	56	15	17	0	2	1	2	8	3	0	.375
15 yrs.	107	130	.451	4.29	459	238	65	1920.1	2003	735	897	7	20	18	19	578	102	0	.176

J. W. Porter

PORTER, J. W. (Jay)
B. Jan. 17, 1933, Shawnee, Okla.
BR TR 6'2" 180 lbs.

	G	AB	H	2B	3B	HR	HR %	R	RBI	BB	SO	SB	BA	SA	Pinch Hit AB	Pinch Hit H	G by POS
1952 STL A	33	104	26	4	1	0	0.0	12	7	10	10	4	.250	.308	1	0	OF-29, 3B-2
1955 DET A	24	55	13	2	0	0	0.0	6	3	8	15	0	.236	.273	8	2	1B-6, OF-4, C-4
1956	14	21	2	0	0	0	0.0	0	3	0	8	0	.095	.095	10	0	OF-2, C-2
1957	58	140	35	8	0	2	1.4	14	18	14	20	0	.250	.350	17	4	OF-27, C-12, 1B-3
1958 CLE A	40	85	17	1	0	4	4.7	13	19	9	23	0	.200	.353	17	3	C-20, 1B-4, 3B-1
1959 2 teams	WAS	A	(37G –	.226)	STL	N	(23G –	.212)									
" total	60	139	31	7	0	2	1.4	13	12	12	20	0	.223	.317	6	2	C-53, 1B-3
6 yrs.	229	544	124	22	1	8	1.5	58	62	53	96	4	.228	.316	59	11	C-91, OF-62, 1B-16, 3B-3

Gary Peters

PETERS, GARY CHARLES
B. Apr. 21, 1937, Grove City, Pa.
BL TL 6'2" 200 lbs.

	G	AB	H	2B	3B	HR	HR %	R	RBI	BB	SO	SB	BA	SA	Pinch Hit AB	Pinch Hit H	G by POS
1959 CHI A	2	0	0	0	0	0	–	0	0	0	0	0	–	–	0	0	P-2
1960	2	0	0	0	0	0	–	0	0	0	0	0	–	–	0	0	P-2
1961	3	3	1	0	0	0	0.0	1	0	0	1	0	.333	.333	0	0	P-3
1962	5	0	0	0	0	0	–	0	0	0	0	0	–	–	0	0	P-5
1963	50	81	21	4	1	3	3.7	12	12	3	19	0	.259	.444	1	0	P-41
1964	54	120	25	7	0	4	3.3	9	19	2	29	0	.208	.367	15	4	P-37
1965	42	72	13	1	0	1	1.4	2	6	2	15	0	.181	.236	7	3	P-33
1966	38	81	19	3	2	1	1.2	12	9	0	19	0	.235	.358	5	1	P-30
1967	48	99	21	0	2	2	2.0	10	13	2	23	0	.212	.313	6	1	P-38
1968	46	72	15	3	1	2	2.8	10	8	6	13	0	.208	.361	14	2	P-31
1969	37	71	12	4	0	2	2.8	9	4	2	15	0	.169	.310	0	0	P-36
1970 BOS A	37	82	20	3	1	1	1.2	12	11	8	11	0	.244	.341	0	0	P-34
1971	53	96	26	4	0	3	3.1	7	19	3	20	0	.271	.406	18	5	P-34
1972	33	30	6	2	0	0	0.0	2	1	1	7	0	.200	.267	0	0	P-33
14 yrs.	450	807	179	31	7	19	2.4	86	102	29	172	0	.222	.348	66	16	P-359

◆ INDEX ◆